Penn. Avenue Bridge.　　　Observatory　　　National Gallery　　　War Department.　White House.

THE CITY OF
Washington

Treasury Department.   Patent Office.   Post Office.   Washington Mon.ᵗ Ent.ᶜᵉ to Long Brᵈ.ᵍ City Hall.   Smithsonian Institute. Armory

U S Capitol   Navy Yard   Arsenal   Insane Asylum

AN ILLUSTRATED HISTORY

THE CITY OF
Washington

by The Junior League of Washington

Edited by *Thomas Froncek*

Alfred A. Knopf   NEW YORK   1977

Panorama illustration on pages 1, 2 and 3

View from 1860 *Soldier's Guide Book*

Kiplinger Washington Collection

THIS IS A BORZOI BOOK
PUBLISHED BY ALFRED A. KNOPF, INC.

Grateful acknowledgment is made to the following for permission to reprint previously published material:

E. P. Dutton & Co., Inc.: Excerpts from *Leaves From an Old Washington Diary, 1854–1863* by Elizabeth Lindsay Lomax, edited by Lindsay Lomax Wood. Copyright 1943 by Lindsay Lomax Wood.

Harper & Row, Publishers, Inc.: Excerpts from pages 112, 115–116, 126, 127, 204 of *Never a Dull Moment: The Memoirs of Countess Marguerite Cassini.* Copyright © 1956 by Marguerite Cassini.

McGraw-Hill Book Company: Excerpts from *Carp's Washington* by Frank G. Carpenter.

Manufactured in the United States of America.

First Edition

Library of Congress Cataloging in Publication Data

Junior League of the City of Washington.
  The City of Washington.

  1. Washington, D.C.—History. I. Title.
F194.J8 1977   975.3   77-75008
ISBN 0-394-40812-8

Original by C. S. Reinhart

Visitors on the terrace of the Capitol.

Contents

Taking Off . . .
An Introduction

"Sir: We have agreed that the Federal District shall be called the 'Territory of Columbia' and the Federal City 'The City of Washington'." In this message to Major Pierre L'Enfant of September 9, 1791, the Commissioners charged with its founding gave the city its name.

Impressions of this area have been recorded in drawings and paintings and in the accounts of explorers, travelers and residents for over 350 years. They have been collected for this book to give a deeper understanding, enjoyment and pride in Washington. With a look into the past, the names on the land, the rivers, the roads, the familiar sights and neighborhoods take on new meanings. This is about the beginnings of Washington and the people who built the city, believing in the promise it holds.

This illustrated history grew from Douglas Sprunt's idea that the Junior League of Washington should collect some early pictures and maps for a "lively and affectionate history." She and several other former League presidents and long-time members with special interests in the city joined to investigate the possibilities.

The San Francisco League's preservation book, "Here Today," gave us courage, and, like our own adventurous founder, Elizabeth Noyes Thompson Hempstone, seated on the left of the picture, we too took flight into the unknown.

Encouragement came from potent sources: Clement Conger said we could avail ourselves of the treasures under his surveillance as curator at the White House and the Diplomatic Reception Rooms of the Department of State; publisher Austin Kiplinger said we could copy what we wished of the extraordinary Kiplinger Washington collection of paintings, prints and photographs. On a positive note of encouragement from Ashbel Green of Alfred A. Knopf, Inc., we moved ahead. We brought to the task assorted professional backgrounds and formidable experience in the world of volunteers. We had produced television shows, horse shows, guided tours through museums and galleries, raised money and spent it on projects in almost every health, welfare and educational institution in town—but we had never written an illustrated history of the city.

The Junior League voted funds to pay for reproducing pictures, and William Edmund Barrett became our chief photographer. Our distinguished mentor John Newton Pearce started us off with lectures on local history. About one hundred past and present League members, assisted by friends and well-wishers throughout the city and elsewhere, set to work on a great fishing expedition that was to last some four years. Immensely helpful to us was the goodwill engendered by the Washington League's seventy years of steadfast purpose that requires its members' involvement in community affairs through volunteer work. Many doors were opened because the work on this book was being done entirely by volunteers. Any royalties will be returned to the community in Junior League projects.

Every picture in this book recalls somebody's helpful suggestion, a stranger's kindness, a friend's generosity with a family heirloom. Every quotation represents pleasurable hours in private and public libraries and reminds us of sudden happy pairings of pictures with contemporary descriptions of the same subject. We delighted in the smell and feel of eighteenth- and nineteenth-century letters, drawings, family reminiscences and scrapbooks that scattered little crusts of newsprint when a page was turned. In this supposedly transient place we found descendants of almost all the early families.

The vision of a modest collection of pictures dimmed as we amassed upward of 2,000 photographs. The piles of typed-out quotations from the past grew from inches to feet, great stacks proliferating across the house where the research poured in. Judy Frank was the Junior League editor and principal writer. As the months went by our names were dropped from committee lists. We were missing from board tables, card tables and dinner tables. Family and friends faded away, worn out by our one-track minds and conversation.

Finished at last, the manuscript filled two huge suitcases and was carted to New York by some of our stronger co-workers. After a year with our able and tactful editor, Thomas Froncek, and months in the hands of Jos. Trautwein, Lucille Ogle and Jeanette Mall at Vineyard Books, it emerged—the book we had hoped it would be.

While we regret the lack of space for many endearing anecdotes, family memories, treasured objects, it consoles us to know our research will be added to the growing files of local history.

"There are two Washingtons—political Washington and the real Washington made up of friends and neighbors," said Benjamin McKelway, editor of the *Evening Star*, in 1951. The peculiar mixture of public and private Washington and of great and small events has always been a delight and fascination to those of us lucky enough to call Washington home. "The Secretary of State was seen one morning at an early hour floating down the Potomac, with a black cap on his head and a pair of green goggles on his eyes," wrote Stratford Canning, the British envoy, of that famous swimmer John Quincy Adams. Beyond the marble city of the postcards there has always been another city that we have tried to capture in this book. "For shopping we would take the stage to Georgetown, or, for something special, the ferry to Alexandria," an old lady who lived on G Street used to tell her granddaughters. There are stories of President Benjamin Harrison with a market basket on his arm and Daniel Webster carefully directing the butcher how to prepare his roast. Webster, an ardent fisherman (whose Washington descendants still own his rod), "would often leave the Department of State for a day of piscatorial enjoyment at the Great Falls of the Potomac . . . throw off public cares and personal pecuniary troubles to cast his lines with boyish glee," wrote Benjamin Perley Poore. Even today a certain Cabinet officer of the 1970s regularly pulls on his waders and catches bass with his fly rod near the Potomac's fall line.

We have delighted in discovering how much of our past is present. Those of us who have worked on this book want to share these discoveries with our readers.

1 The Patawomeck: Site for a City (before 1790)

Chapin Library, Williams College, Williamstown, Massachusetts

Captain John Smith

"Regain therefore your old spirits, for return I will not until I have found the Patawomeck."

—Captain John Smith to his crew, 1608

The site chosen by the Founding Fathers for the District of Columbia lies at the felicitous spot where the foothills of the Appalachians roll down to the lowlands of the Tidewater—as far up the Potomac as a ship could sail. The Potomac passed through the geographic center of the seaboard colonies. It also offered the advantage of a relatively short portage to the Mississippi. Situated here, just below the river's fall line, the Federal City promised to be the commercial gateway to the interior of the vast continent.

When the area was first sighted by Europeans—probably in 1608 by Captain John Smith and his men—the Algonquin Indians lived here in great numbers, drawn by the quartzite and soapstone quarries, the fertile soil, the fish and waterfowl of the Potomac, the flesh and hides of buffalo and deer. With the coming of the Europeans a commerce in beaver pelts rapidly developed to meet the fashionable taste for beaver hats. And tobacco became the great cash crop.

Ownership of the new land was dispensed at the King's pleasure to English court favorites.

Virginia was at first settled by the London Company of Adventurers. The Palatinate of Maryland was carved out of Virginia for Lord Baltimore. By about 1700 all of what became the Federal City was in private hands, much of it being used for agriculture. The Indians disappeared into the Blue Ridge, which was the western frontier for almost half of America's history. But although the Indians' dwellings and their way of life vanished, evidence of their former presence can still be found. Some of their trails became the irregular "Roads" of the modern city (as distinct from the neatly geometric streets and avenues). And in the valley of Rock Creek Park anyone with a knowing eye can find evidence of the stone quarry and workshop where the woodland Indians dug quartzite and then chipped, flaked and polished the stone into weapons and tools.

Near the 1585 Roanoke Island settlement promoted by Sir Walter Raleigh, John White depicted Indians of that area. His drawings also offer valuable insights into the way of life of tribes at the Potomac fall line. Prints based on White's drawings were published in 1590 in a promotional brochure designed to attract settlers. This rendering of the "Indian Town of Secota" shows, among other things: (C,D) a ceremonial feast; (E) tobacco fields; (F) a cornfield with a watchtower for guarding against marauding beasts and birds "for which cause the watchman maketh continual cryes and noyse"; and (I) a garden "used to sowe pompions" (pumpkins and squash). Said White: "This people voyde of all covetouness lyve cherfullye and at their harts ease."

Library of Congress, Rare Book Room and Special Collections

Captain John Smith's sketch maps and descriptions provided the basis for this map which was published in 1612.

John Smith, adventurer, had no intention of turning back to Jamestown in spite of a bad storm and the petitions of his frightened crew.

In 1606, at the age of twenty-seven, he had joined the London Virginia Company and crossed to the New World with the first permanent English colonists. Now, in 1608, he was to become the first known Englishman to captain a boat up the Potomac River and to reach what was from most evidence the fall line, the site chosen for the Federal City 182 years later.

The trip was made, said a crew member:

"to search for a glistering metal the savages told us they had from Patawomeck, also to search what furs, and what other minerals, rivers, rock, na-

tions, woods, fishings, victuals, and what other commodities the land afforded, and whether the bay were endless or how far it extended."

There was also the hope of finding the keenly sought passage to the South Seas.

Smith and his men met with mixed receptions at Indian villages along the Potomac, but the Indians they found on the Anacostia, who called themselves the Nacotchtankes, were friendly. Smith later wrote in his *Historie*:

"The river above this place maketh his passage downe a low pleasant valley overshadowed in manie places with high rocky mountains; from whence distill innumerable sweet and pleasant springs."

10

The ship continued up the Potomac to what is believed to be Little Falls. Here a crew member describes their search for gold:

> "Having gone so high as we could with the boat, we met divers savages in canoes, well loaded with the flesh of bears, deer and other beasts, whereof we had part. Here we found mighty rocks growing in some places above the ground as high as the shrubb, trees and divers other solid quarries of divers tinctures; and divers places where the wa-ters had fallen from the high mountains, they had left a tinctured, spangled scurf that made many bare places seem as gilded."

The explorers returned to Jamestown without finding either gold or the route to the South Seas. But their descriptions of their voyage, together with Smith's detailed sketch maps of Virginia, make an invaluable record. They were used as late as the nineteenth century in boundary discussions between Maryland and Virginia.

In the detail an arrow indicates the site of present-day Washington. According to recent research, Indian names correspond to later sites: Tauxenet (Mount Vernon), Assaomeck (Alexandria), Nameroughquend (the Pentagon), and Nacotchtanke (Anacostia).

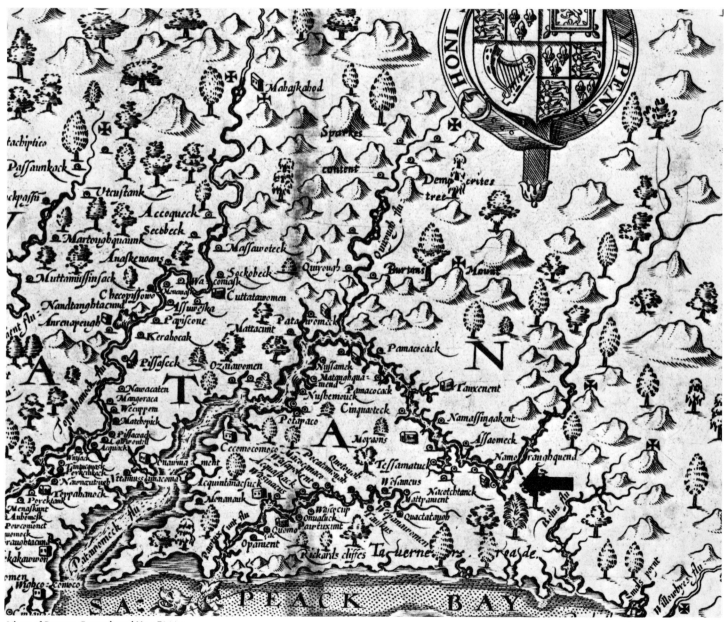

11

A Land of Abundance

John Smith was an explorer, but for Henry Fleete, son of an English barrister, the adventure was trade. The Potomac teemed with beaver, which the Indians ignored, "they themselves haveinge noe use at all for it, beinge not accustomed to take paines to dresse it & make coats of it."

Fleete knew the hazards of trading. In 1623 he had been a crew member in an expedition up the Potomac that had ended in disaster. Fleete survived but remained five years with the Nacotchtankes. When he returned to England to seek financial aid for a new trading expedition an English journalist wrote:

> "Here is one, whose name is Fleete, newly come from Virginia, who having been lately ransomed from the Indians, with whome he hath long lived, till he hath left his own language, reporteth that he hath oftentimes been within sight of the South Seas, that he hath seen Indians besprinkle their paintings with powder of gold, and that he has likewise seen rare precious stones among them, and plenty of black fox, which of all others is the richest fur."

Returning to Virginia, Fleete arranged that

> "all the Indians . . . in the River of Patowmack will take paines this winter in the killinge of Beavers and preserve the furres for mee now that they beginne to finde what benefit it may accrew to them hereby."

He also provided that the Nacotchtankes were to donate twenty beaver skins yearly, at the "going away of the geese," in homage to the King of England.

When Governor Calvert arrived to begin the colonization of Maryland, Henry Fleete was in the group that met him and advised him that the Indians were friendly at Yowaccomoc (St. Mary's). Fleete later served in the Maryland Assembly and when he moved to Virginia was elected to the House of Burgesses. He has many descendants in Virginia, and the town Fleeton on the Rappahannock River is named in his memory.

John White's 1585 watercolor of an Indian fishing party illustrates the abundance of wildlife that attracted red men and white to the Potomac and other Chesapeake waterways.

For the Indians, a valuable resource found near the Potomac was stone for making weapons and tools. The stones shown here were recently found at the site of a quarry and workshop in Rock Creek Park near a stream called Piney Branch. Anthropologists think these stones may have been fashioned by Indian workmen as much as 5,000 years ago.

The gentleman below is dressed in a beaver hat, as fashion demanded. The rendering of a thriving beaver pond (right) was printed in 1684 in *New Voyages to North America* by L. A. Lahontan.

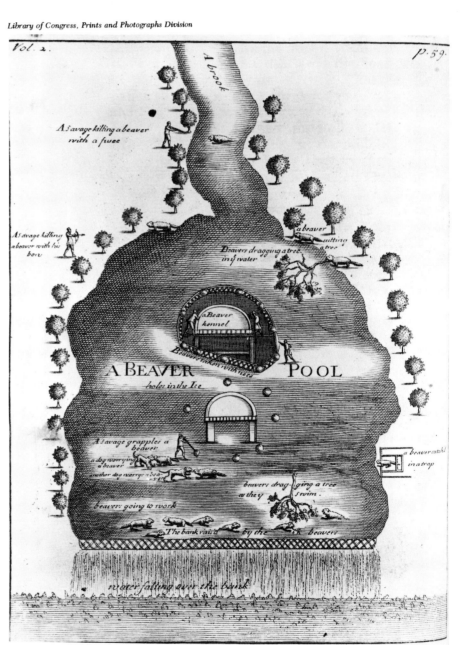

George Calvert, the first Lord Baltimore, who is shown here in a portrait by Daniel Mytens the Elder, was Secretary of State to James I. He converted to Catholicism in 1625, resigned his office and was named Baron Baltimore in the Irish peerage. A member of both the Virginia and New England companies, he visited Newfoundland, encouraging settlement there and in Virginia. A charter was drawn up conveying him broad proprietary powers north of the Potomac on both sides of the Chesapeake Bay, but he died before the instrument passed the seals.

Patents from the King

Out of Virginia came Maryland, by way of a request from Lord Baltimore to King Charles I. Writing from Newfoundland (where he held the royal patent of Avalon), Baltimore petitioned the King for land in a warmer climate. The letter is dated August 19, 1629:

> "From the midst of October to the midst of May there is a sad face of winter upon all this land, both sea and land so frozen for the greatest part of the time as they are not penetrable no plant or vegetable thing appearing out of the earth until it be about the beginning of May, nor fish in the sea besides the air so intollerable cold as it is hardly to be endured. . . . I am determined to commit this place to fishermen that are better able to encounter storms and hard weather, and to remove myself with some 40 persons to your Majesty's dominion of Virginia, where if your Majesty will please to grant me a precinct of land with such privileges as the King your father my gracious master was pleased to grant me here, I shall endeavour to the utmost of my power to deserve it and pray for your Majesty's long and happy reign. . . ."

In 1632 King Charles complied with Baltimore's request. The new palatinate was carved out of Virginia and named for Charles's wife, Henrietta Maria. Baltimore and his heirs were made absolute lords of Maryland. As noted by Richard Blome, an English traveler of the period, the Proprietors had

> "power of enacting Laws, Martial Laws, making of War, and Peace, pardonning of offences, Conferring of Honours, Coyning of Money, etc. And in acknowledgement thereof, yielding and paying yearly to his Majesty his Heires and Successors, two Indian arrows at Winsor Castle in the County of Berks, on Easter Tuesday; together with the fifth part of all the Gold and Silver oare that shall be found there."

Cecil Calvert, the second Lord Baltimore, became the first "Proprietary" of Maryland and so realized his father's dream of American colonization. Outfitting two ships, the *Ark* and the *Dove*, he enlisted some 200 "adventurers" to settle the colony, which they began to do in 1634. His liberal religious views led to Maryland's unique Act of Toleration in 1649. Fearful that jealous investors in Virginia might undermine Maryland's development, Cecil remained in England all his life to protect his interests and sent his younger brother, Leonard Calvert, to govern the colony. In this portrait Cecil Calvert and his namesake-grandson hold a map published in 1635 to promote the colony.

Younger brother of the child Cecil, who died young and so never held the title, Benedict Leonard Calvert, the fourth Lord Baltimore, survived his father by only a few months. He was estranged from his father at the time of the third lord's death because he had publicly renounced the Roman Catholic faith, probably to court royal favor. As soon as his father died, Benedict Leonard Calvert petitioned George I for restitution of political control of Maryland. This was granted to his sixteen-year-old son, who was his successor. In this portrait by an unknown artist, the fourth lord wears the robes of a peer. His plumed hat adorns a table carved with the armorial bearings of the Lords Baltimore from which derives the Maryland flag, the only state emblem showing the arms of a colonial founder.

Forests, fields and houses line the waterways in this remarkable map of Maryland and Virginia in 1670. Published in London in 1673, the map was surveyed and drawn by Augustin Herrman, a Bohemian by birth, who settled in Maryland at Bohemia Manor on the Bohemia River (both named by him).

Herrman rendered every existing building. Studying the Potomac–Maryland area, a concentration of settlers' houses can be seen at Cape Lookout and northwestward along the mouth of the Potomac. But habitation stops well short of the future site of Washington (marked by the words "Turky Buzard Point," below the large "A"). As Herrman has indicated, this area of the future District of Columbia was in Charles County.

In his "Report on Plantations" of 1678, the third Lord Baltimore described the pattern of settlement shown on Herrman's map:

> "The principal place or town is called St. Maries, where the General Assemblies and Provincial Court are kept, and whither all ships trading there doe in ye first place resort, but it can hardly be called a town, it being in length by the water about five miles and in breadth upwards towards the land not above one mile in all which space excepting only my own house and buildings wherein the said courts and public offices are kept, there are not above 30 houses, and these at considerable distances from each other, and the buildings as in all other parts of the Province very mean and little, and generally after ye manner of the meanest farm houses in England. Other places we have none that are called or can be called towns, the people therein effecting to build near each other but so as to have their houses near the waters for convenience of trade and their lands on each side of and behind their houses, by which it happens that in most places there are not fifty houses in the space of 30 miles."

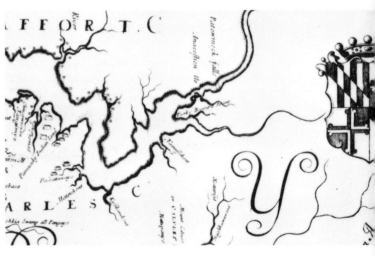

This detail of the rare Herrman map shows the vicinity of the future site of Washington, including "Potowmeck Falls," "Anacostien Ile" (the site of an Indian village) and "Turky Buzard Point." "Anacostia" derives from the Nacotchtanke tribe.

17

This deed of 1712 (above), which conveyed land from one Virginian to another, invokes the name of "The Right Honorable Catherine Lady Fairfax Baroness Dowager of Cameron in Scotland the Only Daughter and Heir of Thomas late Lord and Marguritte late Lady Culpepper Dec.d and sole proprietor of the Northern Neck" of Virginia. Upon the death of Lady Catherine, the Fairfax titles and property passed to her son, Thomas, Sixth Lord Fairfax, who appears (left) in a portrait by Reynolds.

In his youth, Thomas Fairfax was "the petted darling of London's gilded court circles and the victim of unrequited love," which kept him a bachelor all his life. In middle age he emigrated to his American lands, moving into the Belvoir household of his cousin, Colonel William Fairfax. He ended his days in seclusion at Greenway Court, some ten miles south of Winchester, Virginia, and his title went to a younger brother. Thomas Fairfax is best remembered for the kindness he showed to a sixteen-year-old boy who was his fox-hunting companion at Belvoir in 1748. The boy was George Washington, whom Fairfax hired as a surveyor and took west to the mountains.

Throughout the seventeenth century, while the British Crown was struggling to survive the Puritan Revolution, Virginia remained loyal to the King. But in his return to power Charles II ran up heavy political debts. Thus, in 1673, Thomas Lord Culpepper and Henry Bennet, Earl of Arlington, were granted vast acreage in Virginia—acreage to which loyal Virginians already held claim. When the Virginia Assembly sent agents to England to protest the grants, Culpepper and Arlington agreed to relinquish their claims so long as they received profits from various kinds of taxes. By 1677 Culpepper was Governor of Virginia, and in 1681 he bought out Arlington's share. Culpepper's daughter Catherine brought these holdings to her marriage to the Fairfax family. The Fairfaxes rarely pressed their claims to landownership. This light hand led many squatters to claim Fairfax lands as their own, with later resultant lawsuits that were among the reasons Virginia was termed "the most litigious of the colonies."

Colonel William Fairfax, Thomas, Lord Fairfax's cousin and his agent in Virginia, built Belvoir about 1740. Besides supervising the vast Fairfax lands, he served as collector of customs, was in the House of Burgesses and was a member of the "Council of State." His daughter Sara married Colonel John Carlyle, who built the Carlyle House in Alexandria. His daughter Anne married Lawrence Washington, elder half brother of George Washington.

18

This map (below) shows the lands owned by Thomas, Lord Fairfax in 1745, at about the time he came to America. The western boundary of his property, marked by the diagonal dotted line at left (above the words "Augusta County"), was located in what was still an unsurveyed wilderness. Young George Washington, sent to survey these western wilds, wrote:

> "I have not slept above three or four nights in a bed, but after walking a good deal all the day, I have laid down before the fire upon a little hay, straw or fodder, or a bearskin, whichever was to be had, with man, wife and children, like dogs and cats and happy is he who gets the berth nearest the fire. Nothing would make it pass off tolerably but a good reward. A doubloon is my constant gain every day that the weather will permit of my going out, and sometimes six pistoles [a Spanish coin widely circulated in the colonies]."

His early travels in the Virginia wilderness made Washington acutely aware of the commercial and political importance of America's frontier regions.

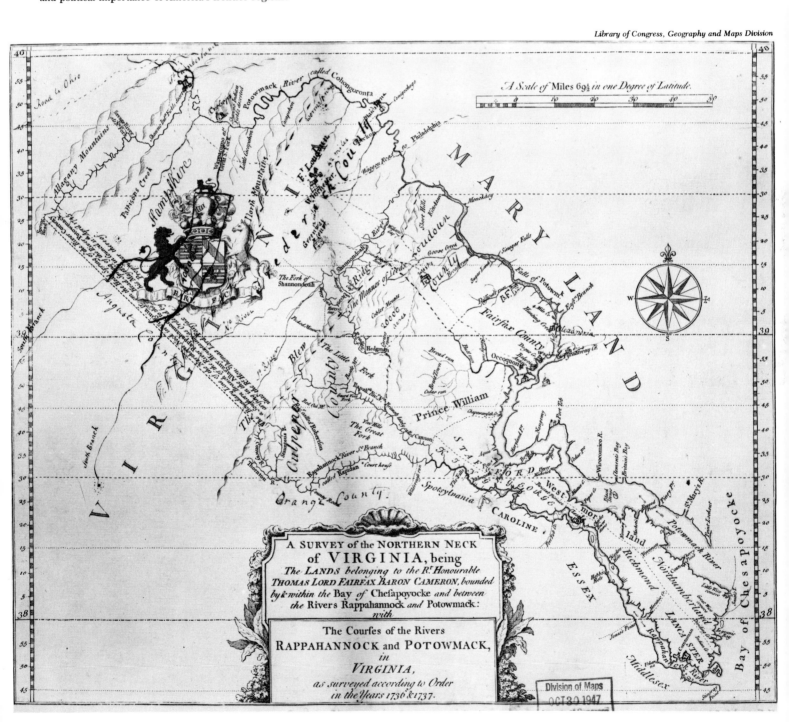

19

Christophle De Graffenried (signature)

Christophle De Graffenried, whose portrait and signature are reproduced here, was a Swiss baron who founded the colony of New Bern in North Carolina. Restless to start another colony, the baron explored the Potomac River well above Great Falls. Despite his enthusiasm no colony was founded. But his travels produced a journal and a map (drawn in 1711) that are valuable early records of the history of the area.

The De Graffenried family Bible (below), owned by DeGraffenrieds living in Washington today, is opened to the page that records the baron's marriage in 1684. One of his present-day Washington descendants bears the first name Tscharner, which was the maiden name of the baron's wife.

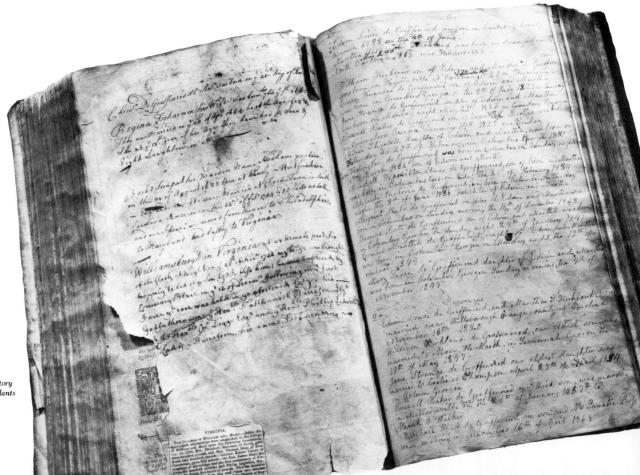

From a family history owned by descendants

On this, the French version of his map (there was also a German version), De Graffenried noted the houses of early settlers in the Washington area—Ninian Beall ("Coll. Bells"), John Addison and Notley Rozier. Sugarloaf Mountain, which he is said to have named, is here transcribed as "Mont de Sugarlove." Following are excerpts from De Graffenried's alphabetical code to the map, along with his comments on points of special interest.

"A. [Little Falls] At the foot of this fall, to the side we wished to build a house and establish a plantation in order to cart merchandise from there. The greatest merchant vessels can sail up to within a half of a quarter of a league of this fall, which is very convenient for commerce.

B. Just below the falls, there is caught a prodigious quantity of the best fish. In the month of May they come there in such numbers that they kill them with a stick.

C. [Theodore Roosevelt Island] This island is all cut out of rock. Above it is a very fine and good soil, sufficient to support a whole family. Indians live there. One could make an impregnable fort of it. . . .

D. [Georgetown] Plantation of Colonel Bell [sic], eight hundred acres of land to sell for 168 Sterling. Very suitable and convenient for our design. . . .

Q. [Just above Little Falls] Charming island of very fine land and trees, on one side steep rocks, on the other an approach suitable for boats. This place with the plantation of Colonel Bell would have suited us well."

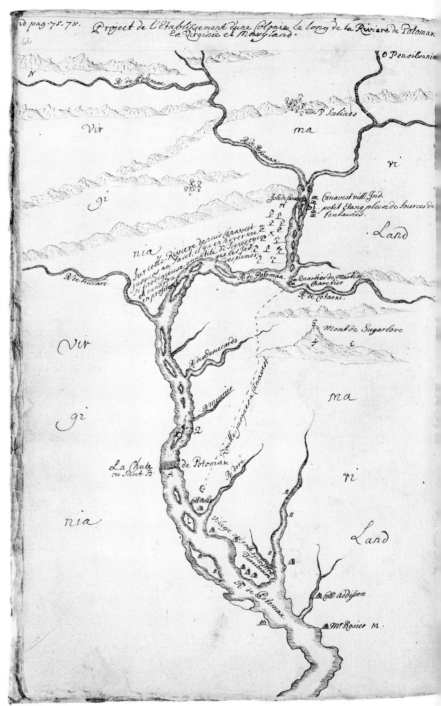

From De Graffenried's Relation du Voyage d'Amérique (1716); Burgerbibliothek, Bern

"*I believe that there are scarcely any places in the world, more beautiful and better situated than this of the Potomac. . . . There is a very pretty island [today's Theodore Roosevelt Island] of very good ground, and facing it, an angle between the great Potomac River and another little river named Gold Creek [now Rock Creek] . . . suited to receive everything which comes up the river, the greatest merchant vessels being able to sail there as well as that which comes down from above the falls or from the surrounding country.*"

—Baron De Graffenried, 1716

21

Colonel Joseph Belt, who owned the land that later became the site of Chevy Chase, was a member of the Maryland House of Burgesses, and during the French and Indian War he served as a colonel of the Prince George County militia. In 1747, on part of his 560 acres, Belt built a frame farmhouse, which, with 218 acres, was acquired in 1814 by Abraham Bradley. Bradley had moved from Philadelphia with the government in 1800 and served as Assistant Postmaster. The Bradley farmhouse (above) survives as part of the Chevy Chase Club. Sections of "Belt Road" are found today between Tenleytown and the Brookeville Road.

Ninian Beall, whose signature and seal are reproduced above, served nearly fifty years as Ruling Elder of the Patuxent Presbyterian Church, keeping it going during fourteen years when it had no minister. In 1704 he gave land for a church at Marlborough, and in 1707 he donated the silver communion service (below). Thought to be the oldest such Presbyterian silver in America, it is presently owned by the Hyattsville Presbyterian Church, which grew out of the Patuxent congregation.

The Landowners

NINIAN BEALL, the "Coll. Bell" of De Graffenried's map, is the best known of the seventeenth-century landowners whose holdings in time became the Federal City. A tall, redheaded Scot, Beall fought for Charles II at the Battle of Dunbar, was captured and was sent first to Barbados and then to Maryland, where he was indentured for five years. When he was freed he was given fifty acres. From then on, as Indian fighter, public figure and landowner, his name was written large in Maryland history. To him was patented, in 1687, a 1,503-acre tract called "Inclosure," which is now part of the National Arboretum. He also owned "Beall's Levels," comprising 255 acres in the area where the White House was later built, and "Rock of Dumbarton," a 795-acre tract named for a Scots landmark. For his acts of bravery and public service he was granted warrants for perhaps 25,000 acres, far more than he took up.

A planter, grist-mill operator and iron-foundry operator, Beall also served in numerous public offices (as many of his descendants do today). But most of all he was a military man who raised companies of rangers to patrol plantation borders, negotiated with the Indians, and kept the peace—by force when necessary. At seventy-four, he was named to the highest military post in the colony, Commander-in-Chief of the Provincial Forces of Maryland.

Ninian Beall and his wife are thought to have had twelve children. Their youngest son, George, owned "Rock of Dumbarton" when it was surveyed in 1752 as part of the new port town of Georgetown. George's son, Thomas, was the Mayor of Georgetown who met with George Washington in 1791 to discuss terms of the town's incorporation into the District of Columbia. Today, Ninian Beall's descendants number as many as 70,000 people, including a recent U.S. Senator and four Maryland governors.

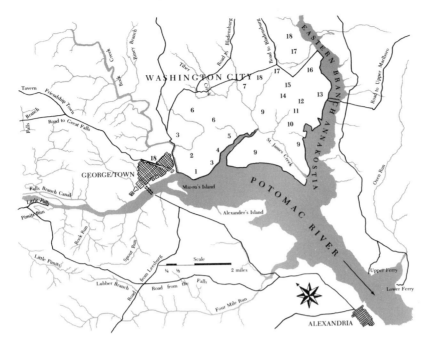

ORIGINAL PATENTEES
OF WASHINGTON
EARLY LANDOWNERS

1. William Hutchison
2. John Watson
3. John Langworth
4. John Lewger
5. Richard and
   William Pinner
6. John Peerce
7. Francis Pope
8. Robert Troope
9. George Thompson
10. Walter Houp
11. Walter Thompson
12. Andrew Clarke
13. Zachariah Wade
14. Richard Evans
15. William Atcheson
16. Walter Evans
17. Henry Jowles
18. Ninian Beall

Between 1663 and 1703, all the lands which became the city of Washington were acquired, by grant or purchase, by the people listed on this page. The numbers on the map indicate the general location of each man's property. The map and the information about the landowners are based on research published in 1936 by Bessie Wilmarth Gahn.

1. WILLIAM HUTCHISON, owner of "The Vineyard" (1689), was founder and vestryman of Piscataway Parish, 1693, and member of the House of Burgesses for Charles County. A leading negotiator with the Indians, he donated 1,000 pounds of tobacco for a free school at Annapolis.

2. JOHN WATSON, owner of "Newbottle" (1687), owned 300 acres subject to a yearly rent of twelve shillings sterling. He was a member of the vestry of William and Mary Parish, St. Mary's County, and of the Assembly. As a Justice of the "Provincial Court of St. Marie's Citty" he was paid 1,840 pounds of tobacco for twelve days' attendance and two days' travel.

3. JOHN LANGWORTH, owner of "Widow's Mite" (1664). His 600 acres, "on the north side of an inlett called Tyber," extended north to what is now 18th Street and Columbia Road. The tract probably included the White House grounds and was later owned by Ninian Beall. Langworth had come to America in 1637, indentured and had later moved into Charles County. In 1666 "Mrs. Langworth's children" were killed by the Indians. At her death the land went to her husband's nephew, William Langworth.

4. JOHN LEWGER owned "Layton Stone" (pre-1666) but never registered his patent. Born in London in 1602, Lewger arrived in Maryland in 1637. By 1644 he was Secretary of the Province, Attorney General, Judge of All Causes Testamentary and Matrimonial, Registrar of the Land Office, and member of the Privy Council.

5. RICHARD and WILLIAM PINNER, owners of "Father's Gift" (1666). Their father Richard came to Maryland in 1638, indentured and later moved from the eastern shore of Virginia to Charles County. He had a warrant for 500 acres due him, which his sons inherited on his death.

6. JOHN PEERCE, owner of "Jamaica" and "Port Royal" (1685), each of which included about 500 acres and extended from the White House area to what is now Florida Avenue. His name is variously spelled Peerce, Pearce or Pierce. His patent states that he is of Calvert County and that his two pieces of land lie in Charles County "in the freshes of potomoke River near the head of Broad [Tiber] Creek." A family named Pearce owned the Lafayette Square section until about 1790.

7. FRANCIS POPE, owner of "Rome" on the Tiber (1663), a 400-

acre tract north of Robert Troop's "Scotland Yard." He was a member of the Assembly in 1642 and Justice of the Peace for Charles County, 1667 and 1670.

8. ROBERT TROOPE, owner of "Scotland Yard" (1663), came to America in 1651. For bravery in battle, Lt. Troope received one of the earliest land grants from Lord Baltimore.

9. GEORGE THOMPSON was owner of three tracts— "Duddington Manor," "Duddington Pasture" and "New Troy" (1663). Thompson's vast tract of 1,800 acres covered what is now Capitol Hill and an area to the north, southwest Washington, the Navy Yard and southeast Washington. This was the first patent granted by Lord Baltimore in the area. In 1691 Thompson sold the land to Thomas Notley for 40,000 pounds of tobacco.

10. WALTER HOUP, owner of "Houp Yard" (1686). The tract comprised 500 acres fronting on the Eastern Branch, between Cerne Abbey Manor and Walter Thompson's "The Nock."

11. WALTER THOMPSON, owner of "The Nock" (1686). These 500 acres, lying along the Eastern Branch, were assigned to Thompson by Ninian Beall.

12. ANDREW CLARKE, owner of "Meurs" (1685), 500 acres assigned by Ninian Beall.

13. ZACHARIAH WADE, owner of "Brother's Purchase" (1670). Wade was an attorney at St. Mary's who served as a Burgess for Charles County and later as a Justice of the Peace.

14. RICHARD EVANS, owner of "Barbadoe" (1685). Son of Obediah Evans, who had been transported to America in 1667, Evans' yearly rent to Lord Baltimore for the grant of 250 acres came to ten shillings sterling.

15. WILLIAM ATCHESON, tract unnamed (1698). The patent for this tract has not been located. Atcheson later owned several other tracts in Charles County.

16. WALTER EVANS, owner of "Nameless" (1698). The deed for 230 acres mentioned three neighbors with adjoining tracts: Richard Evans, Zachariah Wade and William Atcheson. The Evans family lived on the Eastern Branch for many years; Evans Point takes its name from them.

17. COLONEL HENRY JOWLES, owner of "The Grange" (1685). In charge of the Militia of the Province of Maryland in 1682, Jowles received 20,000 pounds of tobacco as a gift for his services in raising troops. In 1694 he was appointed "Chiefe Judge in Chencery and Keeper of the Great Seal of Maryland." A year later, "afflicted with ye Gout and other Indispositions of body," he was relieved of his duties.

23

William Tatham's history of *The Culture and Commerce of Tobacco*, published in London in 1800, included these illustrations of the tobacco trade, which dominated the commerce of Maryland and Virginia for two hundred years. The tobacco leaves were cured by being hung inside sheds (above). The openwork walls of the shed allowed the air to circulate around the leaves, while the roof kept the tobacco dry in wet weather. The cured tobacco was stored in barrels under the roof of a public warehouse (e). A public inspection house is shown at bottom.

"The office of *Inspector* [Tatham noted in his history] is a public office constituted by legislative authority, for the purpose of inspecting, and making diligent search, into the quality and conditions of every hogshead of tobacco which is designed to be put on shipboard, to the end that no imposition should be practised in vending it to incompetent judges of the commodity: and that the best possible security may be held by the merchants in Europe, against the probability of damage arising at sea, either from the carelessness of the packer, or the too moist condition of the plant.

"This office is always to be filled, at each and every inspection warehouse respectively, by two respectable planters, being skilled in the knowledge of tobacco, who are of good repute and responsibility, and men highly respected in their neighborhood. It is an office of high trust and importance in trade; and, to the great credit of the institution; it has scarcely produced an instance of corruption."

The Tobacco Trade

*". . . the general trade of Maryland depends chiefly
upon Tobacco, which being esteemed better for a Foreign
Market than that of Virginia, finds greater vent abroad;
and the planters at home, in exchange thereof, are
furnished by the Merchant with all necessaries, for
himself, his House, Family, and Plantation."*

—Richard Blome, 1672

The Tatham print (below) shows the stages of growth of the tobacco plant: the bud (a); the flower in full bloom and in cross section
(b and c); the seed pod (d); and the leaf (e), which has had a hole eaten
in it by a tobacco worm.

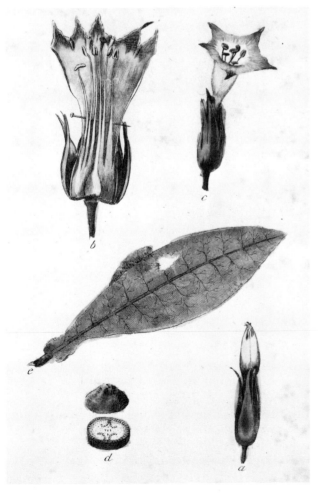

The tobacco was conveyed to market by boat or wagon or was
rolled along the road in special horse-drawn rigs (above). Some of the
roads in present-day Washington were created by such rolling tobacco barrels.

A MAP of
the moſt INHABITED part of
VIRGINIA
containing the whole PROVINCE of
MARYLAND
with Part of
PENSILVANIA, NEW JERSEY AND NORTH CAROLINA
Drawn by
Joshua Fry & Peter Jefferson
in 1751.

Hogsheads of tobacco, being prepared for shipment to England, line the wharf in this cartouche, which decorated a 1751 map of Virginia and Maryland. The map was drawn by Joshua Fry and Peter Jefferson, the father of Thomas Jefferson; they did versions in French and English.

The tobacco inspection station was the core around which grew the two tobacco ports, Alexandria, Virginia, and Georgetown, Maryland. As early as 1730 there was a warehouse at the mouth of Hunting Creek, on the Virginia shore of the Potomac—hence one of the town's early names, Hunting Creek Warehouse. (It was sometimes also known as Belle Haven.) Planters who used this facility petitioned the Virginia Assembly for the creation of a town there, and their request was granted by an act of 1749. On the Maryland shore the tobacco inspection station nearest the Potomac fall line was located where Rock Creek joined the Potomac, at Saw Pit Landing. By 1751 this had become Georgetown.

Both towns grew rapidly during the third quarter of the eighteenth century, which was a time of remarkable profits in the tobacco trade. Sail lofts, rope walks, shipyards, warehouses, grog shops, taverns, inns and wharves proliferated, and so did the houses of those who had come to work in the new towns.

Tobacco Ports on the Potomac

"Public warehouses were established under the kingly government of Virginia, for purposes of receiving and inspecting tobacco, at many places upon the principal rivers, below the great falls thereof."

—William Tatham, 1800

In the aquatint below by G. A. Parkyns, the Georgetown waterfront is seen as it appeared in the early 1790s, shortly after it became part of the District of Columbia. Just visible upstream, in the middle of the Potomac, are the rocks known as The Three Sisters.

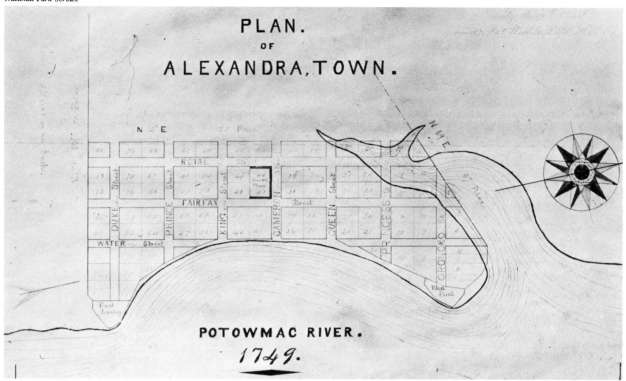

PLAN.
OF
ALEXANDRA, TOWN.

POTOWMAC RIVER.
1749.

Owned by Alexandria descendants

When the Alexandria lots were auctioned on July 13, 1749, Colonel John Carlyle bought the third lot, paying thirty Spanish pistoles for lot #41 and sixteen pistoles for an adjacent lot. Carlyle, who was born in Scotland and emigrated to America in 1740, married the daughter of William Fairfax of Belvoir. He completed his house (below) in 1752. Carlyle's seashell snuffbox (left) still belongs to family members living in Alexandria.

To create Alexandria, some sixty acres were acquired from the Alexander and West families. The ground was laid out in a gridiron of eighty-four half-acre lots by John West, a county surveyor assisted by Lord Fairfax's young protégé, George Washington, who sketched out a similar grid for his half brother, Lawrence, a purchaser of one of the lots. The town's street names reflected Royalist sentiments which prevailed before the Revolution.

At Carlyle House, in 1755, five colonial governors met to take measures with General Edward Braddock against the French and the Indians in the west. From his Carlyle House headquarters the general crossed the Potomac and landed at "Braddock's Rock" in Foggy Bottom. A marker near the Theodore Roosevelt Bridge shows the spot. Other markers show his route along Wisconsin Avenue through Bethesda and Rockville and north to Fort Duquesne (present-day Pittsburgh). Near the fort, Braddock's forces were ambushed and the general himself was mortally wounded. Young George Washington, who had just succeeded his late half brother Lawrence as commander-in-chief of the Virginia Militia, led the survivors back to safety.

William F. Smith Collection

Collection of Government Services Savings & Loan, Bethesda, Maryland

Life in early Alexandria centered around the market square in the foreground of this sketch. Behind it is the City Hall, which was built later.

The Virginia legislature's first reference to Alexandria was an act of 1752 allowing that "two fairs be kept annually—May and October. Two days for space for sale of cattle, victuals, provisions, goods, wares, and merchandise and all persons attending shall be exempt and privileged from all arrests, attachments, executions whatever except in capital offenses, breach of the peace or for any controversy, suit or quarrel that may arise."

The father of the Constitution's Bill of Rights, George Mason, Virginia statesman and planter, lived at Gunston Hall and was among the foremost citizens of Alexandria. This portrait was painted by D. W. Boudet from a lost original done in 1750 by John Hesselius.

Citizens of Alexandria and Fairfax County played a prominent role in shaping colonial opposition to British policies. Foremost among their contributions were the Fairfax Resolves, which stated principles later incorporated into the young republic's philosophy of government. Written by Alexandrian George Mason, who later wrote the Constitution's Bill of Rights, the Resolves were passed at Alexandria Courthouse on July 18, 1774, at a meeting chaired by George Washington:

> "1. RESOLVED that this Colony and Dominion of Virginia can not be considered as a conquered Country; and if it was, that the present Inhabitants are the Descendants not of the Conquered, but of the Conquerors. That the same was not settled at the national Expence of England, but at the private Expence of the Adventurers, our Ancestors, by solemn Compact with and under the Auspices and Protection of the British Crown. . . .
>
> 2. RESOLVED that the most important and valuable Part of the British Constitution . . . is the fundamental Principle of the People's being governed by no Laws, to which they have not given their Consent, by Representatives freely chosen by themselves. . . .
>
> 3. RESOLVED that . . . the legislative Power here can of Right be exercised only by [our] own Provincial Assemblys. . . .
>
> 4. RESOLVED that . . . no Argument can be fairly applyed to the British Parliament's taxing us."

The Resolves went on to pledge Virginia's support to Massachusetts, then suffering "ministerial Vengeance" and a virtual blockade as a result of the Boston Tea Party. They called on the other colonies to join in sending food and money to Boston and to appoint deputies to a Congress "to concert a general and uniform Plan for the Defence and Preservation of our common Rights." Two months later, September 5, 1774, the First Continental Congress met in Philadelphia.

Wearing the Continental "buff and blue," which evolved from the uniform of the Fairfax County Militia, George Washington takes command of the American Army in Cambridge, Massachusetts, on July 3, 1775, in this print by Currier & Ives. Washington's famous white horse, Blueskin, seen in this and in other of his Revolutionary War portraits, was borrowed from an Alexandria neighbor. Washington was the most prominent commander of the French and Indian War who was still young enough to lead an army at the time of the Revolution. Congress hoped that appointing him head of the Continental Army would tighten the bond between southern and northern colonies.

31

Owned by Washington descendants, photograph courtesy of Frick Art Reference Library

Another prominent Alexandrian who fought in the Revolution, Henry Lee joined the Continental Army at nineteen, the year the Revolution began. He fought in New York, Pennsylvania and New Jersey. As a major in command of the cavalry unit called "Lee's Legions," "Light-Horse Harry" Lee served in South Carolina under General Nathaniel Green. After the war he became governor of Virginia, and later he served as a Congressman from Alexandria. He was a friend of Washington, whose adopted son's daughter married Lee's son, Robert Edward. More than a dozen Alexandria houses are associated with the early Lees; one stands at the center of the photograph (below). The large house next to it belonged to the Fairfax family. Christ Church is at the end of the street.

Collection of William F. Smith

32

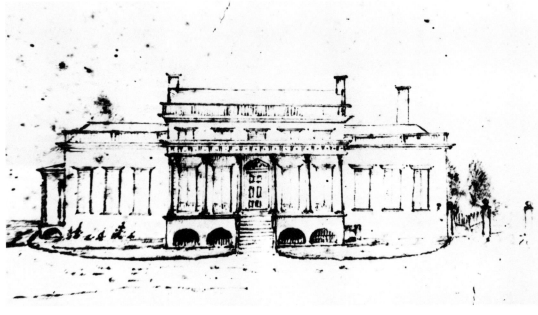

General Washington presents his best respects to Mrs. Dulany with the horse Blueskin; which he wishes was better worth her acceptance. —

Marks of antiquity have supplied the place of those beauties with which this horse abounded in his better days. Nothing but the recollection of which, & of his having been the favourite of Mrs. Dulany in the days of his courtship, can reconcile her to the meagre appearance he now makes. —

Mrs. Washington presents her Compliments and thanks to Mrs. Dulany for the Roots of Scarcity. —

Friday past 2 OClock

When the Revolution ended, George Washington returned the horse Blueskin to Mrs. Benjamin Dulany. Dulany descendants still own the wry note of thanks (above) that Washington wrote when he returned the horse. ("Scarcity," mentioned in the last line, was a beetlike vegetable.) Elizabeth French Dulany was George Washington's godchild and the ward of both Washington and George Mason, the executor of her father's estate. The Dulanys' country house (below) was on Shuter's Hill, where the Masonic Temple now dominates the Alexandria skyline.

Collection of William F. Smith

The Glebe (left) is an Arlington house built on the 1775 foundations of an earlier residence for the rector of the Falls Church and Christ Church, Alexandria, who lived midway between his two parishes. A "glebe" is farmland attached to church property; this one gave its name to Glebe Road. The house is still standing. As Bishop Meade noted:

"The vestry-book commences in 1765. At that time there were two churches in the new parish of Fairfax—one at the Falls, called, as the present one is, Little Falls Church; the position of the other—the Lower Church—is not known. . . .

"In the year 1766, it is determined to build two new churches—one at the Little Falls, very near the old one, and one in Alexandria, to contain twenty-four hundred square feet, and to be high-pitched so as to admit of galleries. [The church was not completed until 1773.] The ten pews are now sold, and General Washington, though having just been engaged in the erection of Mount Vernon Church, which was finished the same year, and having a pew therein, gives the highest price for one in Christ Church, which was occupied by him and his family during his life, and has been by some of his name and family ever since."

This view of Alexandria was printed in 1845, in Peter Force's *Guide*. Bishop Meade, in his 1857 history of the *Old Churches, Ministers and Families of Virginia*, wrote:

"At the close of the last or beginning of the present century [Alexandria's] population was ten thousand, and its commerce greater than it now is. So promising was it at the close of the war, that its claims were weighed in the balance with those of Washington as the seat of the National Government. It is thought that, but for the unwillingness of [George] Washington to seem partial to Virginia, Alexandria would have been the chosen spot, and that on the first range of hills overlooking the town the public buildings would have been erected."

Shuter's Hill (see page 33) was supposed to have been chosen for Capitol Hill.

The Virginia and Maryland lands below the Potomac fall line were not the scene of any stirring battles during the American Revolution. Yet the war severely affected the life of the area. The tobacco trade fell off, and the overall decline in transoceanic trade hurt both Georgetown and Alexandria. In the long run, however, the war triggered the chain of events that eventually turned ten miles square of farmland, forest, and river ports into the capital of the emerging nation.

Instrumental in this development was George Washington's continuing interest in the western lands and in Potomac navigation. In 1784, shortly after resigning as Commander in Chief, Washington made a 650-mile trip by horseback to the Ohio "to obtain information of the nearest and best communication between the Eastern and Western waters." He wrote to Governor Harrison of Virginia:

> "I need to remark to you Sir, that the flanks and rear of the United States are possessed by other powers, and formidable ones, too; nor how necessary it is to apply the cement of interest to bind all parts of the Union together by indissoluble bonds, especially that part of it, which lies immediately west of us. . . . what troubles may we not apprehend, if the Spaniards on their right, and Great Britain on their left, instead of throwing stumbling-blocks in their way, as they now do, should hold out lines for their trade and alliance? What . . . will be the consequence of their having found close connections with both or either of those powers in a commercial way? It needs not, in my opinion, the gift of prophecy to foretell.
>
> The western settlers . . . stand as it were upon a pivot. The touch of a feather would turn them any way."

Thomas Jefferson concurred.

Soon after the war ended, he wrote to Washington to warn that Virginia must move quickly lest New York (which would soon have the Erie Canal) capture the bulk of western commerce. Jefferson urged Washington, who was president of the Potomac Canal Company, to revive and enlarge his earlier plans for the Potomac. "What a monument to your retirement that would become," Jefferson wrote. Since the canal would cross state boundaries and involve the inland navigation projects of several states, the "Mount Vernon Conference" was called for the purpose of "keeping up harmony in the commercial relations" between the states and to smoothe the administrative path of the waterway. This interstate cooperation laid the groundwork for the Constitutional Convention.

This romantic view of the city of Washington, as seen from the heights above Georgetown, is among the earliest known views of the city. Previously unpublished, it was painted by George Jacob Beck, circa 1795–97. It is the original source for several later (and more commonly known) renderings of the city.

Among those who found the charms of Georgetown irresistible was General Edward Braddock. Passing through town in 1755, on the way to his ill-fated campaign against the French and Indians, Braddock wrote to a lady in England:

> "... never have I attended a more complete banquet, or met better dressed or better mannered people than I met on my arrival in George Town, which is named after our gracious majesty. The men are very large and gallant, while the ladies are the most beautiful that my eyes have ever looked upon. ... The habitations of these genial folk ... are stately buildings that have no superiors in England, and the interior decorations are things of beauty. ... In fact, dear madam, I might sum up everything by declaring George Town is indescribably lovely and I am loath to leave it and its hospitable people."

"Last Thursday passed through this town on his way to New York the most illustrious, the President of the United States of America," reported the Georgetown *Times and Potomac Packet* on April 23, 1789. The paper continued:

> "His Excellency arrived at about 2 O'Clock on the bank of the Potowmack, escorted by a respectable corps of gentlemen from Alexandria where the George Town ferry boats, properly equipped, received his Excellency and suit, safely landed them, under the acclamation of a large crowd of their grateful fellow citizens—who beheld his Fabius, in the evening of his day, bid adieu to the peaceful retreat of Mt. Vernon, in order to save his country once more from confusion and anarchy."

By 1789, when the President passed through, Georgetown had become a thriving port with a busy life of its own and with a ferry crossing which, since 1738, had linked the seaboard states.

The site of the proposed Federal City was still undecided, but Georgetown and the Potomac area were high on the list of probabilities.

Georgetown was originally part of Prince George's County, Maryland, but was included in Montgomery County when that county was established in 1776. The first mayor of Georgetown, appointed in 1790, was Robert Peter, who came from Scotland to Bladensburg and moved to Georgetown in 1754. The factor for a tobacco importing firm and a successful merchant, Peter was a major landowner both in Georgetown and across Rock Creek in the area which became the Federal City. His lands there reached from the Potomac in Foggy Bottom in a wide arc, following Boundary Street (then the road to Bladensburg, now Florida Avenue) to Vermont Avenue. His will provided firewood for his widow from his farm at Franklin Square (13th and K streets NW).

"George-Town . . . is a pleasant Village situated on the waving Hills on the N. Side of the Potomack . . . the Hills on the back of the Town which are improved & improving with handsome Country seats & which in some situations will now sell for 50 guineas an acre, command a noble view of the Town, of the City of Washington & of the Potomack quite down to Alexandria. Mason's Island in front of the E. End of the Town adds much to the Beauty of the view. The Houses are exceedingly well built of Brick. The Town may contain 150 families & between 30 & 40 very good brick Buildings. At the Peace [1783] this Place had not above 1 doz. Houses."

—James Kent, 1793

This early plan of the city of Washington, with Georgetown appearing at upper left, is from Tobias Lear's *Observations on the River Potomack*, a pamphlet published in 1793. The plan shows the city as it was envisioned by French architect Pierre L'Enfant. Little of the plan had yet been realized in 1793, but James Kent, newly arrived from New York, found enough interest in Georgetown and the surrounding area to warrant the handwritten annotations that he added to the margins of this copy of Lear's map:

"1. Masons Island
2. Travers Tavern in Georgetown where I lodged December 1793.
3. Ferry Road to Alexandria
4. Hotel
5. Notley Young's old brick house where I dined. It had a fine view down to Alexandria even to Mount Vernon.
6. Colonel Forest's house where I dined say 2 miles North of Georgetown. It stands on the hills, and commands a fine view over the city and down the river.
7. Academy in Georgetown stands on a hill with a fine prospect. The whole of Georgetown is on waving hills, the most delightful."

Washington, as sketched by John Trumbull in 1794.

The Georgetown Presbyterian church at M and 30th streets, built in 1782, was enlarged in 1793 and 1801. Its founder, Stephen Bloomer Balch, served as pastor for fifty-two years. "Let us resolve to be social rather than fashionable, and generous instead of extravagant" he exhorted his congregation. The church moved to P Street in 1878.

The first Georgetown church was built by a German Lutheran congregation in 1770, at Wisconsin Avenue and Volta Place. Today a Lutheran church stands on this same corner. In 1769, when an addition was made to the original boundaries of Georgetown, landowners Charles Beatty and George Fraser Hawkins specified: "Four of said lots we give to public uses, to wit: one for building on, a church for the use of the Church of England, one of a Calvinist church, one for a Lutheran church, and the other for a market house." Methodism came to Georgetown in 1772; and the Scots tobacco factors who founded Georgetown built their Presbyterian church there in 1782. Soon, churches and schools of other denominations were also being built in Georgetown, includ-

John Carroll of Maryland, who founded Georgetown University in 1789, was the first American archbishop. He was appointed the Prefect Apostolic by the Holy See in 1784, with a prefecture extending from Canada to Louisiana. His "Proposal for Establishing an Academy at George-Town, Patowmack-River, Maryland" appealed "to all liberally inclined to promote the Education of Youth" for "Students of EVERY RELIGIOUS PROFESSION." Contributions and students came from both Catholic and Protestant families. Two of George Washington's nephews enrolled. The university was the first Catholic institution of higher learning in the United States. In the early view of the university (above), the oldest campus building, "Old South," is the one on the right with the three dormer windows.

ing the Roman Catholic academy that later became Georgetown University. As James Kent noted in 1793:

St. John's Church

"There is a little Presby. Church partly finished, & a plain brick Roman Chapel at the W. End with a clumsy Steeple to it. They have an Academy here under the Direction of a President & vice-President who are Romish Priests. The House now used is a large square 2 story brick building on a most salubrious & commanding Eminence at the W. End of the Town—a new Building is begun near the same place—Tho the Academy is but of two years old they have now between 80 & 90 scholars drawn from all quarters, & principally from Roman Catholic families. The Protestants don't relish it. . . . This academy contemplates to give degrees. It gives great attention to the Scholars . . . & it is growing rapidly."

St. John's, founded in 1796, was the first Episcopal parish in Georgetown. The building, dated 1804, is considered, in part, the design of William Thornton, architect of many houses and public buildings in the District of Columbia, including the Capitol. The founder of the parish, the Reverend Walter Dulany Addison, came to Georgetown in 1794. Until St. John's was built, he held services in Georgetown's Presbyterian Church.

Kiplinger, Washington Collection

The twentieth-century sketch (above) is of the Old Stone House, perhaps Georgetown's oldest surviving building. The colonial Georgetown houses (below) were sketched in 1882 by deLancey Gill. They were located at 3250 M Street and have since been demolished.

Owned by the artist's descendants

The location of a permanent residence for Congress was debated for years. In 1783 Congress chose a situation on the Delaware River, near Trenton, New Jersey, and two weeks later added a second site on the Potomac near Georgetown, planning not one but two Federal Cities. The government was to alternate between them, leading one wit to suggest putting the government building on wheels. But the plan for two capitals was defeated, and competition between other cities and sections was resumed. The possibility was strong, however, that the Federal City might come to the banks of the Potomac, and hopes, and land values, remained high. In a letter to President Washington, dated September 17, 1790, Thomas Jefferson and James Madison reported on a conversation with an important Georgetown-area landowner on the pressing issue of finding a site for the Federal City:

"In the course of the visit we made the day we left Mount Vernon, we drew our host (General John Mason of Analostan Island) into conversation on the subject of the federal seat. he came into it with a shyness not usual to him. whether this proceeded from his delicacy as having property adjoining George town, or from what other motive I cannot say. he quitted the subject always as soon as he could. he said enough however to shew his decided preference of George-town. he mentioned shortly, in its favor, these circumstances, 1. its being at the junction of the upper & lower navigations where the commodities must be transferred into other vessels: (and here he was confident that no vessel could be contrived which could pass the upper shoals and live in the wide waters below his island.) 2. the depth of water which would admit any vessels that could come to Alexandria. 3. the narrowness of the river & consequent safeness of the harbour. 4. its being clear of ice as early at least as the canal & river above would be clear. 5. its neighborhood to the Eastern branch, whither any vessels might conveniently withdraw, which should be detained through the winter. 6. its defensibility, as derived from the high & commanding hills around it. 7. its actual possession of the commerce, & the start it already has.

"He spoke of George town always in comparison with Alexandria. when led to mention Eastern branch [the Anacostia River] he spoke of it as an admirable position, superior in all respects to Alexandria."

The Bank of Columbia (right) was organized early in 1794 to handle the extensive real-estate transfers through which Benjamin Stoddert (below, right), together with William Deakins, Jr., privately purchased sites for the Federal City at the request of George Washington, who wanted to avoid speculation that would drive up land costs. The bank building stands today on M Street west of Wisconsin. The street elevation is drastically changed from this early photograph.

Among the bank's shareholders was "Old Yarrow." Long a familiar figure in Georgetown, he was a slave who earned his freedom through an arrangement with his master and became a Georgetown property owner.

41

This portrait of Benjamin Stoddert's children was painted in 1789 by Charles Willson Peale. The detail from the painting (left) shows the tobacco warehouses and waterfront of Georgetown, with Roosevelt Island and the river. Although it is romanticized, the view is the earliest known of the port of Georgetown.

"Tho the Wharfs are few & indifferent I observed 2 ships here, & am told that George-Town on an average ships annually 5,000 hogsheads of Tobacco—From 150 to 160,000 bbls. of Flour, & between 3 & 400,000 Bushels of Wheat, & that Alexandria doubles it as to both the Cotton articles, tho in Tobacco George-Town more nearly rivals it as its Inspection is better &c."

—James Kent, 1793

"The articles you requested me to buy for you I now send by the Captain, as per order & i trust that they mite meet your approbation; the silver fringe, i have not been able to procure, as it has been sold but 3 yds. I can not find any other under two pounds a yd, and i have been to all the shops. As this tambor muslin is a yd. short of your Order, you can have it for two shillings a yd. or Return it and the owner will take it back. Captain Quander has a bolt of yellow China silk, which he will sell you for two Pound ten shillings. I hope that you will be down here to see us all before summer, and I remain your very dear friend Grace."

—Miss Grace Miller of Georgetown
     to "Olivia," in Philadelphia, March 30, 1775

The original eighteenth-century dependency at the back of the house called Mackall Square (above) is one of Georgetown's oldest buildings. A "telescope house," Mackall Square was built from back to front with the brick part added in 1820. Today the old-fashioned gardens and lane leading to the house still suggest the country atmosphere that characterized old Georgetown.

Dumbarton House (right), formerly called Bellevue, was built in 1799 and was one of the first houses on the Heights above the river in Georgetown. Most of these early estates were small farms. As late as 1930 some of them still had a few horses, a cow or two, and some fruit trees, as well as formal gardens.

The history of successive sales of the property where Dumbarton House stands, traced in 1930 by Miss Cordelia Jackson for the Columbia Historical Society, indicates the speedy turnover of land as the Federal City emerged. In 1796 the land passed from Thomas Beall (grandson of Ninian Beall) to Peter Casanave and then to Uriah Forrest. In 1797 it belonged to Isaac Pollock; in 1798, to Samuel Jackson (who built the house); in 1805, to Joseph Nourse. During the War of 1812 it was owned by Charles Carroll of Bellevue (brother of Daniel Carroll of Duddington), who rescued Dolley Madison from the White House when the British attacked Washington in 1814. It was in this house that she took refuge. Today, the restored Dumbarton House is open as a house and museum. It is the headquarters of The National Society of the Colonial Dames of America in the District of Columbia.

Georgetown's original northern boundary was Prospect Street, on the hilltop above the harbor. The street was named for "Pretty Prospect," the country property of Benjamin Stoddert and Uriah Forrest. Here, where they could enjoy the commanding view of the river, a number of Georgetown's prosperous citizens built substantial houses toward the end of the eighteenth century. Among them was Stoddert's own Halcyon House at 34th Street, built in 1787. Stoddert, who became Secretary of the Navy under John Adams, was an important figure in the commercial and political life of Georgetown. Tradition has it that from the south windows Stoddert used to watch with his telescope for the return of the ships that he and his business partners sent to distant ports. His view of the harbor is shown on pages 42 and 43.

2 The Nation's Capital (1790–1814)

"No nation had ever before the opportunity offered them of deliberately deciding on the spot where their Capital City should be fixed . . . the plan should be drawn on such a scale as to leave room for that aggrandizement and embellishment which the increase of the wealth of the nation will permit it to pursue at any period however remote."

—Pierre Charles L'Enfant to George Washington, 1789

This previously unpublished view (below) of early Georgetown and Roosevelt Island was painted by Rebecca Wister Morris Nourse. It shows the Frederick Road, once an Indian trail, later a rolling road and now Wisconsin Avenue. Many early travelers, including President John Adams, caught their first glimpse of the new city from this point.

The brightest names of the American Revolution were instrumental in the founding of the nation's capital. Washington fastened on the Potomac site as the commercial gateway to the interior, and his prestige helped to carry the point. Jefferson, as Washington's agent, imposed his classical vision on the city, intending that the visible reality should manifest the greatness of the emerging nation. Adams was the first President to preside in the new Federal City.

Jefferson, who was Secretary of State at the time, explains the famous compromise of 1790, by which the Potomac shore was selected as the future site of the Federal City, in return for passage of Alexander Hamilton's bill (favored by the North), which authorized federal assumption of war debts incurred by the states:

> "This measure produced the most bitter and angry contests ever known in Congress, before or since the union of the States. . . . The Eastern members particularly . . . threatened a secession and dissolution. Hamilton was in despair. As I was going to the President's one day, I met him in the street. He walked me backwards and forewards before the President's door for half an hour. He painted pathetically the temper into which the legislature had been wrought, the disgust of those who were called the Creditor states, the danger of the secession . . . . I proposed to him . . . to dine with me the next day, and would invite another friend or two, bring them into conference together, and I thought it impossible that reasonable men, consulting together cooly, could fail, by some mutual sacrifices of opinion, to form a compromise which was to save the union. . . . It was finally agreed . . . the vote [against Hamilton's bill] should be rescinded. . . . But it was observed that this pill would be peculiarly bitter to the Southern States, and that some concomitant measure should be adopted to sweeten it a little to them. There had before been propositions to fix the seat of government either at Philadelphia, or at Georgetown permanently afterwards, this might . . . calm in some degree the ferment. . . . So two of the Potomac members [Alexander White and Richard Bland Lee] agreed to change their votes, and Hamilton undertook to carry the other point [that of establishing the capital on the Potomac]."

Ever the down-to-earth man of finance, Washington dickered with local farmers so that the city could be founded with little capital outlay.

The area for which he negotiated was a ten-mile-square diamond laid out on a north-south axis with the town of Alexandria at the southern tip. The other points reached far into the farmlands, forests and small settlements surrounding the confluence of the Potomac and its Eastern Branch (the Anacostia River): to the east near Oxon Hill, to the north near present-day Silver Spring and to the west at Falls Church.

At about the center of the diamond, next to Georgetown, the Federal City was laid out. The original plans for the city, ambitious as they were, covered only the area from the Eastern Branch to Rock Creek, with Boundary Street (now Florida Avenue) forming the northern limits. The city was soon known as "Washington," the ten-mile-square as "The District of Columbia." With the designs for the White House and the Capitol chosen by open competition, the government paid 25 pounds for each acre used for parks and public buildings. The rest of the land was surveyed and divided into lots. The original proprietors were given back every other lot, presumably having been made richer by the federal presence even after the loss of so much of their land. The alternate lots, now federal property, were raffled, auctioned—anything to raise cash to pay for the federal buildings.

The plan of the city was undertaken by a Frenchman whom Washington had known in Revolutionary days as a member of the Corps of Engineers. In laying out the streets, Pierre Charles L'Enfant drew on the magnificence remembered from the Versailles of his boyhood. Jefferson, self-schooled as a city planner during his European tour, guided L'Enfant's hand, urging wider avenues, broader vistas—in short, a city that would convey the most spacious, resounding statement about the nation's intentions. It was to recall Greek love of beauty, the republican simplicity of early Rome.

Eyes fixed on this higher reality, the first Washingtonians slogged through swamps, struggled through forests, shot game in fields near the White House. Visitors from the cultivated capitals of Europe and from the settled splendors of New York, Philadelphia and Boston laughed at the pretensions of this raw wilderness that called itself a capital city. But the harshness was softened by the camaraderie among those who moved here when the federal government came down from Philadelphia in the summer of 1800.

Every year, more and more private houses replaced the primeval forests. Yet the capital remained a modest, almost tentative city. Its burning by the British in 1814 was largely due to indifferent defenses. Everybody believed that if the British came ashore they would put the torch to a more important place, such as Baltimore.

Surveying the Site

Ellicott and Banneker surveyed the boundaries of the District of Columbia using the instruments shown here: a Transit and Equal Altitude Instrument (made by Ellicott) and a compass.

On January 22, 1791, George Washington appointed three commissioners to manage the surveying of the site, "reposing" (as he wrote) "special trust and confidence in the integrity, skill, and diligence of Thomas Johnson and Daniel Carroll, of Maryland [a relative of Daniel Carroll of Duddington], and David Stuart, of Virginia." The men appointed to conduct the survey were two Marylanders, Andrew Ellicott and Benjamin Banneker. Washington's instructions for the survey were:

> "Beginning at Jones's Point, being the upper cape of Hunting Creek in Virginia, and at an angle in the outset of forty-five degrees west of the north, and running in a direct line ten miles for the first line: Then beginning again at a right angle with the first, across the Potomac ten miles, for a second line; thence from the termination of said first and second line, running two other lines of ten miles each, the one crossing the eastern branch aforesaid and the other the Potomac and meeting each other in a point."

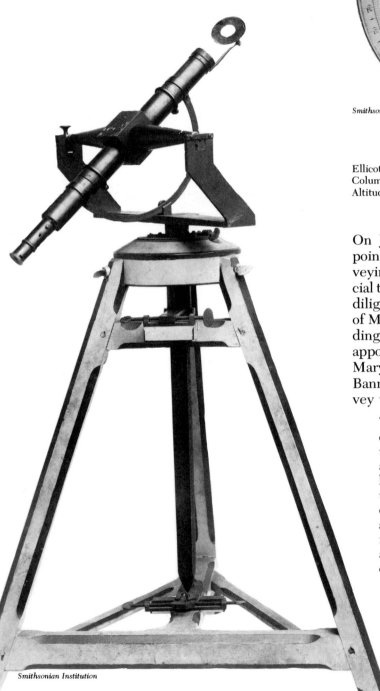

48

Major Andrew Ellicott (1754–1820), who was unofficially styled the "geographer general of the United States" after he began his survey of the District in 1791, was from the prominent Quaker family for whom Ellicott City, Maryland, is named. A veteran of the Revolutionary War, he had surveyed the western portion of the Mason–Dixon Line and some of the boundaries of Pennsylvania and New York. In the following letter to his wife, Ellicott describes the environs of Washington as they appeared to him while he was surveying the District boundaries:

"The Country thro' which we are now cutting one of the ten-mile lines is very poor; I think for near seven miles on it there is not one House that has any floor except the earth; and what is more strange, it is in the neighborhood of Alexandria, and George-Town.

"This country intended for the Permanent Residence of the Congress, bears no more proportion to the country about Philadelphia and German-Town, for either wealth or fertility, than a crane does to a stall-fed Ox!"

The only known likeness of Benjamin Banneker that was produced during his lifetime appeared as the frontispiece for his 1795 almanac. In an earlier edition of the almanac the author was described this way by James McHenry (later a Maryland Senator):

"Benjamin Banneker, a free black . . . is about fifty-nine years of age; he was born in Baltimore county; his father was an African, and his mother the offspring of African parents [although his maternal grandmother was an English indentured servant].—His father and mother having obtained their freedom, were enabled to send him to an obscure school, where he learned, when a boy, reading, writing, and arithmetic as far as double position; and to leave him, at their deaths, a few acres of land upon which he has supported himself ever since. . . . [His] facility in calculation . . . was often serviceable to his neighbours, and at length attracted the attention of the Messrs. Ellicotts, a family remarkable for their ingenuity and turn to the useful mechanics. It is about three years since Mr. George Ellicott lent him Mayer's Tables, Ferguson's Astronomy, Leadbeater's Lunar-Tables, and some astronomic instruments, but without accompanying them with either hint or instruction, that might further his studies, or lead him to apply them to any useful result. These books and instruments, the first of the kind he had ever seen, opened a new world to Benjamin, and from thenceforward he employed his leisure in astronomical researches."

"Wednesday evening arrived in this town, Major Longfont, a French gentleman, employed by the President of the United States to survey the lands . . . where the federal city is to be built."

— *Georgetown Weekly Ledger, March 12, 1791*

"I have the Honor of Informing you of my arrival at the place where I could not possibly reach before Wednesday last and very late in the evening after having traveled part of the way on foot and part on horse back leaving the broken stage behind.

"On arriving I made it my first care immediately to wait on the mayor of the town in conforming with the direction which you gave me–he appeared too much surprised and he assured me he had received no previous notice of my coming nor any instruction relating to the business I was sent upon–however next day–yesterday morning, he made me a kind offer of his assistance in procuring for me three or four men to attend me in the surveying and this being the only thing I was in need of every matter has been soon arranged. I am only at present to report that an heavy rain and thick mist which has been incessant ever since my arrival here has put an insuperable obstacle to my wish of proceeding immediately to the survey."

— *L'Enfant to Jefferson, March 11, 1791*

Pierre Charles L'Enfant (1754–1825), above, grew up at the Court of Versailles and was trained as an architect. He came to America in 1777 to serve in the Corps of Engineers. In 1783 Baron von Steuben asked him to design the insignia for the Society of the Cincinnati. In 1791 the Society's first president, George Washington, officially invited him to lay out plans for the national capital. In a letter to L'Enfant, dated August 18, 1791 (detail below), Thomas Jefferson expresses his ideas for a map of the city. L'Enfant adopted his suggestion for drawing the map in such a way that there would be "no waste in the square sheet of paper." But the architect greatly expanded Washington's and Jefferson's idea of the city.

L'Enfant's artistic temperament and his insubordination eventually alienated the Commissioners. As he planned the streets, L'Enfant found that the houses of two of the most influential proprietors of the city, Notley Young and Daniel Carroll, were in the way. He announced to them that the houses must come down. Two days later Mr. Carroll complained to Washington:

"Major L'Enfant has proceeded with his hands to the demolishing of my building, which he has in great measure effected, having entirely destroyed the roof, and thrown down the greater part of the upper story, in fine the building is ruined. This appears to be the most arbitrary act ever heard of."

Washington followed up Carroll's letter on December 1 with his own to the Commissioners:

"I receive with real mortification the account of the demolition of Mr. Carroll's house, by Major L'Enfant, against his consent. . . . You are as sensible as I am of his value to us:—But this has its limits: and there is a point beyond which he might be over-valued."

The next day Washington wrote to L'Enfant, enjoining him "to touch no man's property without his consent, or the previous order of the Commissioners." Washington wrote:

"I wished you to be employed in the arrangements of the Federal City.—I still wish it: but

do I would suggest to you the idea of doing it on a square sheet to hang corner upwards, thus ◇ the outlines being N.W. N.E. S.E. & S.W. the meridians will be vertical as they ought to be; the streets of the city will be horizontal & vertical, & near the center, the

It was the Commissioners, not the President or Congress, who gave the city its name and designated the lettering and numbering system of the streets. Their intentions were laid out in a letter to L'Enfant, whose job included planning the grid for the city's streets.

only on condition that you can conduct yourself in subordination to the authority of the Commissioners."

Washington was reluctant to press L'Enfant too hard. "If . . . he should take miff and leave the business," Washington wrote to the Commissioners, "I have no scruple in declaring to you (though I do not want him to know it) that I know not where another is to be found who could supply his place." Finally, however, even Washington had to agree that L'Enfant was becoming intolerable. Not only did the architect fail to produce a map on time, but he even had the temerity to ask that the Commissioners be replaced. This was too much. "To change the Commissioners *can not be done* on grounds of propriety, justice or policy," Washington wrote to L'Enfant in February 1792. L'Enfant was dismissed—less than a year after he had been hired. Afterward Washington wrote to the Commissioners (on March 6, 1792):

"Matters are at length brought to a close with Maj. L'Enfant. . . . I am convinced, Gentlemen, that in your transactions with Major L'Enfant, you must have suffered much from his temper; and if my approbation of your conduct in this business can afford you pleasure, you may be assured you have it—even if I had no corroboration of the fact, I should be persuaded, from what I have known of his disposition . . . there would scarcely be a possibility of action harmoniously in concert with him."

Not all who were involved in the dispute with L'Enfant were disposed to feel unkindly toward him. After he was dismissed, the landowners of the area (excluding Daniel Carroll and his kinsman, Notley Young) wrote to Major L'Enfant to "lament extremely" the loss of his services. The proprietor Samuel Davidson wrote: "I Pray God to realize your hope and my fervent wish, by the return of Major L'Enfant . . . and to remove by a halter, or otherways, those blockheads of Commissioners now in authority there, who do everything in their power to prevent the prosperity and establishment of that City." Although L'Enfant continued to live in the Washington area, he received only one more commission from the government.

After Ellicott and Banneker completed the L'Enfant plan for the city it was given to two engravers. Both produced maps that were widely reproduced. In Philadelphia, the firm of Thackara and Vallance came up with a version that was even reprinted as a handkerchief (below). The Boston firm of Samuel Hill made a similar engraving. A proof sheet was sent to Thomas Jefferson, who forwarded it from Philadelphia to the Federal City Commissioners on July 11, 1792, noting:

> "I observe the soundings of the creek & river are not in it. it would be well to know of Mr. Ellicot whether they were in the original sent to Boston. if not, you will probably think it adviseable to insert them in this proof sheet, and send it to Boston . . . to Mr. Blodget, under whose care the engraving is going on."

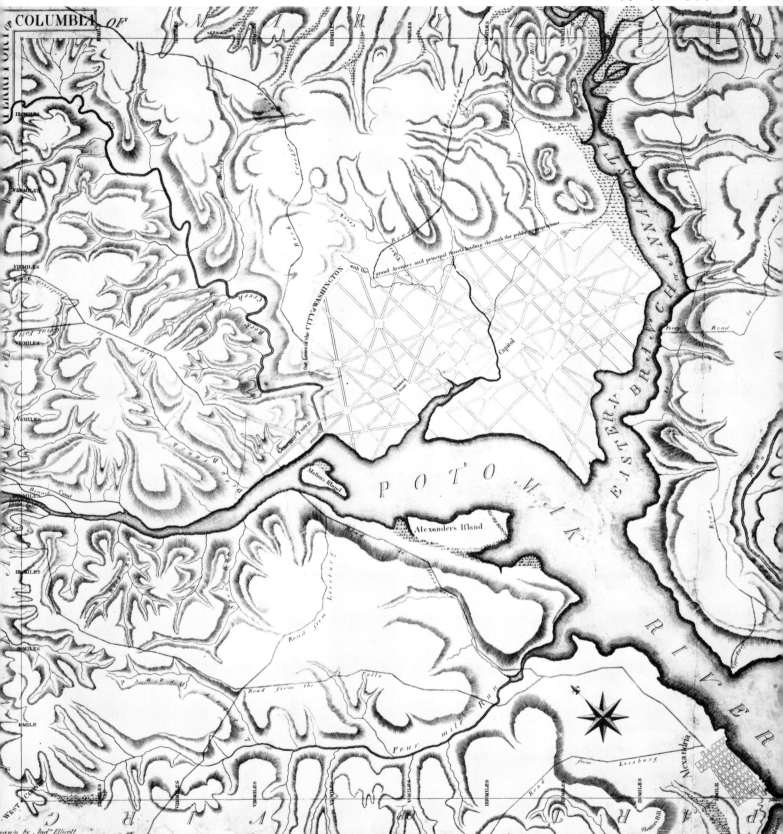

Ellicott's topographic map (above) was the first map of the District (here styled "Territory") of Columbia to be published after the site was selected in 1790. Probably engraved by Thackara and Vallance of Philadelphia in 1793 or 1794, it was published by Joseph T. Scott in 1794. The map shows the bounds and boundary stones of the District, its topography and the roads then in use, as well as incorporating Pierre L'Enfant's plan for the Federal City.

Since 1916 the Daughters of the American Revolution have preserved and maintained the District boundary stones. Today thirty-seven of the original forty remain. They may be found along Western, Eastern and Southern Avenues, which form the District boundaries, and in Virginia, following King Street. The location of Alexandria's Jones Point boundary stone, at the southernmost corner of the District, is shown in the map below, which is the only eighteenth century engraved plan of the town. The map was drawn in 1798 by Colonel George Gilpin, a director and an associate of George Washington in the Potomac Canal Company. The following report of the Jones Point boundary stone installation appeared in the Alexandria *Gazette*, April 21, 1791:

> "The mayor and the commonality, together with the members of the different lodges of the town, at 3 o'clock waited on the commissioners at Mr. Wise's, where they had arrived. After drinking a glass of wine to the following sentiment, viz., 'May the stone we are about to place in the ground remain an immovable monument of the wisdom and unanimity of North America,' the company then moved on to Jones Point. . . .
>
> "When Mr. Ellicott had ascertained the precise point from which the first line of the District was to proceed, the Master of the Lodge . . . assisted by some of the other brothers, placed the stone; after which a deposit of corn, wine and oil was made upon it and the following observations were delivered by the Rev. Muir:
>
> " 'Of America it may be said as it was of Judea of old, that it is a good land and large, O America, and prosperity within thy palaces. May jealousy . . . be buried deep under the work which this day we have completed, brethren and gentlemen.' "

Magnum Weeks

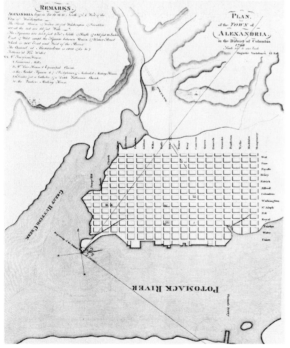

Martin Luther King, Washington Collection

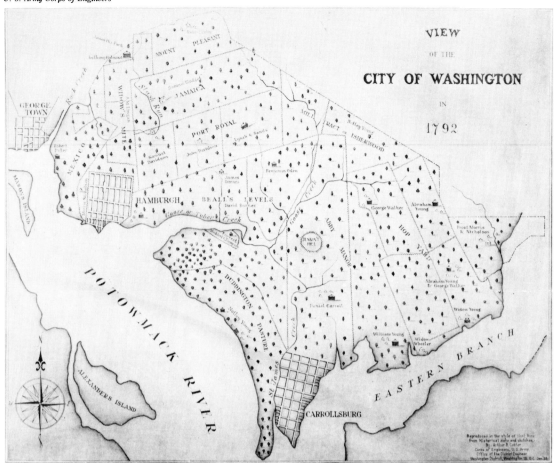

The names of those who owned property in the Federal City in 1791, and the location of their houses, are shown on this map. The map, produced in 1952 by Arthur B. Cutter of the Army Corps of Engineers, is based on the original research and map of 1874 by Dr. Joseph N. Toner, a Washington physician and historian. Jenkins' Hill eventually became the site of the capitol building. Hamburg and Carrollsburg were little more than paper towns, for which plans were drawn, a few lots sold and even fewer buildings erected. Both "towns" reflected the ambitious hope of landowners that Washington would become a great trading center.

Reproduced here is a certificate signed by the Commissioners of the Federal City, acknowledging the purchase of a lot by L'Enfant. The government reserved some lands for public uses and expected the sale of others to pay for all improvements that would eventually be made. Lot sales were slow and disappointing, and for many years the finances of the Federal City remained precarious.

56

AT a public Sale of Lots in the City of WASHINGTON, *Peter Charles L'Enfant of George Town Maryland* became purchaser of Lot number *thirty* in square number *one hundred twenty seven* for the consideration of *ninety nine pounds current Money of Maryland* on the terms and conditions published at the same sale: And he hath accordingly paid one-fourth part of the said consideration money, and given Bond, with security, for the payment of the residue; on the payment whereof, with interest, according to the said Bond the said *Peter Charles L'Enfant* or his assigns will be entitled to a conveyance in fee.

18 October 1791
Square No 127. Lot No 30

Th Johnson
D d Stuart } *Commr*
Dan l Carroll

199

Land for the Federal City

When the Federal City was founded the area consisted largely of farmlands held by nineteen families. Throughout the eighteenth century these properties had been changing hands through inheritance or sale, usually within the same small circle of people. Many of these people were related by marriage. Most of them seem to have known each other and to have shared the bonds of civic office, militia service and church responsibilities. Most of the proprietors have descendants living in the city today. The map shows, however, that by 1792 many farm properties had been bought up by financiers and speculators who had been drawn to the area by the prospects of the new city. New owners of choice lands were Samuel Blodgett, John Davidson, Samuel Davidson, Prout, and Morris and Nicholson.

The terms by which private lands were to be purchased by the federal government for parks, public buildings and streets and alleys were laid out by George Washington in the following letter to Thomas Jefferson, dated March 31, 1791:

"All the land from Rock-creek along the river to the eastern-branch and so upward to or above the ferry including a breadth of about a mile and a half the whole containing from three to five thousand acres is ceded to the public on condition that when the whole shall be surveyed and laid off as a city (which Major L'Enfant is now directed to do) the present Proprietors shall retain every other lot; and for such of the land as may be taken for public use, for squares, walks, &ca, they shall be allowed at the rate of Twenty-five pounds per acre—The

Tobias Lear (1762–1816) frequently acted on behalf of the President and served as his private secretary. The builder of one of the principal docks in the new city, he was also the author of *Observations on the Potomack*, which he wrote to stimulate interest and investment in the area.

Public having the right to reserve such parts of the wood on the land as may be thought necessary to be preserved for ornament &ca. The Landholder to have the use and profits of all their ground until the city is laid off into lots and sale is made of those lots which by the agreement become public property. No compensation is to be made for the ground that may be occupied as streets or alleys.

"To these conditions all the principal Landholders have subscribed . . . even the obstinate Mr. Burns has come into the measure."

On March 29th, Washington had noted in his Diary: "Finding the interests of the Landholders much at variance . . . Dined at Colo. Forest's today with the Commissioners and others." Forrest gave the dinner in the house now numbered 3350 M Street. This same diary entry says: "the business was brought to a happy finish."

Department of State

This is the seal that President Washington requested the Secretary of State, Thomas Jefferson, to use in making official the agreement with the proprietors of the land between the Potomac and Anacostia rivers. The design was the result of a resolution passed by Congress on July 4, 1776: "That Dr. Franklin, Mr. J. Adams and Mr. Jefferson, be a committee, to bring in a device for a seal for the United States of America." Jefferson suggested a cloud by day and a pillar of fire by night leading the children of Israel through the wilderness. Franklin preferred Moses dividing the Red Sea for his people while drowning the Pharaoh, with the motto "Rebellion to tyrants is obedience to God." Six years and two committees later they agreed on this design, which remained in use until 1841, when it was replaced by a less griffinlike eagle and a wider shield. From the first it has been in the safekeeping of the Secretary of State as senior member of the Cabinet.

The house above belonged to the "obstinate Mr. Burnes," who held the first deed to be issued in the newly designed District of Columbia. David Burnes was a successful farmer and county magistrate. In 1792 he advertised land "in the most eligible situations. . . . A purchaser may combine prospect, commercial advantage, and vicinity to President's Palace." A notice Burnes published five years later suggests something of what the land near the White House—and David Burnes's temper—was like:

> "I Hereby forewarn all persons from hunting with Dog or Gun, within my inclosures or along my shores;—likewise, cutting down Timbers, Saplings, Bushes, of Wood of any kind, carrying off and burning Fence logs, any old wood on the shores; or in the woods;—If I should find any person trespassing as above I will write to my attorney and suits will be commenced against the tresspassers in the general court."

After Burnes died in 1799, his house, probably built in 1750, was preserved by his daughter. It was finally demolished in 1894, and the Pan American Union was later built on the site.

David Burns's daughter Marcia (left) was his only child. According to Christian Hines, who published his *Early Recollections of Washington City* in 1866, Miss Burns (or, just as often, Burnes)

> "was, perhaps, more talked of than any other female in the District of Columbia at that time [about 1798]. Almost every person heard of the rich young heiress . . . and many young men were desirous of making her aquaintance, but most of them lacked the courage. . . .
> "At this time there were but few places in the city suitable for members [of Congress] to board at. . . . The discontent which prevailed among them was so great that it was feared that the seat of the government would be removed from Washington. In fact, I believe the attempt was made, but fortunately failed. . . . Among the families to which the members [of Congress] would resort of an evening . . . to spend a few hours in social conversation, was that of Davy Burns. Here would assemble mostly the young and single members, nearly all of them being attracted thither by the charms of . . . Marcia Burns. Among these was a young member from New York, by the name of John P. Vanness, a person of prepossessing appearance and fine manners, who proposed marriage to Miss Burns, was accepted, and married her; and thus became the husband of Miss Marcia Burns, the rich heiress of her father, Davy Burns, and possessor of the vast number of lots in the city of Washington, which were formerly styled Burns' farm."

Rock Hill, the house seen here in a watercolor painted after the Civil War, was built about 1750 by Anthony Holmead II, who owned much of what is now Northwest Washington, mainly above Boundary Street. Holmead had come from England to take up the family claim to lands probably obtained in 1727. The original settler, James Holmead, is listed in records of 1726 as being a Vestryman of Rock Creek parish and paying an extra tax because he was a bachelor.

Anthony Holmead began building his first house, a log cabin, in about 1740. The cabin eventually grew to become Holmead Manor, which was located at what is now the 3500 block of 13th Street. Rock Hill was Holmead's "Mill Seat," where he stayed when supervising work at his mill on Rock Creek. It was near S and 24th streets NW and was later renamed Kalorama. By the time this painting was done the original Rock Hill had been changed often and had suffered a bad fire. Family members—many of whom still reside in Washington—believe the center part of the house, except for the roof, originally looked as it does here.

Loveday Holmead (1774–1852), who became Mrs. Thomas W. Pairo, was born at Rock Hill and inherited a large part of the Holmead estate. Christian Hines recorded that during the Revolution a portion of the French army forded Rock Creek near the site of the paper mill and camped on the Kalorama grounds, making the Rock Hill kitchen their headquarters. Mrs. Pairo told him that she, "being then a child, would go to the kitchen door and peep through the chink at the officers, and that her mother was alarmed for fear the French soldiers would steal her chickens, but that none of them were stolen by them."

Until her death in 1764 Ann Rozier (left) was the sole owner of the lands that today include Capitol Hill as well as all of Southeast and Southwest Washington. As the only child of Notley Rozier, she inherited the Capitol Hill property from her father, who had inherited it from his godfather, Thomas Notley. Originally the land had been part of 1,800 acres that had been granted to George Thompson in 1663 by the Second Lord Baltimore—combining the three tracts known as Duddington Manor, Duddington Pasture and New Troy. Thomas Notley had bought the tracts from Thompson in 1691 for 40,000 pounds of tobacco.

Ann Rozier was married twice. She first married Daniel Carroll, from Annapolis, by whom she had a son, Charles Carroll of Duddington, and a daughter, Mary. Her second marriage was to Benjamin Young, by whom she had another son, Notley Young (whose portrait appears below, along with that of Mrs. Young). As inheritors of Ann Rozier's lands, Notley Young and Charles Carroll's son Daniel became the last private owners of those great tracts of land. On March 30, 1791, they joined the other proprietors in signing the agreement that established the Federal City. As recollected by John Cotton Smith in 1800:

> "There appeared to be but two really comfortable habitations, in all respects, within the bounds of the city, one of which belonged to Daniel Carroll, Esquire, and the other to Notley Young, who were the former proprietors of a large proportion of the land appropriated to the city, but who reserved for their own accommodation ground sufficient for gardens and other useful appurtenances."

James Kent, who met the Young family during his visit to the Federal City in 1793, noted that "Notley Young's old brick house where I dined . . . had a fine view down to Alexandria even to Mount Vernon." Built in 1756, the plantation house stood on a bluff overlooking the Potomac at what is now G and 10th streets SW. In the Young chapel the first services of the Roman Catholic Church in Washington were held, and it was the custom for everyone to stay for dinner after Mass. George C. Henning, who lived there as a child, recalled that in one wing of the house the lower floor was used "as the servants' dining room, where the commonalty were dined after Mass . . . while the gentry were dined above."

When planning the Federal City, L'Enfant found that the Young house lay directly in the path of one of his avenues. Writing to the Commissioners, he asked that it be removed as "a nuisance to the city." But George Washington intervened and the house was allowed to stand. It remained on the site until 1856, when it was demolished.

Notley Young's grist mill, shown in a previously unpublished painting by August Köllner, was the only mill within the bounds of the original Federal City. Called at various times the Casanave, the Fenwick, the Pearson and the Logan mill, it was located on a branch of the Tiber near the south side of N Street, between First and Second streets NE. Designed by Benjamin Latrobe, it was, according to local historian James Croggon, "an old-fashioned grist mill fed by the waters of the Tiber, an overshot after an undershot wheel being used. It was of frame, and during its existence, as the population increased, business demanded its enlargement."

Casanovia, sketched by William G. Newton, was built by Peter Casanave and his wife Ann, who was Notley Young's daughter. Married in 1791, the couple lived briefly at Bellevue (now Dumbarton House) in Georgetown before moving into this house, which stood on a hill near Delaware Avenue between M and N streets NE.

Peter Casanave and his wife lived here only a few years. Casanave died in 1796, and Ann returned to her father's home. But a glimpse of Casanave can be found in the following excerpts from a letter (now owned by a Washington descendant), which he wrote to Ann's father in June 1791, asking for her hand:

"You Sir as a good prudent & tender Father I make no doubt you will wish to know whome I was before you knew me in George Town & my present Situation in Live for the suport of the State I

have So long wish to enter to with your Daughter, for this reason I thought best to Inclose you a Exact Statement of all my affairs by the Contence of which you will be able to See what I am know worth more then Five Thousand pounds after paying all my Debts in this World.

"By Birth I am the 13th Son of Barthelemy Casanave whose profession was a farmer of his own ground & he Carried allso a considerable trade by a Tan House Near the Town of Navarreux pprovince of Navarre . . .

"I was about [16] years of age when my Oncle . . . place me into the Counting Room [of] one of the First Mercantil Houses in [Valencia] where I remain for about 4 years, 2 of [them] in the Capacity of Book Keeper & Casier. Being desiros to see more of the country I left that place & House & went to the City of Madrid with the aprobation of my Oncle, & as Soon as I got to that Capital, I was placed in to the House of Messrs. Lucet & Co. Banquere. . . .

"An offer was Made to me by Messrs Lacase Mercy & Sons at that time one of the most reputable Houses in [Cadiz], to Come to America where they Carried great Business & where I should be Established & advance by them, . . . No sooner I got to Baltimore then my Friend Mr. Toey promise me that I should be the first man Interested in the Establishment of a House he was about forming in Virginia but before this took place Misfortunes on Misfortunes hapen to the House of Cadiz from the effects of the ware which disappointed all our Expectations & nothing was done for me by them but a compensation of about £200. Cash for what Services I had done to the House of Toey Brothers & Co. for about 16 months labour with which sume or a Little better I quit the House & Came to George Town [in] April 1785."

Charles Carroll of Duddington and Carrollsburg and his sister Mary, painted by John Wollaston the Younger, were the second generation of Carrolls to live on and own what eventually became Capitol Hill. They were the two oldest children of Daniel Carroll and Ann Rozier, the great landholder, from whom Charles Carroll acquired the Capitol Hill estate known as Duddington. His Carrollsburg designation derives from the port town he planned to develop on his lands at the mouth of the Anacostia. His house was one of the earliest in the Anacostia area. Built in 1759, when Carroll acquired the property, the house was located near the present Navy Yard, at the intersection of South Capitol Street, Que Street and Georgia Avenue. Mary Carroll married Ignatius Digges, whose family estates included the land opposite Mount Vernon, where Fort Washington was later erected.

Charles Carroll's grandfather, for whom he had been named, had been the first Carroll to settle in Maryland. A lawyer, a Catholic and an Irish gentleman, he had come to Maryland in 1680, after being appointed Attorney General of the colony by the Second Lord Baltimore. He became one of the largest landholders in Maryland and was deeply involved in the colony's political and social life. One of his two sons became the father of Charles Carroll of Carrollton, who lived near Baltimore and was a signer of the Declaration of Independence. The other son, Daniel Carroll, married Ann Rozier and was the first of the Carrolls to own Capitol Hill.

In 1791 Daniel Carroll of Duddington, son of Charles Carroll, was the proprietor of lands crucial to the planning of the Federal City. He was therefore in a commanding position and became a leading spokesman for the interests of the Carroll family and of the other proprietors.

Born in his father's house, Duddington, near the Anacostia River, Daniel Carroll had entered into the shipping business early in life and had important connections with prominent firms on both sides of the Atlantic. As a kinsman had written in a letter of introduction dated at "Baltr. 30 July 1785":

> "The Bearer Mr. Daniel Carroll is a young gentleman of this country of the first Family and Fortune here, he is my particular Friend and Name Sake. Therefore I introduce him to your Friendship and request you may show him every attention of civility in your power.
> "He goes to Europe merely for his improvement and proposes visiting Flanders, will accompany his cousin . . . Charles Carroll to the college at Liege where he remains for his education."

Fine Arts Commission, photo number 66-G-1B-53 in the National Archives

Daniel Carroll's own Duddington (right) was occupied by 1793, even though the building was still unfinished. Benjamin Latrobe finally completed it in 1797. First erected in what was to become New Jersey Avenue—to the extreme displeasure of Major L'Enfant—the house was subsequently rebuilt in the location shown in the plan (below). It was demolished in 1886.

Carroll and the other proprietors of lands in the area assumed that the selection of the Potomac site for the new Federal City would make them all rich men. Recalling those times, Daniel Carroll wrote in 1837 that the results were other than expected:

> "I perfectly remember that the general opinion was that so great was the gift that the citizens never would be subject to taxation for the improvement of the streets having relinquished every alternate lot to the Government. Instead some were so wild as to suppose . . . that the Government might pave the streets with ingots of gold or silver. After nearly half a century the result is now fully known: the unfortunate proprietors are generally brought to ruin and some with scarcely enough to buy daily food for their families."

Library of Congress, Geography and Maps Division

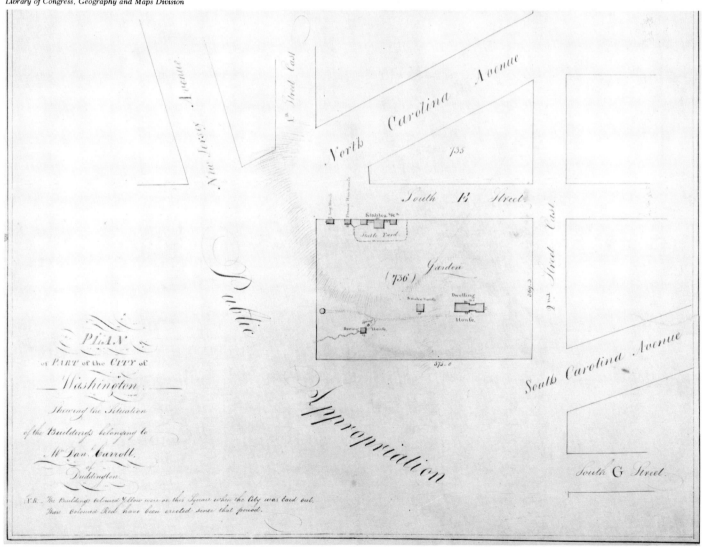

"None more elegant"

"The plans of the public buildings were obtained by public advertisement offering a reward for that most approved by Genl. Washington. General Washington knew how to give liberty to his country, but was wholly ignorant of art. It is therefore not to be wondered, that the design of a physician, who was very ignorant of architecture was adopted for the Capitol, and of a carpenter for the president's house. The latter is not even original, but a mutilated copy of a badly designed building near Dublin."

—Benjamin Henry Latrobe, 1806

Erroneously attributed to Abraham Faws, "A.Z." was the pseudonym for Thomas Jefferson. Either because he did not want to prejudice the decision, or because he was aware his design would not carry the day, Jefferson entered the President's House competition anonymously. The classical design was modeled after Palladio's Villa Rotonda near Vicenza.

Originally the job of designing the President's House and the Capitol Building was left to L'Enfant. As Washington wrote when he dismissed the architect from service, "five months have elapsed and are lost, by the compliment which was intended to be paid to you in depending *alone* upon your plans for the public buildings instead of advertising a premium to the person who should present the best." Having no designs from L'Enfant, the Commissioners resorted to holding a competition.

The competition to design the President's House was in time won by James Hoban (right), an Irish architect who had practiced for ten years in Charleston, South Carolina, and had designed the state capitol in Columbia. Hoban also designed Blodgett's Hotel in Washington and was actively involved in the city as a member of the Washington City Council from 1820 until his death in 1831. Hoban's original elevations for the White House closely resembled the 1810 drawing below which is probably by Samuel Blodgett. The design has often been compared to that of Leinster House in Dublin.

White House Collection

65

An Irishman, James Diamond, entered both the President's House and Capitol competitions unsuccessfully. Though often derided for the oversized rooster adorning the dome, Diamond's design indicates his awareness of classical architectural motifs, which he probably derived from pattern books.

As the site for the Capitol, L'Enfant selected "Jenkin's Heights," which may have been named after a farmer who leased land nearby. L'Enfant explained his reasons in a letter to George Washington:

> "After a minute search for other eligible situations, I may assert without apprehension of appearing prejudiced in favor of a first opinion, that I could not discover one in all respects so advantageous . . . for erecting the Federal House [as] the western end of Jenkin's Heights [which] stands ready as a pedestal waiting for a superstructure & I am confident were all the ground cleared of wood, no other situation could bear competition with this."

The award for the design of the Capital was not so easily determined. A newspaper advertisement was placed by the Commissioners in principal towns of the United States for both the President's Palace and the Capitol: "A premium of a lot in the city of Washington . . . and $500 shall be given by the Commissioners of the Federal Buildings to the person who before the 15th of July, 1792, shall produce to them the most approved plan for a Capitol to be executed in this city." As the deadline approached, however, an exasperated Washington wrote to Commissioner David Stuart (on July 9, 1792) that "if none more elegant than these should appear on or before the 10th instant, the exhibition of architecture will be a very dull one indeed."

Right up to the close of the competition, the designs of Stephen (Etienne) Hallet (opposite) were given the most favorable consideration, and he was led to believe that he would win the award. As Washington wrote to the Commissioners:

> "Some difficulty arises in respect to Mr. Hallett, who as you know was in some degree led into his plan by ideas we all expressed to him. This ought not to induce us to prefer it to a better; but while he is liberally rewarded for the time and labor he has expended on it, his feelings should be soothed as much as possible. I leave it to yourselves how best to prepare him for the possibility that the Doctor's [William Thornton's] plan may be prefered to his."

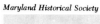

Because of the attention given to the windows and doorframes, it is likely that Phillip Hart was a carpenter or builder by trade and was unaccustomed to working on such a grand scale. The grotesque figures in his plan (above) are part of the original design.

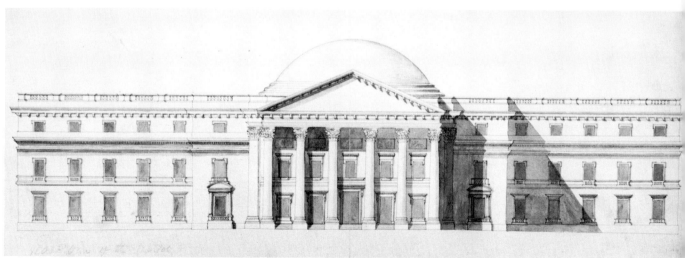

The winning design for the Capitol was acclaimed by George Washington for its "grandeur, simplicity, and beauty." It was submitted by Dr. William Thornton (left), a graduate in medicine from Edinburgh, who came to Philadelphia from the West Indies in 1787. Thornton later wrote that he "lamented not having studied architecture and resolved to attempt the grand undertaking and study at the same time." The design above, believed to be his original plan for the Capitol, is called the Tortola Scheme because it was drawn on that West Indies island. The fold over the right-hand wing offers an alternative façade.

After his arrival in Philadelphia, Thornton realized the inadequacy of his entry and radically altered the monumental design to suit Jefferson's stated preference for the architecture of classical antiquity. Jefferson's influence in selecting the final design was paramount, for as Washington himself admitted: "I profess to have no knowledge of Architecture."

Thornton went on to become a major figure in early Washington. He was architect of several important buildings, and he held numerous offices, including Commissioner of the Federal City, first superintendent of the Patent Office and vice-president of the D.C. Medical Society. As Mrs. Thornton wrote in her diary:

"His search after knowledge was perhaps too general, as it embraced almost every subject; . . . he cou'd have attained perfection in any art or science had he given up his mind solely to one pursuit—philosophy, politics, Finance, astronomy, medicine, Botany, Poetry, painting, religion, agriculture, in short, all subjects by turns occupied his active and indefatigable mind."

Thornton was noted as the author of a treatise on teaching the deaf and dumb and claimed to have collaborated with John Fitch on the invention of the steamboat. He was described by a contemporary as "a man of infinite humor—humane and generous . . . his company was a complete antedote to dullness."

In this drawing by Benjamin Latrobe (right) George Washington is shown being escorted by his fellow Masons to the laying of the cornerstone of the Capitol on September 18, 1793. According to the *Columbia Mirror and Alexandria Gazette* (September 23, 1793): "The procession marched . . . in the greatest solemn dignity, with music playing, drums beating, colors flying and spectators rejoicing, from the President's square to the Capitol." The trowel he used is exhibited in the Masonic Temple in Alexandria.

Alexandria–Washington Lodge No. 22, A.F. & A.M., Alexandria, Virginia

69

"Great Improvements are contemplated"

"The Avenues are all cut thro the woods, & these, together with the Basement Stories I have mentioned, & and here and there a House & Hut scattered, being excepted, this City, so splendid already in the exaggerating Tales of Fame consists of woods, Swamps & naked Hills of apparently thin sandy soil. But great Improvements are contemplated next Spring. House Lots (not water Lots) are held up high, say £100 & are offered for Sale in Europe at £150. In September 1793 the wealthy and enterprising James Greenleaf purchased 3000 lots of ground at 25 Maryland currency and this gave a sudden and amazing spring to the importance of the city. In Dec. 1793 Mr. Greenleaf associated Robert Morris and John Nicholson of Philadelphia both men of large capital and fertile minds with him in his speculations and purchased for Mr. Morris 3000 lots in the city at 34 M.C. a lot. The purchasers are bound to erect yearly a small number of houses on each 3rd lot for 7 years. Here then are 6000 lots owned by this powerful company, & great and immediate improvements are in contemplation. . . ."

—James Kent, 1793

Wheat Row, located at 1313 4th Street SW, was constructed in 1794–95 and was among the earliest Washington row houses. Built by James Greenleaf and his associates, Morris and Nicholson, Wheat Row's red bricks were purchased from Daniel Carroll. The row, which is still standing, takes its name from its owner and first occupant, John Wheat.

"In America, where, more than in any other country in the world, a desire for wealth is the prevailing passion, there are few schemes which are not made the means of extensive speculations; and that of the erecting of Federal-City presented irresistible temptations, which were not in fact neglected.
"Mr. Morris was among the first to perceive the probability of immense gain in speculations in that quarter; and in conjunction with Messrs. Nicholson and Greenleaf, a very short time after the adoption of the plan purchased every lot he could lay hold on, either from the commissioners or individual proprietors; that is to say, every lot that either one or the other would sell at that period."

—"Notes on the District,"
Duke de la Rochefoucauld-Liancourt, 1797

The corner building (left) belonged to a row known as the Seven Buildings and stood at 1901 Pennsylvania Avenue, NW. Started in 1794–95, the row was reputed to have been another venture of the over-extended Morris-Nicholson real-estate syndicate. At one time, this building was known as the house of 1,000 candles because of a celebrated evening reception given by Dolley Madison in honor of Andrew Jackson.

The Six Buildings (above), which were occupied by the Department of State, were built by Isaac Pollock, an important investor in the early city. Grandson of a founder of Truro Synagogue in Newport, Rhode Island, he was a man of education and means and was probably the first Jew to play an important role in city affairs. Pollock brought his family to Washington in 1795 and bought land and built in several locations. Pollock and Thornton, who had adjoining farms near Wisconsin Avenue and Bradley Boulevard, had many building projects in common. But like most early speculators, Pollock lost almost his entire fortune through property investments. One of his Six Buildings still stands on the north side of Pennsylvania Avenue near 21st Street.

The sketch map below was included in a letter written in 1796 by Nicholas King, a surveyor who was seeking to persuade a Philadephia friend to purchase a lot in the Federal City. The property, wrote King, was located on B Street, "on the summit of the Capitol Hill and will always command a view of the Mall, & public Gardens." The price was "about 400 Dollars" for approximately one-third of the block where the Longworth House Office Building now stands.

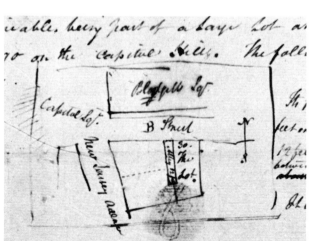

To demonstrate his confidence in the Federal City, President Washington built a double townhouse near the Capitol that was to be used as a boardinghouse. Attached houses were generally cheaper to build than houses built separately and at different times. In 1799 Washington wrote to William Thornton:

> "Although my house, or houses (for they may be one or two as occasion requires) are I believe, upon a larger scale than any in the vicinity of the Capitol, yet they fall short of your wishes. . . . The houses are three flush stories of Brick, besides Garret rooms;—and in the judgement of those better acquainted in these matters than I am, capable of accommodating between twenty and thirty boarders.—The buildings are not costly, but elegantly plain."

A plaque between the Capitol and Union Station marks the location of the houses, sketched above.

Elizabeth Parke Custis, granddaughter of Martha Washington, was married in 1795 to Thomas Law, a wealthy Englishman. Of the new Mrs. Law, the Duke de la Rochefoucauld-Liancourt, who stayed in the Law house during a 1797 visit to the city, observed that she was "an amiable woman, who unites accomplishments, sweetness of manner and a charming figure to a sound understanding, and all the qualities that contribute to make the married life happy."

Dumbarton House

This compote, a Custis family heirloom, was used in the Laws' house, which was a center of Washington social life.

Law had become deeply involved in real-estate speculation in the Federal City, having bought more property from the Morris–Nicholson syndicate than anyone else. Although Law was a member of a prominent British family and the former holder of high administrative offices in India, George Washington wrote at the time of the engagement: "Mr. Law, so far as I have obtained any knowledge of his character, is a respectable man and much esteemed . . . he is a stranger . . . prudence requires, and as a man of honor he cannot refuse to make a settlement upon her previous to marriage;—of her own fortune, if no more." His foresight protected Mrs. Law's Custis inheritance when their marriage ended in 1804. The following account, from William Faux's *Memorable Days in America*, appeared that same year:

> "Mr. Law settled on her, in case they parted, 15,000 a year. The event which seemed thus to be anticipated, soon after occurred; for Mr. Law visiting England soon after his marriage and leaving his wife in America, she, during his absence, eloped with a young dashing officer in the Army. Mr. Law returned only to part with one of the most accomplished ladies in the land. She lives in high style, and her house is the resort of the most fashionable parties."

In a letter to a friend, architect William Thornton described Mrs. Law shortly after her separation:

> "Mrs. Law has dashed in a very high military state lately, and I suppose will beat up for Amazonian Volunteers. My wife said she would write to your good Lady, and as all the dear Creatures like a little Tincture of Extravagance I am confident she will describe [Madame] Law in colours that even a Description of Cleopatra's Gala Suit could not touch. I shall leave Mrs. Law therefore on Horseback to be *taken off* by the Ladies, although attended by seven officers."

The Laws' separation led, several years later, to the city's first divorce. Mrs. Law resumed her maiden name. Afterward, writing in his former wife's defense, Law noted that "No elopement took place"; the separation was the result of a "disagreement in disposition." He added that he "always paid tribute correctly due to Mrs. Law's purity of conduct, which I never did empeach."

Honeymoon House, sometimes called the Law House, was rented by Thomas and Eliza Law during their honeymoon and the first year of their marriage. One of the city's earliest speculation houses, it was built in 1796 and still stands at 6th and N streets SW.

Thomas Law was one of many early investors who lost fortunes in speculative housing and real estate. The failure of the syndicates, such as Morris and Nicholson, was a severe blow, morally and financially, to the prestige of the city. The following impressions were recorded in 1806 by a visitor, Charles W. Jansen:

"Speculation, the life of the American, embraces the design of the new city. Several companies purchased lots and began to build, with an ardor that soon promised a large & populous city. Before they arrived at the attic story, the failure was manifest. . . . Except some houses uniformly built, with some public-houses, and here and there a little grog shop, this boasted [Pennsylvania] Avenue is as much wilderness as Kentucky. Some half-starved cattle browsing among the bushes present a melancholy spectacle to the stranger, whose expectation has been warmed up by the illusive descriptions of speculative writers. So very thinly is the city peopled that quails and other birds are constantly shot within a hundred yards of the capitol."

As another observer, Robert Sutcliff, wrote in 1804:

"We only need here houses, cellars, kitchens, scholarly men, amiable women, and a few other such trifles, to possess a perfect city. In a word, this is the best city in the world to live in—in the future."

Closely associated with many great occasions in George Washington's life, the ballroom at Gadsby's Tavern (above) in Alexandria was one of the largest public rooms in Colonial America, when buildings were distinguished by disciplined elegance rather than vast size. Here Washington's birth-night balls were annually held. As George Washington Parke Custis noted in his diary:

> "The birth-night balls were instituted at the close of the Revolutionary War and its first celebration, we believe, was held in Alexandria. Celebrations of the birth-night soon became general in all the towns and cities, the twenty-second of February, like the Fourth of July, being considered a national festival. . . . The last birth-night ball attended by the venerable chief was in 1798. Indeed he always appeared greatly to enjoy the gay and festive scene exhibited at the birth-night balls, and usually remained to a late hour."

The boys of Georgetown College, dressed in uniforms like this one, greeted General Washington when he visited Georgetown in 1798. As Christian Hines recalled, large crowds lined the town's streets to catch a glimpse of the general as he passed on his way to the house of Thomas Peter (where he spent his last night in the city):

> "On each side of Water Street, from the foot of High street . . . to the bridge, the citizens were ranged on either side while General Washington walked between them, uncovered and bowing to the people as he passed along. . . . The Georgetown College boys . . . were dressed in uniforms consisting in part of blue coats and red waistcoats, and presented a fine appearance."

"First in the hearts of his countrymen"

George Washington died at sixty-seven, in the last month of the last year of the eighteenth century, after he caught a chill while riding over his farms in a storm. He dismissed Dr. James Craik's efforts with "I feel myself going. I thank you for your attentions but I pray you to take no more trouble about me. Let me go off quietly." He gave Tobias Lear, his secretary, instructions about his funeral and died, after a four-day illness. Because of the storm, the funeral was held not at Christ Church, where Washington had been a vestryman, but at Alexandria's Presbyterian Church (below), which had been established by the Scots who founded the port town and which is still the site of a Presbyterian meetinghouse. The New York *Spectator* recorded the funeral oration that Alexandria Congressman "Light Horse Harry" Lee delivered before a joint session of Congress, in which Lee eulogized Washington as "First in war, first in peace, and first in the hearts of his countrymen."

"The reminiscences which the Alexandrians most cherish [wrote William Morrison in his 1844 *Guide* to Washington and vicinity] are those which associate their town with the domestic attachments and habits of [General] Washington. The reader of his letters and addresses will remember that he constantly speaks of them as his old and valued fellow-citizens, his kind and cherished neighbors and associates. Writing from York Town, he assures them that, 'amidst all the vicissitudes of time and fortune, he should ever regard with particular affection the citizens . . . of Alexandria.' . . . This friendly interest was manifested on every occasion, and a legacy of £1,000 to a free school in the town, testifies that it ceased only with his life."

At the 1800 parade honoring George Washington's birthday, the first after his death, this nine-year-old Alexandrian, Samuel Arell Marsteller, whose grandfather was one of George Washington's pallbearers, wore the uniform of the Boys Corps of Alexandria. Painted by Jacob Frymire, August 8, 1800.

75

Martha Parke Custis, nicknamed "Patsy," married Thomas Peter of Georgetown in 1795 and built Tudor Place, at 31st and Que. William Thornton, commissioned to design the house, presented drawings that included the design for the south façade that is shown here. The family thought this plan too elaborate and chose a simpler one, also by Thornton. The house is still in the family.

The heirs of Washington's affections—if not his blood—maintained a continuing presence in the city named in his honor. Houses lived in by all four of his wife's grandchildren still stand within twenty miles of the Capitol: Honeymoon House in Southwest Washington, where Elizabeth Parke Custis and her husband, Thomas Law, lived during part of their brief marriage; Tudor Place in Georgetown, built by Martha Parke Custis and her husband, Thomas Peter; Woodlawn, near Mount Vernon, built by Eleanor Washington Parke Custis and her husband, Lawrence Lewis; and Arlington (the Custis–Lee Mansion), built by George Washington Parke Custis and his bride, Mary Lee Fitzhugh.

Martha Washington's four grandchildren were the surviving children of Eleanor Calvert and John Parke Custis, the son of Martha Washington and her first husband, Colonel Daniel Parke Custis of Arlington. When John Parke Custis died of "camp fever" at the battle of Yorktown in 1781, the two youngest children, Eleanor and George, were taken to Mount Vernon, where they were adopted by George and Martha Washington. The two older girls continued to live with their mother, who later married Dr. David Stuart, one of the first three Commissioners of the Federal City. Stuart visited Mount Vernon often, and the two households stayed in close touch. The names of Elizabeth and Martha Parke Custis appear in Washington's diaries almost as often as those of the Mount Vernon children, Eleanor and George.

George Washington Parke Custis, seen here in an 1808 portrait, was referred to all his life as "The Child of Mount Vernon." But in 1802, when Martha Washington died, Mount Vernon went to the General's nephew Bushrod Washington. The will left to Washington Custis the "tract on Four Mile Run in the vicinity of Alexandria containing 1200 acres." On this site young Custis immediately began to build Arlington, which was to be called "one of the earliest and most notable of the houses of the Greek Revival." A wing was built first, and to this little house in 1804 Custis brought his sixteen-year-old bride, Mary Lee Fitzhugh. Designed by architect George Hadfield, the building was not completed until 1820.

Throughout Custis' life the house was very much a shrine to the first President. Mount Vernon furnishings filled the house, and the campaign tent from Valley Forge was set up on the riverside on festive occasions. When Custis died in 1856 Arlington went to his only child, Mary Anne Randolph Custis, who lived there as the wife of Robert E. Lee. In the spring of 1861, when Virginia seceded, the Lees left Arlington. The house, now called the Custis–Lee Mansion, was eventually restored by the National Park Service; its grounds became Arlington Cemetery. Wrote Sarah E. Vedder in her *Reminiscences of the District of Columbia* (1830–51):

> "Arlington . . . was daily visited by strangers, and many were the picnic parties enjoyed there in the lovely woods surrounding the mansion. . . . Mr. Custis had two or three pavillions built to accommodate the parties, either to set the tables or to dance. Frequently he would come down to the grounds and participate in their amusements. He has been known to take his violin and play for the dancers."

The Government Arrives

"About this time, 1800, the seat of Government was being removed from Philadelphia to Washington City. The vessels in which was brought the furniture, &c., landed and discharged their cargoes at Lear's wharf, and as the vessels were unladen, their contents were carted away to the War and Navy offices, the only two that were built at the time. Some of the furniture was stored away in the stone ware-house and afterwards taken away in wagons, it being too bulky to be removed in carts. Wagons were rather scarce in Washington then, and our cart was engaged with others in removing the boxes of books, papers, &c."

—Christian Hines, 1866

This unpublished 1801 watercolor view by J. Benford shows Washington's Potomac shore as it looked at about the time the government was moved to the District from Philadelphia. It shows the riverfront from Georgetown on the left almost to "Turky Buzzard" Point—the tip of land where the Anacostia River originally met the Potomac. The center cluster of buildings is Lear's Wharf, which was built and operated by George Washington's secretary, Tobias Lear. The first bridge over Rock Creek, at M Street, is seen at left. In a print similar to this at the Library of Congress, the large building on the hill on the right is identified as Duddington, the house on the river as Thomas Law's. Above that on the right, Wheat Row, and left of the Law house, up the hill, is the insignificant two-story building that was the Capitol in 1800.

Stagecoaches, horses and private carriages kept the roads leading to Washington busy in 1800 as government officials and their families came to the new capital. In mid-May, Benjamin Stoddert, the Secretary of the Navy, wrote to a Georgetown friend to inform him that President John Adams would soon be arriving in town on a brief inspection trip. In his letter, Stoddert urged that the President be given a warm reception:

> "He proposes to stay but a little while. I wish he would remain longer. This and other good things will depend on the manner of employing his time. I request, therefore, that setting Bashfulness at defiance, you will urge the Pres. to go to the balls, to ride with you in your coach. . . . Let [him] be pleased with the attention and with the country."

On June 3, Mrs. Thornton noted in her diary that "the President has arrived." The next day she wrote:

> "The president came bye about three O'clock, Dr. T. had a horse got ready, & with some other Gentlemen accompanied him to the Capitol. He stopt first at his house & the Treasury Office. He travels in a Chariot & four. and is going to Lodge at Tunnicliffe's Tavern on the Capitol Hill."

In November Abigail Adams traveled to Washington—with a considerable entourage—by way of the Post Road from Baltimore to join her husband. In a letter to her sister she described the last leg of the journey:

> "Having lost my way in the woods on Saturday in going from Baltimore, we took the road to Fred-

Most travelers came to Washington by way of Bladensburg (opposite), the main stop on the Post Road from Baltimore. Writing of an inn there, Thomas Twining noted that "over the fireplace in the dining room was a plan of Washington, with the streets, squares, and public buildings of the intended city minutely detailed." Abigail Adams, for one, found more comfortable lodgings a few miles up the road at "Montpelier" (below), which Major Thomas Snowden built for his wife, Ann Ridgely. The house still stands today. At right: the box in which the much-traveled John Adams kept his beaver hat.

Privately owned

erick and got nine miles out of our road. You find nothing but a Forest and woods on the way, for 16 and 18 miles not a village. Here and there a thatched cottage without a single pane of glass, inhabited by Blacks. My intention was to have reached Washington on Saturday. Last winter there was a Gentleman and Lady in Philadelphia by the Name of Snowden whose hospitality I heard much of. They visited me and were invited to dine with us, but did not, as they left the city before the day for dinner. They belong to Maryland, and live on the road to this place 21 miles distant. I was advised at Baltimore to make their House my stage for the night, the only Inn at which I could put up being 36 miles ride from Baltimore. . . . I set out early, expecting to make my 36 miles if possible; no travelling however but by daylight; We took a direction as we supposed right, but in the first turn, went wrong, and were wandering more than two hours in the woods in different paths, holding down and breaking bows of trees which we could not pass, until we met a solitary black fellow with a horse and cart. We inquired of him our way, and he kindly offered to conduct us, which he did two miles, and then gave us such a clue as led us out to the post road and the Inn, where we got some dinner. Soon after we left it, we met the chariot then 30 miles from Washington, and 20 from our destination. We rode as fast as the roads would allow of, but the sun was near set when we came in sight of the Majors. I halted but could not get courage to go to his House with ten horses and nine persons. I therefore ordered the coach man to proceed, and we drove rapidly on. We had got about a mile when we were stopped by the Major in full speed, who had learnt that I was coming on; and had kept watch for me, with his Horse at the door; as he was at a distance from the road. In the kindest, and politest manner he urged my return to his House, represented the danger of the road, and the impossibility of my being accommodated at any Inn I could reach; A mere hovel was all I should find. I plead my numbers. That was no objection. He could accommodate double the number. There was no saying nay and I returned to a large, Handsome, Elegant House, where I was received with my Family, with what we might term true English Hospitality, Friendship without ostentation, and kindness without painful ceremony. . . . I need not add that they are all true federal Characters. Every attention possible was shown me and the next morning I took my departure, having shared in the common bounty of Major Snowden's hospitality, for which he is universally celebrated—I arrived about one o'clock at this place known by the *name of the city*, and the Name is all that you can call so. As I expected to find it a new country, with Houses scattered over a space of ten miles, and trees and stumps in plenty with a castle of a House—so I found it—The Presidents House is in a beautiful situation in front of which is the Potomac with a view of Alexandria. The country around is romantic but a wild, a wilderness at present."

Privately owned

81

"The entrance or avenues, as they are pompously called, which lead to the Am. seat of gov't, are the worst roads I passed in the country. . . . Deep ruts, rocks, and stumps of trees every minute impede yr. progress and threaten yr. limbs with dislocation."

—Charles W. Janson, 1806

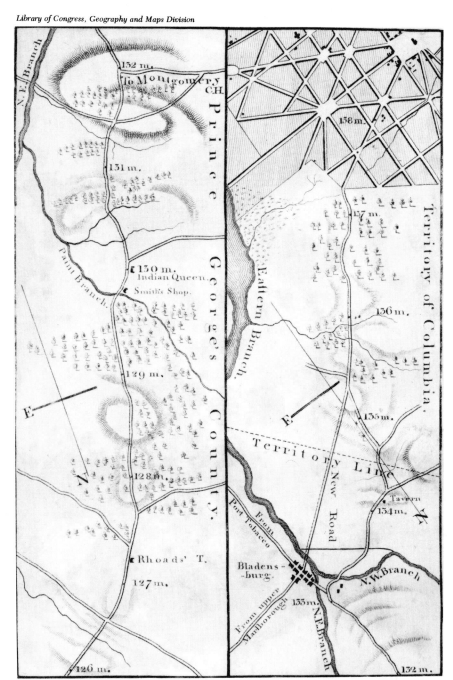

The last twelve miles of the Post Road into Washington from Philadelphia are shown in the map at left, circa 1802. The Post Road was one of the most frequently traveled roads into the capital. The Duke de La Rochefoucauld-Liancourt, who entered the city in 1797 by taking a ferry across the Eastern Branch (the Anacostia River), wrote that the crossing was made "in a tolerably good boat, a little too flat, and a great deal too small for the quantity of horses which are taken into it. I passed in this boat with ten horses and a carriage, and was uneasy till I arrived on the other side."

Virginia Congressman John Randolph, riding to Washington in the middle of December 1821, left this account of fording the Accotink, near Alexandria, after traveling six days on the main road from Richmond:

"Very cold. . . . Waters out. . . . As I pressed my little mare on [I] found the water-mark under water. Pohick, a most dangerous ford at all times . . . was behind me, and no retreat and no house better than old Lear's hovel, except the church, where [there] were no materials for a fire. When I reached Accotink the sand bank in the middle of the stream was uncovered, but for near a mile I was up to the saddle-skirts. A great price, my good sir, for the privilege of franking a letter and the honor of being overlooked by the great men [of Congress], new as well as old."

Chain Bridge near Georgetown was painted by Benjamin H. Latrobe in the early 1800s. The first bridge across the Potomac (a ferry ran by Analostan as early as 1720), Chain Bridge was first built in 1797, when the toll was ten pence. Repeatedly washed away by floods and ice storms, the bridge was rebuilt many times. John Shippen of Philadelphia, who traveled to Washington in 1801, described the bridge this way:

"Three miles from Georgetown just at the head of tide water & at what are called the little falls, a bridge of single arch crosses the Potomac. It is composed of wood. Erected by one Palmer of Connecticut I was told that it was framed by him in Connecticut & shipped round in its multiplicity of pieces. The abuttments are a huge pile of mossy square stones bolted together with great iron pins & melted lead, a novel sight to me and I take it completely resistable of the most swollen floods of water. The Virginia side a high bank, Maryland side low base of immoveable large deep rocks. Here the Potomac is narrow and deep."

A vivid picture of the capital city as it appeared in 1803 was recorded by an English visitor in this letter, made available by Walter Muir Whitehill:

"Well we got here from Baltimore early on tuesday morning, having travelled the greatest part of the night. . . . The first notice you have of this embryo London (or to be more in tone with the American modesty this embryo Rome) is a small stone between two stumps of trees upon which is inscribed "The boundary of the City." This is proper enough for you have got about two miles to go before you fall in with a single inhabitant to tell you so. Immediately upon leaving this stone you rise a hill and come upon a large plain . . . and then first see the Capitol, a ponderous unfinished mass of brick and stone . . . one or two brick buildings with corresponding sheds, half a dozen stragling houses or fragments of houses fill up the view till you get there which now being the highest ground gives you a complete command of the Potomack with both its branches, together with George Town—I can compare the cite upon which the Capitol stands and about a mile in circumference to the top of a Quakers hat and the rest of this imperial city comprised on its brim. . . . Directly opposite . . . and distant about two hundred yards is half a dozen handsome brick houses . . . fitted up for boarding lodgers and an hotel—a few irregular paltry single houses and hovels make up the rest of this side. On the South between the crown and the brim to follow my old metaphor Mr. [Thomas] Law has built half a row of houses from eight to ten much like the other ones mentioned before and somebody else has been goose enough to follow his example and fill up the same space on the opposite side of the street—this is about a quarter of a mile from the Capitol and the only spot till you get to George Town (three miles,) which can be called anything like a street. There now only remain the N and W sides. The first will soon be finished as there are not above ten buildings over the whole space and those a moderate walk from one another on the West.

84

This watercolor by William R. Birch shows the Capitol in 1800, when only one wing of the building had been completed. The map below, published about two years later, shows the extent of settlement in the city at the time. A list of Washington buildings drawn up in November 1801 showed a total of 621 houses standing on private land—almost double the number that had existed eighteen months before. Of these, 207 were of brick and 414 of wood. Thomas Twining, who arrived in the city in April 1796, noted that

"Although no habitation of any kind was visible, I had no doubt but I was now riding along one of the streets of the metropolitan city. I continued in this spacious avenue for half a mile, and then came out upon a large spot cleared of wood, in the center of which I saw two buildings on an extensive scale and some men at work upon one of them . . . the plan which I had seen hung up in the dining-room at Bladensburg had prepared me for something rather more advanced."

Library of Congress, Geography and Maps Division

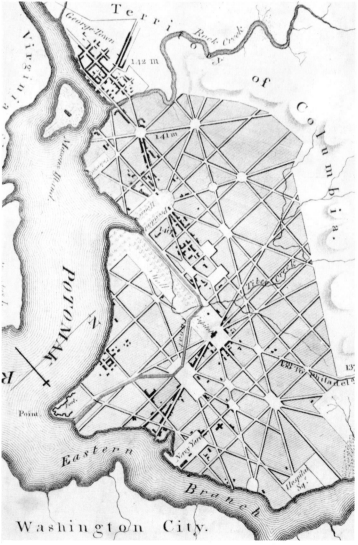

After having got down into my brim there is a most noble raised road with foot paths on each side with a row of poplars . . . which last the whole way to the Presidents palace—a distance of about a mile and three quarters. On this road the number of Citizens may amount to about fifty families. The Palace is . . . without any fence but a few broken rails upon which hang his excellencys stockings and shirts to dry and his maids blue petticoat—acting almost as wings to this stone building are two immense brick piles which contain the public offices such as Secretary of State Treasury and post office—from here as you approach the Rock Creek you find a thicker settlement but it is not till you cross the creek and get to George Town which was meant as it were only to the Western suburbs to this magnificent city that you can possibly conceive yourself to be in even a country town. It is curious to observe that in spite of all the governments plans to force the population towards the center of the Town that it has uniformly resisted, and is now progressing in a contrary direction."

85

Buildings were far apart and farm animals roamed the streets when the watercolor above was painted, about 1803, by surveyor Nicholas King. The President's House can be seen in the distance (left of center), while at right is the Patent Office, originally built to be Blodgett's Hotel, at 8th and E streets NW. The hotel was designed by James Hoban as the grand prize in a lottery scheme. Here, in 1800, Washington's first theatrical performance was held. "The building, at the time, was not finished," recalled Christian Hines. "The floor was but temporarily laid with rough boards. The seats, also, were all rough boards, laid down to serve as benches." The hotel was never finished and the lottery prize never awarded. Instead, the building was used to house various civil and governmental offices and was purchased by the government in 1810. It burned in 1837.

Of the President's House at this time, Benjamin Ogle Tayloe noted: "The house and grounds remained in an unfinished and neglected state, the latter wholly unimproved, and enclosed only by a post and rail fence of wood, which assimilated with the democratic simplicity of the day." Yet the house was still too imposing for Thomas Jefferson. Moving in 1801, he found it "big enough for two emperors, one pope, and the grand lama." He did add colonnaded wings on each side for servants quarters, an ice house, workshops, storage for provisions, a wine cellar, and a henhouse. However, a visitor from Ireland, Thomas Moore, observed that Jefferson, in his "philosophical humility . . . inhabits but a corner of the mansion himself and abandons the rest to a state of uncleanly desolation, which those who are not philosophers cannot look at without regret."

Department of State

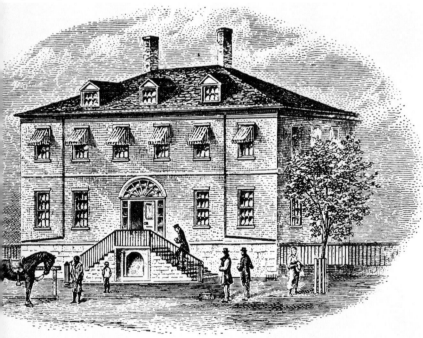

The Treasury Building is seen here as it appeared in 1800, when Washington became the seat of government. At the time the city had a population of 3,000, and the federal government consisted of five departments: State, Treasury, War, Navy and Post Office, employing a total of 137 clerks. Washington was still a small town, with a small town's intimacy. Christian Hines remembered seeing President John Adams for the first time

"when the Treasury office was on fire. When the alarm of the fire was given, several brothers and myself ran up F street to where the fire was. We were informed that the President was in the line, and was busy in aiding to pass the buckets to and from the burning building. So curiosity to see the President induced us to go up where he was, and there, sure enough, we saw him in the line engaged as above stated. . . . At that time, 1800, we had no hose; consequently, we had to fill our engines with leather fire-buckets by forming two lines to the pump,—one line to pass the full buckets to the engine, and the other line to pass them back to be filled again."

"Our local situation is far from being pleasant or even convenient. Around the Capitol are seven or eight boarding houses, one tailor, one shoemaker, one printer, a washing woman, a grocery shop, a pamphlets and stationery shop, a small dry goods shop and an oyster house. This makes the whole of the Federal City as connected with the Capitol."

—Secretary of the Treasury Albert Gallatin,
January 15, 1801

Newly arrived government officials—most of whom came to Washington without their families—usually found lodging in the city's hotels and boardinghouses. According to a contemporary newspaper account, the boardinghouse brought "together around the common mess-table, kindred spirits," who were often from the same section of the country and often voted as a bloc in Congress.

For some newcomers, life in a boardinghouse was a grim prospect. Oliver Wolcott, Jr., Secretary of the Treasury under John Adams, wrote in July 1800:

"I do not perceive how the members of Congress can possibly secure lodgings, unless they will consent to live like scholars in a college or monks in a monastery, crowded ten or twenty in one house, and utterly secluded from society. The only resource for such as wish to live comfortably will, I think, be found in Georgetown, three miles distant, over as bad a road, in winter, as the clay grounds near Hartford."

Vice President Thomas Jefferson, who moved into a Capitol Hill boardinghouse in November 1800, had no such qualms. As noted by one Washington chronicler, Margaret Bayard Smith, Jefferson

"lived on in perfect equality with his fellow boarders, and ate at a common table. Even here, so far from taking precedence of the other members of Congress, he always placed himself at the lowest end of the table. Mrs. Brown, wife of the senator from Kentucky, suggested that a seat should be offered him at the upper end, near the fire, if not on account of his rank as vice-President, at least as the oldest man in the company. But the idea was rejected . . . and he occupied during the whole winter the lowest and coldest seat at a long table at which a company of more than thirty sat down."

Mr. Jefferson, however, stayed at the boardinghouse for only four months. In March 1801 he became President and moved to the White House.

Carroll Row (left) stood near the Capitol, on what is now the site of the Library of Congress. It was built in 1805 by Daniel Carroll, who leased it to Pontius D. Stelle, a local innkeeper. Mr. Stelle advertised his new place of business as "a building about 100 feet front and containing fifty rooms [which] enables the subscriber to offer every accommodation to members of Congress and travelers."

Fine Arts Commission, photo number 66-G-23N-18 in the National Archives

"The private houses are all plain buildings; most of them have been built on speculation, and still remain empty. The greatest numbers, at any one place, is at Green Leaf's Point, on the main river, just above the entrance of the eastern branch. This spot has been looked upon by many as the most convenient one for trade. . . . Some build near the capitol, as the most convenient place for the residence of members of Congress, some near the President's House; others again prefer the West end of the city, in the neighborhood of Georgetown, thinking that as trade is already established in that place, it must be from thence that it will extend into the city."

—Isaac Weld, an English visitor, 1795

With the arrival of the government came men of means to build prominent private houses. Among them was Timothy Caldwell of Philadelphia, who, in 1802, purchased the property at 2017 I Street NW and set out to erect the "handsomest house in the Capital City." His house, seen at left, was afterward occupied by James Monroe and his family prior to his Presidency. Since 1915 it has served as the home of the Arts Club. Robert Brent, who was appointed by Thomas Jefferson to be Washington's first mayor, built his house (below) in 1809, at the corner of 12th Street and Maryland Avenue SW. Brent, who married Notley Young's daughter, built the "House Next to the Corner" for his son.

"Mr. J. Tayloe, of Virginia, has contracted to build a house in the City near the President's Square of $13,000 value," wrote architect William Thornton to George Washington in April 1799. John Tayloe III, seen above in a portrait by St. Memin, built his house at 1741 New York Avenue NW for twice as much as Thornton estimated. The watercolor of The Octagon (top right), with the White House in the background, was painted between 1830 and 1840 by John Ross Key (a grandson of Francis Scott Key). The Octagon's elaborate hip roof was probably added around 1818.

In the room at right President James Madison signed the Treaty of Ghent, which ended the War of 1812 and formed the basis of the present-day alliance between the United States and Great Britain. The President and Mrs. Madison had made The Octagon their temporary residence after the British burned the President's House in 1814. One of the city's finest examples of Federal architecture, The Octagon today is part of the headquarters of the American Institute of Architects.

Business . . .

About 1798 "business was beginning to be pretty brisk in Washington," recalled Christian Hines. This rare drawing, done in that same year, is a plan by Nicholas King for a shop that was to be erected at the corner of South Capital and N streets NW. As Hines wrote:

"Some of the public buildings were nearly finished, and others were in a state of advancement. People began to talk about settling here, and selected such lots as would suit best the business they were engaged in respectively. . . . I remember that, sometime previous to this, a few friends assembled at my father's house for the purpose of consulting with each other as to where would be the most suitable place to settle. Among these gentlemen were Mr. Stettineus, a bookbinder, and Nicholas Sparrow, a tailor. . . . On [the] square between H and I and Vermont [were] two two-story brick houses called the 'Two Sisters,' one of which was occupied by Captain Andrews and the other, to the north by a Mr. Middleton, as a cabinet makers' shop. In this house some of the first mahogany desks were made for congress in 1800, [before] the first session . . . in Washington."

Washington's first market stood on the President's Square, almost opposite the White House. In January 1801 the citizens moved to get rid of the random sheds and stalls and to build a proper market house on Pennsylvania Avenue between Seventh and Ninth streets. The site chosen became "Market Square," an important center in the life of the city for the next 130 years. Beginning on Tuesday, December 15, 1801, when the Center Market opened, Tuesdays, Thursdays and Saturdays were Market Days. David Ballie Warden wrote in 1816: "Two of the luxuries of life, pine-apples and ice, are found at Washington at a cheap rate. The former, imported from the West Indies, are sold at twenty-five cents each. The latter article is purchased, throughout the summer, at half a dollar per bushel."

and Pleasure

Horseracing, cockfighting and the theater were traditional in Virginia and Maryland. Racing provided occasions for lively social gatherings, often led by John Tayloe III, who was the founder of the Jockey Club. As William Plummer wrote in 1803:

"Annually when John Tayloe, famed for his wealth, his beautiful residence, the Octagon House, and his blooded horses, entered his trotters at the Jockey Club meets, the halls of Congress emptied, no matter what important public business was pending. At the track laid out in a field north of the city 'persons of all descriptions from the president and chief officers of state, down to their negro slaves . . . collected together, driving full speed about the course, shouting, betting, drinking, quarrelling and fighting.' "

According to Christian Hines, Washington's first racecourse was located near Washington Circle, "somewhere between F & K and Twenty-first and Twenty-third streets. At times the sport of cock-fighting was indulged in here also." There were other racecourses near Franklin Square (13th and K streets NW) and in Mt. Pleasant.

Games of chance also offered popular entertainment. On July 5, 1803, Samuel Harrison Smith wrote: "By the by, what do you think of my going to such an extent as to win 2Doll. at Loo the first time I ever played the game, and being the most successful player at the table? I confess I felt some mortification at putting the money of Mrs. Madison and Mrs. Duval into my pocket."

Theater came to the "10 miles square" as early as 1768, when road companies from major American cities and England visited Alexandria. Performances were given in local taverns and halls. Then, in 1798, Liberty Hall, Alexandria's first theater, was built. A year later, in Georgetown, a theater was opened in Mrs. Suter's ballroom in Union Tavern; and in August 1800 the first regular place of amusement in the new city, the United States Theater, was opened in Samuel Blodgett's hotel. The Washington Theater, the first building erected in the capital as a theater, was built by subscription in 1804 and opened on September 11, 1805. For the next sixteen years The Washington presented a variety of fare ranging from light comedy to Shakespeare. Rebuilt after a fire, it reopened in 1822 as the City Assembly Rooms and long remained a fashionable gathering place for Washington society.

THE CELEBRATED ENGLISH *RUNNING HORSE* CLIFDEN,

WILL stand the ensuing season at my Farm in Prince Georges county, about 5 miles from Queen Ann, 9 from Bladensburg, the same distance from Upper Marlborough, and about 15 from the city of Washington, at 2 DOLLARS the season; but 20 DOLLARS will be received in FULL if paid within the season; which will commence in March and end on the 1st of August. Good pasture will be furnished gratis, as soon as the grass is good,

The advertisement above appeared in *The National Intelligencer* of April 15, 1807. Below is *The Intelligencer's* account of the opening night of The Washington Theatre in September 1805.

On Monday the Theatre was opened with Wives as they Were, and the Sprigs of Laurel. In conformity to our expectations the House is fitted up with great neatness. The ornaments are few, but are plain and elegant. There is a distinct view of the whole stage from every quarter of the house ; and the seats are placed at a convenient distance from each other. The *coup d'œil* impresses the eye very agreeably, by presenting the appearance of harmony, unity, and accommodation. The whole house, the stage as well as that part occupied by the audience, appears like one elegant room, happily proportioned and neatly furnished. And what is of the first importance, the spectator receives every word uttered by the actor.

The National Intelligencer,
AND
WASHINGTON ADVERTISER.

Vol. I. WASHINGTON CITY, PRINTED BY SAMUEL HARRISON SMITH, NEW-JERSEY AVENUE, NEAR THE CAPITOL. No. LXXXI.

FIVE DOLLS. PER ANN.   FRIDAY, MAY 8th, 1801.   PAID IN ADVANCE.

America's first national newspaper, *The National Intelligencer*, began publication in 1801, shortly after the government moved to the Federal City. Founded by young Samuel Harrison Smith, a twenty-eight-year-old Philadelphian who was the son of a member of the Continental Congress, the paper was published three times each week and cost $5 per year. One of its employees, Joseph Gales, was the only reporter covering Senate proceedings between 1807 and 1820; he sat beside the Vice President and shared his snuffbox.

In 1810 Gales bought the *Intelligencer* from Smith. Gales's brother-in-law, William Seaton, joined him as co-editor and co-owner in 1812, and in the following year they made the paper a daily. Long the city's only newspaper, the *Intelligencer* enjoyed government support and was recognized as the official voice of the Adams, Jefferson and Madison administrations. Despite the loss of official patronage it lasted until the Civil War. In the meantime, Gales and Seaton also published twenty-nine volumes of the *Register of Debates in Congress*, 1825–1837; *Annals of Congress* (published intermittently through 1856); and thirty-eight volumes of the *American State Papers*, 1832–1861.

Charles Lanman, recalling the Gales-Seaton partnership of 1812, wrote in 1860:

> "From this period, of course, their stories, like their lives, became united, and merge, with a rare concord, into one. They have had no bickerings, no misunderstanding, no difference of view which a consultation did not at once reconcile; they have never known a division of interests; from their common coffer each has always drawn whatever he chose; and, down to this day, there has never been a settlement. What facts could better attest not merely a singular harmony of character, but an admirable conformity of virtues?"

The office of *The National Intelligencer*, pulled down by the British in 1814, is shown here as it appeared after it was rebuilt. The building stood at the corner of 9th and E streets NW.

92

Joseph Gales, Jr., co-owner and co-editor of *The National Intelligencer* and mayor of Washington from 1827 to 1830, is shown here in a portrait by Charles Bird King. British by birth, Joseph Gales was singled out for special enmity by Britain's Admiral Cockburn during his attack on Washington in 1814. Margaret Bayard Smith, wife of the founder of the *Intelligencer*, recorded the event in her diary:

> "When [Admiral Cockburn] went to burn Mr. Gales office, whom he called his 'dear Josey,' Mrs. Brush, Mrs. Stelle and a few citizens remonstrated with him, assuring him that it would occasion the loss of all the buildings in the row. 'Well,' he said, 'good people I do not wish to injure you, but I am really afraid my friend Josey will be affronted with me, if after burning Jemmy's palace [James Madison's White House] I do not pay him the same compliment, —so my lads, take your axes, pull down the house, and burn the papers in the street.' "

This was accordingly done. He also ordered that all the C's in the type case be destroyed so that future editions could not vilify his name.

This silver cup, owned by family descendants, was, according to the inscription, awarded at a fair as a prize for

> "the fattest Swine
> to J. Gales, Jr.
> Tendered by the hands of La Fayette
> November 1824."

A middle-aged William W. Seaton, co-owner and co-editor of *The National Intelligencer* and mayor of Washington from 1840 to 1850, photographed by Mathew Brady.

"The state of female society at Washington does great honour to the sex. . . . They are certainly superior women, highly gifted in mental, as they are adorned with personal endowments."

—David Ballie Warden, 1816

Washington's two most important early diarists were Mrs. Samuel Harrison Smith and Mrs. William Thornton. Margaret Bayard Smith came to Washington from Philadelphia in 1800 as the bride of the founder of *The National Intelligencer*. Through the remaining forty-four years of her life she kept the same interest and pleasure expressed in her novel, *A Winter in Washington*:

> "I cannot hope to infuse into others the enthusiasm I felt on my first arrival in the metropolis of our empire; an enthusiasm excited rather by the association of ideas, than by the existing scene. The Tiber ! The Capitol ! were words which imparted a charm to every surrounding object; and never can I forget the emotions which I felt the first time I climbed the hill on which the Capitol is built."

Margaret Bayard Smith's diaries, letters and published works chronicled the growth of the city. The beginnings of schools, churches, charities, city government, the arrival of artists, the establishment of theaters, the erection of new buildings both public and private were duly noted. From her prolific pen come some of our warmest pictures of early Washington.

Margaret Bayard Smith

Anna Maria Brodeau, the wife of Dr. William Thornton, the architect, began her Washington diary on January 1, 1800. The Thorntons' F Street house, midway between the Capitol and the White House, served as a message center. On March 22 she writes that "Messrs Law, Lear & Lewis stopped at the door, on their way to and from George Town." On June 30 she notes that "Mr. Law called while we were at breakfast. Mr. Fitzhugh called. Genl Lee stopped at the door. Genl Marshall's brother also was at the door. Dr. T. went to the office." Her diary continues:

> "[January 4] . . . thence to the Capitol, where we staid for some time by a fire in a room where they were glazing the windows—while Dr. T-n laid out an Oval round which is to be the communication to the Gallery of the Senate Room
> "[January 7] After dinner we Walked to take a look at Mr Tayloe's house [The Octagon] which begins to make a handsome appearance
> "[February 5] Dr. T—at work all day on the East Elevation of the Capitol.—I assisted a little 'till Evening then worked at my netting.
> "[March 20] After breakfast we walked with Dr. T. to the ground behind the President's House, which he is going to have inclosed &c laid out for a garden—it is at present in great confusion, having on it old brick kilns, pits to contain Water used by the brick makers, rubbish &c &c.

Anna Maria Brodeau Thornton, by Gilbert Stuart

"[December 20] Bought a wooden tray of a Negro Man, who has purchased his freedom by making them & bowls at his leisure time. . . . Did all I cou'd with Dr. T's directions to the plan of the Capitol. Waggon came with hay &c"

The wives of the *Intelligencer*'s co-owners and editors were leaders in Washington's early social life and official hostesses when their husbands served as mayors. Sara Juliana Maria Lee, niece of "Light-Horse Harry" Lee, married newspaperman Joseph Gales, Jr., in 1813. She played a dynamic part in his career. As her niece wrote:

> "The stenographic report of that speech [the Webster–Hayne states-right debate] was made by Mr. Joseph Gales, Jr., himself; but in order that the speech of Mr. Webster should appear in the National Intelligencer without delay, on his return from the Capitol, Mr. Gales from his stenographic notes, dictated the text to Mrs. Gales who wrote it out in a beautiful English hand, and the speech duly and punctually appeared, to Mr. Webster's great satisfaction."

In town, the Gales lived, variously, at Ashburton House (see page 131) and the house west of Blodgett's hotel (see page 86). Eckington, their country house, was designed by Charles Bird King. It was northeast of the city near the Smiths' place, formerly called Turkey Thicket. The Smiths' house was incorporated into Catholic University's first building. The Seatons also had a farm nearby. Their name, Turkey Thicket and Eckington all survive as place names in that part of town.

Juliana Gales Seaton was the sister of one Washington editor and mayor and the wife of another. The Seatons' house on E Street, near that of the Gales's, was the scene of a ball for Lafayette on December 15, 1824. The next day Mrs. Seaton wrote in her diary:

> "Last night had the high gratification of entertaining and welcoming Lafayette in our own house, being the only private individuals so honored, as yet. Three hundred and sixty persons took leave of him last evening, being within a score of those invited; and although a very crowded party, I hope not an unpleasant one to the Old General. He is very lame, and we contrived to keep him seated as much as his extreme politeness would allow. . . . My chamber and the large nursery were *deranged* and *arranged* for the occasion, serving as card and supper rooms. We danced in the dining and drawing rooms."

At right, Sara Juliana Maria Lee, the wife of Joseph Gales, Jr., and, below, Juliana Gales Seaton and her children. Both are shown in portraits by Washington artist Charles Bird King.

95

The Jefferson Stable School, at 14th and G streets NW, was remodeled from the White House Stable built in 1800. It was used as a school until about 1870. The sampler of a schoolhouse was worked by Julia Ann Crowley in Washington in 1813.

"Dr T-n received a Letter from an old acquaintance wishing to know if he could meet with encouragement here as a Minister & Tutor in a school. —The City is yet too young for a minister to live & too near George Town for a school at present."

—Mrs. Thornton, January 5, 1800

"Sincerely believing that knowledge promotes the happiness of men, I shall ever be disposed to contribute my endeavors toward its extension," wrote Thomas Jefferson when he was elected the first president of the Board of Trustees that established the city's public schools. In 1804 Congress authorized the City Council "to provide for the establishment and superintendence of public schools," which were supported by taxes and private subscription. Jefferson gave $200. Thus, the city's Eastern and Western Schools were founded. As *The National Intelligencer* reported in 1805:

> "The academy shall consist of as many schools as circumstances may require, to be limited at present to two, one of which shall be situated east of the Capitol . . . the other within half a mile of the President's house. . . . In these schools poor children shall be taught reading, writing, grammar, arithmetic, and such branches of mathematics as may qualify them for the professions they intend to follow, and they shall receive such other instruction as is given to pay pupils, as the board may from time to time direct, and pay pupils shall, besides be instructed in geography and in the Latin language. The schools shall be open each day, Sundays excepted, eight hours in summer and six hours in winter . . . except during vacation, which shall not commence prior to the first of August, nor continue after the 10th of September."

The first school for the city's black children was apparently founded in 1807 by three slaves: Nicholas Franklin and Moses Liverpool of southern Virginia, who worked as caulkers in the Washington Navy Yard, and George Bell, who was owned by Anthony Addison of Maryland. A free school for black children was run from 1818 to 1822 by the black Resolute Beneficial Society. But most black schools were supported by modest fees from the pupils' parents. Although some schools were run by whites—usually in connection with Sunday schools—most were run by blacks.

One of the oldest churches in the Washington area is Rock Creek Church (St. Paul's Episcopal, in Rock Creek Parish), which is shown here in an early nineteenth-century watercolor by Rebecca Wister Morris Nourse. The church's origins can be traced back to 1712, when the leaders of Piscataway Parish ordered their rector to preach at the "Eastern Branch Church" once a month. At a 1719 meeting to create a chapel-of-ease for parishioners' convenience, Colonel John Bradford donated 1,000 pounds of tobacco and "one hundred Acres of Land" along the Piney Branch of Rock Creek, "whereon is Timber for building said Chappel and necessary houses for a Gleab." The walls of the present church date from 1771, funded by a levy on parishioners of 96,000 pounds of tobacco. Vestryman John Clagett gave land in the parish for a public school "out of sentiments of tenderness and regard for the rising generation."

Christ Church was started in 1794, in Daniel Carroll's tobacco barn. It was located on Capitol Hill at New Jersey Avenue, near D Street SE. Of this church Margaret Bayard Smith wrote:

"At this time [1800] the only place for public worship in our new-city was a small, a very small frame building at the bottom of Capitol-hill. It had been a tobacco-house belonging to Daniel Carroll and was purchased by a few Episcopalians for a mere trifle and fitted up as a church in the plainest and rudest manner. During the first winter, Mr. Jefferson regularly attended service on the sabbath-day in the humble church. The congregation seldom exceeded 50 or 60, but generally consisted of about a score of hearers. [Jefferson] could have had no motive for this regular attendance, but that of respect for public worship, [since] choice of place or preacher he had not, as this, with the exception of a little Catholic chapel was the only church in the new city. The custom of preaching in the Hall of Representatives had not then been attempted, though after it was established Mr. Jefferson during his whole administration, was a most regular attendant. . . . The gay company who thronged the H.R. looked very little like a religious assembly. The occasion presented for display was not only a novel, but a favourable one for the youth, beauty and fashion of the city, Georgetown and environs. . . .

"One of the officers of the house, followed by his attendant with a great bag over his shoulder, precisely at 12 o'clock, would make his way through the hall to the depository of letters to put them in the mail-bag, which sometimes had a most ludicrous effect, and always diverted attention from the preacher. The musick was as little in union with devotional feelings, as the place. The marine-band, were the performers. Their scarlet uniform, their various instruments, made quite a dazzling appearance in the gallery. The marches they played were good and inspiring, but in their attempts to accompany the psalm-singing of the congregation, they completely failed and after a while, the practice was discontinued, —it was *too* ridiculous. . . .

"Preachers of every sect and denomination of christians were there admitted—Catholics, Unitarians, Quakers with every intervening diversity of sect. Even women were allowed to display their pulpit eloquence, in this national Hall."

"An Intellectual Festival"

The arts and sciences flourished in Washington during Thomas Jefferson's eight years as President. Guests at the White House and in the leading drawing rooms included not only statesmen and politicians but also the explorer Alexander von Humboldt and artists Charles Willson Peale, Gilbert Stuart and St. Memin. The poet and statesman Joel Barlow moved to town and persuaded his friend Robert Fulton to make an extended visit. But more important than anyone else in stimulating Washington's intellectual growth was Thomas Jefferson himself. No other President has taken such an active role in city development. Along with his Presidential duties, Jefferson was instrumental in determining the classical style of its early public buildings and was actively engaged in trying to save the city's fine old trees. Charles Willson Peale, who was a guest at the White House in 1804, noted that at the "very elegant dinner . . . not a single toast was given or called for, or politicks touched on, but the subject of Natural History and improvements of the conveniences of Life, Manners of the different nations described, or other agreeable conversation animated this whole company."

The Jefferson portrait (above) was painted by Rembrandt Peale. Jefferson's Sheffield Candelabrum (below, left)—one of a pair still owned by his Washington descendants—was purchased for him in England by John and Abigail Adams. (Adams was U.S. Minister there.) Jefferson, who was then Minister to France, had not only just become a widower but had lost most of his household furnishings in a Paris fire. Jefferson's polygraph (below) was used for making copies of letters. Such a device was brought to him by Charles Willson Peale, who noted in his diary in June 1804:

> "I went to the President's and unpacked the Polygraph and was much pleased on finding very little damage done by the jolting of the stage, and happy to find it pleased the President who is fond of mechanicks & amuses himself very often by working at Cabinet work. He told me that he wanted one or two more made and that he would recommend them to the public offices if he found they performed with correctness and ease."

The program at left appeared in *The National Intelligencer* on December 27, 1805.

"One drum major, one fife major and thirty-two drums and fifes" were specified in the 1798 Act of Congress that established the Marine Band—members of which are seen above. The band played for John Adams at the first White House "musick" on New Year's Day, 1801. Thomas Jefferson, a devoted musician who played his violin as much as four hours a day, asked that the band's skills be upgraded by the recruitment of Italian musicians. Eighteen musicians, led by Gaetano Carusi, were recruited in Sicily; but when they arrived in Washington they learned that the newly appointed Marine Commandant knew nothing of the original orders and "The Italian Band" was dispersed. Its leader became a civilian success as a music and dancing master whose Assembly Rooms at 11th and C streets NW were long famous as Carusi's Saloon, the scene of innumerable festive occasions, including several Inaugural Balls.

The silhouette at left of "Baron Humboldt" was pasted in Mrs. Thornton's diaries. Alexander von Humboldt visited Washington in 1804, fresh from his travels in South America. The baron was warmly welcomed by Jefferson, who had just concluded the Louisiana Purchase and wanted the German scientist's views on the territory. Mr. and Mrs. Samuel Harrison Smith entertained Humboldt during his stay, and Mrs. Smith recorded her impressions of the man in her diary, writing: "Never have I seen a human being who so instantaneously prepossessed every beholder in his behalf . . . his face . . . lighted up with the glow of benevolence and the intelligence of genius. . . . This visit was an intellectual festival for us."

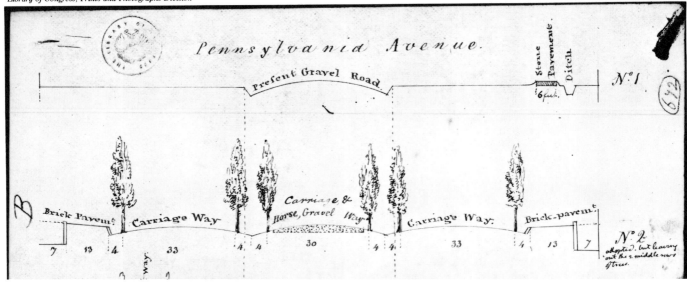

Jefferson had far-reaching plans for improving the appearance of Washington. Prominent among his contributions was the tree-lined approach to Capitol Hill via Pennsylvania Avenue, which was laid out by surveyor Nicholas King in the plan above. The watercolor below, attributed to Benjamin Latrobe, shows fully grown the Lombardy poplars Jefferson suggested for the site. It also shows the Capitol with both wings complete. In March 1803 the superintendent of the city reported to the President on the progress of the poplar planting: "Dr. Thornton, Mr. King and myself, have conversed on the manner of laying off the lines and planting the trees. . . . I shall get the trees from Mount Vernon, and Genl Masons Island & I expect from the samples I have seen they will be of a good size, price twelve & a half cents each."

Jefferson planned that the fast-growing poplars would be replaced eventually by shadier willow oaks, but they were not. In 1816 David Baille Warden complained:

"It is deeply to be regretted that the government or corporation did not employ some means for the preservation of the trees which grew on places destined for the public walks. How agreeable would have been their shade along the Pennsylvania Avenue where the dust so often annoys, and the summer sun, reflected from the sandy soil, is so oppressive. The Lombardy poplar, which now supplies their place, serves more for ornament than shelter."

His care for trees typified Jefferson's concern for the quality of life in Washington. Margaret Bayard Smith recalled

"Nothing affected Mr. Jefferson like . . . wanton destruction of the fine trees scattered over the city grounds. I remember on one occasion . . . his exclaiming, 'How I wish that I possessed the power of a despot . . . that I might save the noble, the beautiful trees that are daily falling sacrifices to the cupidity of their owners, or the necessity of the poor. No, only an armed guard could save them. The unnecessary felling of a tree, perhaps the growth of centuries, seems to me a crime little short of murder, it pains me to an unspeakable degree.'"

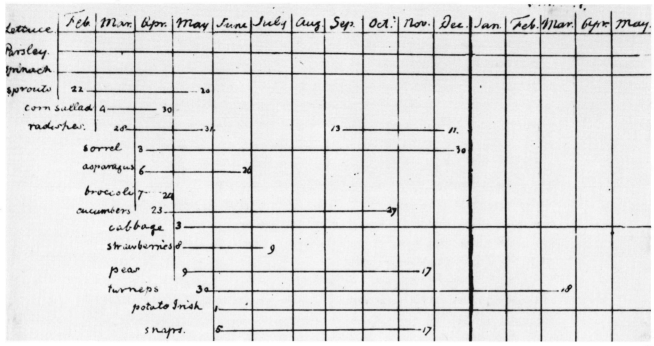

During the eight years of his Presidency, Jefferson made a careful study of the first and last appearance of thirty-seven varieties of vegetables in the Washington market and compiled a chart of his findings (a detail of which appears above). As Jefferson's nineteenth-century biographer Henry Randall wrote:

> "To think of a leader of a great civil revolution—the founder of a new party and creed—the statesman engaged in the pressing cares of a nation—watching with a green-grocer's assiduity, and recording with more than a green-grocer's precision, the first and last appearance of radishes, squashes, cabbages, and cauliflowers in the market—suggests a curious train of reflections!"

Seeing illustrious faces in the humble haunts of the grocery store has been a Washington tradition from the first. Jefferson, as well as his Chief Justice, John Marshall, did their own shopping at the Washington markets. Justice Story recalled that

> "one morning while doing his marketing [Marshall] came across a young Virginia blood who was swearing loudly because he could hire no one to take home his turkey. Marshall stepped up and ascertaining of him where he lived, replied 'That is in my way, and I will take it for you.' When he arrived at the dwelling the young man inquired, 'What shall I pay you?' 'Oh, nothing,' was the rejoinder; 'you are welcome. It was in my way, and no trouble.' 'Who was that polite old gentleman who brought home my turkey for me,' inquired the other of a bystander, as Marshall stepped away. 'That,' replied he, 'is John Marshall, Chief Justice of the United States.' "

John Marshall, portrayed by John Cranch, firmly established the prestige of the Supreme Court and wrote many of its important early decisions during his thirty-five years as Chief Justice. Writing of Marshall, Associate Justice Joseph Story said: "I love his laugh—it is too hearty for an intriguer; and his good temper and unwearied patience are equally agreeable on the bench and in the study."

101

In 1807 Joel Barlow came to Washington at Jefferson's urging, saying that he and his wife had decided "to pitch our tent" after many years of living abroad. In the same year, his popular epic poem, "The Columbiad," was published (with illustrations by his friend Robert Fulton, who also painted the portrait above).

Barlow was the son of a prosperous Connecticut farmer. A graduate of Yale, fluent in many languages, he amassed a fortune in shipping in Europe. His work as a pamphleteer supporting the French Revolution led to his being named a Citizen of France—an honor given to no other Americans except Washington, Hamilton, Madison and Thomas Paine. He served as Minister to France and afterward to the states on the Barbary Coast during the "pirate" years.

Barlow's estate outside Washington, which he purchased in 1805, is seen in the romantic landscape at right by Charles Godman. Located on a hill on the Washington side of Rock Creek, about a mile from the Potomac, the estate had, wrote Barlow, "a most beautiful situation; it wants only the improvements that we contemplate, to make it a little paradise. . . . I find that the name Belair has been already given to many places in Maryland and Virginia, so by the advice of friends we have changed it to one that is quite new—Calorama—from the Greek signifying fine view, and this place presents one of the finest views in America." At right is Barlow's own decoy, which he used on Rock Creek. It is owned by a Washington descendant.

Barlow had little time to enjoy his new home. He died in Poland in 1812 while on a diplomatic mission. (He was trying to reach Napoleon during the Emperor's retreat from Moscow.) But Calorama—or Kalorama—is well known in Washington today as an area of handsome houses and embassies. In 1827 Frances Trollope left this description:

"At about a mile from the town, on the high terrace ground above described, is a very pretty place, to which the proprietor has given the name of Kaleirama. It is not large, or in any way magnificent, but the view from it is charming; and it has a little wood behind, covering about two hundred acres of broken ground, that slopes down to a dark cold little river, so closely shut in by rocks and evergreens, that it might serve as a noonday bath for Diana and her nymphs. . . . this wood is filled with wild flowers, but such as we cherish fondly in our gardens."

Owned by descendants

102

Robert Fulton, best known as the builder and operator of the *Clermont*, the first commercially successful steamboat, was also an artist, engineer, inventor and great friend of Joel Barlow. Hearing that Fulton had tried unsuccessfully to interest the French in his plans for a steamboat on the Seine, Barlow urged him to return to America and to make his home at Kalorama:

> "My project would be that you should pass directly over to England: silent and steady, make Chapman construct an engine 12 inches, while you are building a boat of a proportionate size; make the experiments on that scale, *all quiet and quick*. If it answers, put the machinery on board a vessel and go directly to New York, ordering another engine as large as you please, to follow you. Then secure your patent and begin your operation, first small and then large. I think I will find you the funds without any noise for the first operation in England, and if it promises well, you will get as many funds and friends in America as you want."

Fulton came, and he stayed with the Barlows for some time. The two men are said to have tried out boat models together in Rock Creek.

103

The Lyons' Mill, Bridge and Road are seen from the Georgetown side of Rock Creek in this landscape, painted by William Dougal in the 1800s. The Lyons' (or Federal) Mill was located two miles above the Potomac, at the head of navigation on Rock Creek, and was typical of mills along the creek. In the mill complex, which dated from 1780, was a large mill with three sets of millstones. A half-mile-long millrace extended upstream to Lyons' Dam. There was a barn, a smokehouse, an ice house, a carriage house, a stable and two stone houses: the miller's house near the mill and the eighteen-room Lyons' home on the hill, which overlooked Rock Creek, the Potomac and the growing city of Washington. In 1809 Robert Fulton demonstrated submarine torpedoes to members of Congress at Lyons' Mill Dam. In the great storm of October 1869 Rock Creek swept away Lyons' Dam and left ten feet of water standing in the mill. Although the damage was repaired, the mill was abandoned after the last Lyons died in 1873. In 1913 the mill era ended as Lyons' Mill collapsed with a roar that was heard as far away as Sheridan Circle.

The sketch (left) called "Ruins of the Paper Mill and The Paper Mill Bridge, at P Street," shows the crossing of the main road from Georgetown to Bladensburg, originally a ford. Near here, the British Minister, who rented Thomas Peter's houses at K and 26th streets, wrote that he could "hear his landlord shooting ducks in Rock Creek." This was one of two important mills on the creek built directly below Kalorama. This is a close-up view of the same bridge shown in the picture above.

Until the mid-1800s Rock Creek was navigable as far upstream as P Street. The creek's mouth was one of the sites considered for the Washington Navy Yard. Mills flourished along Rock Creek, especially after grain replaced tobacco on local farms and the Napoleonic Wars drove up the world price of wheat. American farmers prospered and with them the Rock Creek millers, grinding grain in return for a percentage of the flour. The importance of the Rock Creek mills began to decline only after the Chesapeake and Ohio Canal was built through Georgetown in the late 1820s. Bigger and more efficient mill operations soon grew up along the canal, where transportation facilities, as well as large and steady supplies of water, were readily available.

Columbia Historical Society

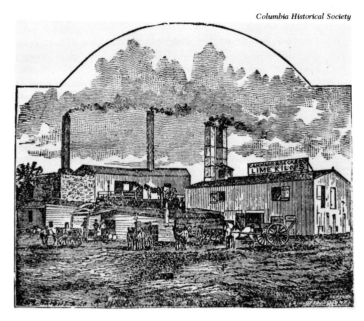

Godey's lime kilns, burning limestone from Harpers Ferry, also stood along Rock Creek. The remains of Godey's kiln are still visible on the east side of the creek near K Street at the end of the C & O Canal. In 1859, as part of a prosperous business reaching from Maryland to North Carolina, 40,000 barrels of lime were produced by fourteen hands at four fires.

The only mill still standing on Rock Creek takes its name from Isaac Peirce (later spelled Pierce), a Pennsylvanian who by 1800 owned some 2,000 acres stretching from the present-day Zoo to Chevy Chase. Pierce built a sawmill, a house and several barns, and in 1820 he and his son Abner built a grist mill later inherited by a nephew, Peirce Shoemaker. In 1890, 350 acres of Pierce land were bought for $250,000 as part of Rock Creek Park. Eighty years later the mill was opened to the public.

National Park Service

John Mason of Analostan, seen in this portrait attributed to Rembrandt Peale, built his family's plantation home in the Greek style—one of the first such houses in the country. The house stood on Analostan (now Roosevelt) Island, just below the mouth of Rock Creek. Originally granted by Lord Baltimore to Captain Randolph Brandt for his valor against the Indians, the island had been bought from Brandt descendants by George Mason of Gunston Hall (see page 30), who willed it, along with adjacent Virginia lands, to John Mason, his fourth son. The seventy-five-acre island is shown as "Mason's I." on the 1818 map below, by Washington surveyor Nicholas King. But Mason himself called it Analostan, a jumbling of the Indian word from which "Anacostia" is derived. In the present century it was renamed to honor Theodore Roosevelt.

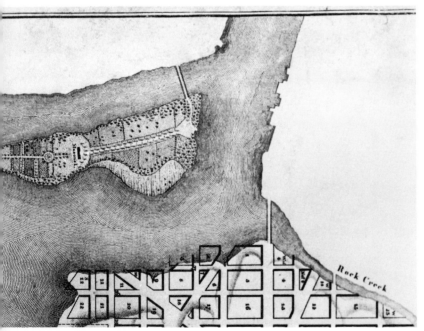

"Annalostan Island, the seat of General Mason, is situated in the river Potomac, opposite Georgetown, and contains nearly seventy acres. A flat boat, of a rude construction, awkwardly impelled by an oar, placed near each extremity, affords a safe conveyance between the island and the main land a distance of about two hundred yards. . . . The highest eminence, on which the house stands, is fifty feet above the level of the river. . . .

"I can never forget how delighted I was with my first visit to this island. . . . We walked to the mansion-house under a delicious shade. The blossoms of the cherry, apple, and peach trees, of the hawthorn and aromatic shrubs, filled the air with their fregrance.

"The house, of a simple and neat form, is situated near that side of the island which commands a view of the Potomac, the President's House, Capitol, and other buildings. The garden, the sides of which are washed by the waters of the river, is ornamented with a variety of trees and shrubs, and in the midst, there is a lawn covered with a beautiful verdure. . . .

"The view from the spot is delightful. It embraces the picturesque banks of the Potomac, a portion of the city, and an expanse of water, of which the bridge terminates the view. Numerous vessels ply backwards and forwards to animate the scene. . . .

"This island has a great variety of trees and shrubs, owing to the seeds brought by the stream from mountainous regions, different species of oak, walnut, mulberry, poplar, locust, ash, willow, the papaw and spindle tree, or burning bush. . . .

"This island is the resort of various reptiles. We found the nest of the terrapin, or fresh-water turtle, in the garden, at the distance of about thirty feet from the water, containing nineteen eggs. . . .

"The deer, wild turkey, canvas-back duck, and wild goose, which inhabited this place about fifty years ago, have all disappeared. This species of duck, so delicious to the taste, was then sold for sixpence."

—David Ballie Warden, 1816

This view of Georgetown from Analostan Island was sketched by Seth Eastman in 1852. "Masons never feel want—nor want feeling" was the toast once raised in Mason's honor. But in time the family wealth declined and the island was sold to pay debts. The house fell into ruins, and the island's meticulous fields and gardens became overgrown. Eventually the island became a public park.

Georgetown. D.C. augt. 6th 1852

An intimate view of life in and about Washington in the early 1800s is found in the letters of Rosalie Eugenia Stier, a Belgian aristocrat who fled the French Revolution and came to Annapolis in the 1790s with her father and brother. She married George Calvert, a banker, businessman and plantation owner (his sister Eleanor married Martha Washington's son; thus he was the uncle of Mrs. Law, mentioned below), and moved to Riversdale, a house that still stands in Bladensburg. Her father and brother eventually returned to Belgium, leaving funds for her to invest. The letters she wrote to her brother were saved by his Belgian descendants.

Privately owned portrait displayed at the Maryland Historical Society

Mrs. George Calvert of "Riversdale," by Gilbert Stuart

"Bladensburg, December 30, 1801. I came back today from the Federal City, where we spent several days with Mrs. Law, who is certainly almost the most charming woman I have met in this country. I was surprised there by Ambassadors and Ministers. Society will be very brilliant this winter. . . . My husband came back today from the 'Federal City' . . . to say that there is nothing new in politics which is at all interesting.

"Riversdale, September 12, 1803. I am very well now, and take much exercise—chiefly on horseback. Mrs. Lewis comes here three or four times a week. We ride together and several 'cavaliers' accompany us. I am sure you would think our habits pretty . . . . Besides our 'beaux' we both have a servant in livery a l'Anglaise who follows us. I have a very fine equipage now with four beautiful brown horses. I go to the Federal City nearly every other day. The road has been made entirely of gravel. Bladensburg has become very brilliant indeed. People come from all directions to drink the waters on Sundays. All Georgetown in particular comes. . . . So many people are dying at Alexandria. . . . I do not know if it is true, but [the

epidemic] has raged from New York, Philadelphia and Baltimore to this place. The drought has been fearful this year which causes the epidemic. We have never been so long without rain.

"January 1807. Society in Washington is very inferior just now! All the government officials, as well as the majority of members of Congress being Democrats and for the most part people of low extraction, so I do not go there often, and employ my leisure hours reading.

"December 3, 1808. Thinking of you continually as I do, dear Brother, how is it that I write to you so seldom? One time Charles has to be soothed,

From The Peter Force Guide, 1845, *Columbia Historical Society*

Bladensburg as it looked in about 1845

which takes a half-hour. Then they come to ask for mustard for a ragout or sugar for a pastry, for you are aware that we American ladies, are, alas! our own house-keepers! Then Caroline must have a reading lesson and George must write. A new coat is brought from the tailor which must be tried on. No, it is not right and a note has to go back with it. The man goes to Georgetown and a long list of details for the household must be remembered. All these occupations seem trifling, and still they prevent me from chatting with you . . . a packet sails in three days. . . . My last letters to Papa were forwarded through Mr. Madison. I hope he received them.

"December 10, 1808. I ride horse-back sometimes, and I bought a very fine horse last year. A good lady's horse is difficult to find, so, as this one was perfect, my husband was induced to give two hundred dollars for him. We always have four fine carriage horses. Our old carriage is very dilapidated and with this new blockade [the Embargo Act] a new one is not to be thought of. Quite a small vehicle serves me to go shopping to Georgetown. . . .

"We work always here without a pause. A lake just finished which looks like a large river before the house on the southern side gives a very beautiful effect, and furnished us at the same time with fish and ice for our ice-house. . . . The old ice-house near the house was not good, as it leaked. We have built a new one in the wood beyond the stables. It is covered with straw and surrounded with great fine trees and looks like a hut. . . .

"We are alarmed from time to time about the national bonds. People dare to speak openly of the dissolution of the union of the States. I am often anxious on this subject. You are all so far away that you cannot be warned of the danger till too late. Perhaps I am a false prophet (and I hope so indeed) but it appears very certain that a government such as this can last only a short time. Every year they change something, the eastern States become daily more bitter against the southern states, and the latter instead of consolidating them do all they can to widen the breach. In short that cannot go on and what will be the result? No one dares to face the issue, but if Madison continues the same system as Jefferson we shall be on the brink of a civil war.

"Riversdale, April 1, 1809. Alas! We are only too well convinced that this government and the Federal Union cannot exist without a respectable navy, but our wretched President is, I fear, one of those wavering weak characters and although in reality an honest man, he will do as much harm as his predecessors. This country has reached a very alarming crisis. Torn by two parties, the eastern

States jealous of the South: Congress enacting Laws she is unable to enforce, and obliged to retract them afterwards only to substitute equally bad ones—our flag insulted at the same time by England and France, and all this the result of the administration of that wretched Jefferson.

"July 23, 1810. My husband . . . says he cannot have anything done properly unless he looks after it himself. . . . He has many duties, above all when we have workmen; then he is director of the Bank of Washington, which takes a day every week; director of a manufacturing company in Georgetown, and principal agent of a road to be made between this place and Washington. Then he has to direct the work of our different plantations, one of which is eighteen miles from here, which takes a day and a half every fortnight. You have no idea how this country has improved since you left. We have all the luxury of Europe and have lost that simplicity which was worth far more. In the towns the change is astonishing. An excellent bridge [Long Bridge] has been made over the Potomac facing the Capital, which shortens considerably the distance to Alexandria. That town does not prosper.

"July 15, 1811. I cannot conceal from you that my fears as to the stability of our constitution augment every moment. I foresee an inevitable revolution and I fear its near approach. Do not think these idle crotchets; the best informed and most weighty people are of my opinion, and it is that of the prominent Senators and Members of Congress. A war with England which our government will provoke will be the preclude, and it is to be anticipated that the Eastern States will put themselves under the protection of that power. What will then become of the Southern States? They will either be torn asunder by the anarchy or fall prey to Napoleon. In whatever way one regards the situation it presents an alarming aspect.

"February 24, 1813. As this time it is nearly impossible to send letters, and I begin this one without the least hope of being able to forward it for a long time. A fleet of two English ships of 74 cannons, and six frigates close the entry to the Chesapeake and Delaware and do not allow the smallest boat to pass. Meanwhile the country is torn assunder by numerous factions and in Congress there is open talk of dissolving the union of the States. In short I do not know how it will all end. . . . The moderation of the English is surprising. We have already taken three of their frigates, there is nothing to prevent their reducing all our ports to ashes (for there is no one to defend them) and still they are content to blockade us."

109

Seth Eastman's 1851 sketch at left shows the bluff where the Tiber met the Potomac. Sometimes known as Braddock's Rock, the bluff is shown on many early maps as a likely site for a fort. The Marines, the first military force to arrive in Washington, camped on this hill in 1800 while waiting for their barracks to be completed.

The Washington Arsenal (left, below) was situated at Greenleaf's Point, the southwestern extremity of Washington, where the Anacostia and the Potomac converge. ("Turky Buzzard Point" is its name on Augustin Herrman's 1673 map, shown on pages 16 and 17.) L'Enfant's plan of Washington called for "a great military works" at Greenleaf's Point "to secure the city from invasion." The original fort became the Washington Arsenal and is now Fort Lesley J. McNair.

The drawing above shows a house just inside the gate on the left. Built about 1800, the building incorporates a farmhouse that is one of the oldest structures in the Federal City. The original house is believed to have been one room deep and perhaps two rooms wide. The rooms on the right-hand side of the drawing are the originals.

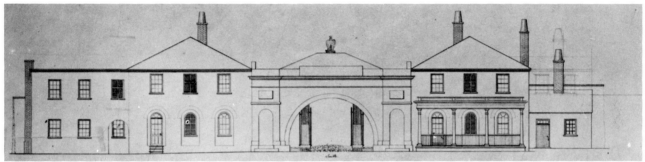

Latrobe's design for the Main Gate of the Navy Yard (above) was mocked by Dr. William Thornton in a poem that provoked a lawsuit (Thornton being ordered to pay Latrobe a penny in damages):

> This Dutchman in taste, this monument builder
> This planner of grand steps and walls,
> This falling-arch maker, this blunder-proof gilder,
> Himself an architect calls.

The arch has not fallen. Altered in 1873, it still serves as the Main Gate.

The view at left, from *Morrison's Guide* of 1842, shows the Washington Navy Yard. The first in the country, the Navy Yard was begun in 1799 on the deep water of the Anacostia, west of Greenleaf's Point. Benjamin H. Latrobe, appointed by Jefferson to be engineer of the Navy Department, designed more than twenty buildings for the Navy Yard.

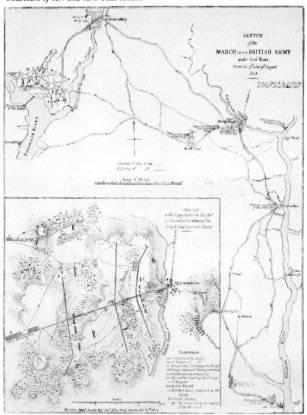

On his way to Washington British Admiral George Cockburn (above, right) anchored his fleet off Alexandria and demanded ransom. The town paid and was spared but earned the scorn of the artist who drew the cartoon above. (The puns on "porter," a kind of ale, and "perry," a pear cider, refer to American naval heroes David Porter and Oliver Hazard Perry.) It was said that the Federal City was offered a similar deal but spurned it. When Cockburn reached the capital he ordered the burning of the White House and other public buildings, and the offices of Joseph Gales' *National Intelligencer*. According to Margaret Bayard Smith

> "Cockburn often rode down the avenue, on an old white mare. . . . He stop'd at a door, at which a young lady was standing and enter'd into familiar conversation. 'Now did you expect to see me such a clever fellow,' he said, 'were you not prepared to see a savage, a ferocious creature, such as Josey [Joseph Gales] represented me? But you see I am quite harmless, don't be afraid, I will take better care of you than Jemmy [James Madison] did!' Such was his manner,—that of a common sailor, not of a dignified commander."

General Robert Ross's map (left) shows his route of attack on Bladensburg and Washington. Richard Rush, an American present during the campaign, wrote:

> "Accounts had come that the enemy was advancing in great force, but whether to enter Washington by Bladensburg or by the bridge at the navy-yard was still unknown. All were anxiously waiting information from the scouts who were coming in in quick succession. The road forked not far from each place, and he might take his choice of either fork. In fact, to keep us longer in the dark, I understood that his whole line, first taking the navy-yard fork, continued in it until the last column got into it. The army then suddenly reversed its front, and marched onward rapidly to Bladensburg."

The City in Flames

During most of the two years of fighting that followed the U.S. declaration of war on Britain in 1812, the chief effect on the capital city was the economic hardship brought on by the British blockade of Chesapeake Bay. But in the summer of 1814 the British fleet under Admiral George Cockburn moved up the bay and began harassing the area. It was widely thought that the rich port of Baltimore would be the British objective. Warned of the enemy's approach, Secretary of War Major John Armstrong replied: "Oh, yes; by God, they would not come with such a fleet without meaning to strike somewhere, but they certainly will not come here. What the devil will they do here? . . . No, no; Baltimore is the place, sir; that is of so much more consequence."

Baltimore was the place, and eventually the British did make an attempt on the city. But first they turned on the capital. In mid-August, Cockburn's ships sailed up the Potomac. At the same time, a force of 4,500 British regulars under General Robert Ross landed at Benedict, Maryland, on the Patuxent, and began marching toward Washington. At Bladensburg they met American forces led by General William Winder and Major Armstrong. The encounter was a half-hour fiasco, derisively nicknamed "The Bladensburg Races." As Margaret Bayard Smith reported, "The enemy march'd on in solid column and attack'd with coolness, and order. The 5th regiment from Baltimore . . . stood their ground firmly, but for a short time only, they were almost destroy'd and our whole troops gave way and began a disor'd retreat." Following up his advantage, General Ross continued toward the capital.

Before the British advance as many as could fled the city. As Margaret Bayard Smith recalled:

> "We were roused on Tuesday night by a loud knocking,—on the opening of the door, Willie Bradley called to us, 'The enemy are advancing, our own troops are giving way on all sides and are retreating to the city. Go, for Gods sake go.' He spoke in a voice of agony, and then flew to his horse and was out of sight in a moment."

The only shots fired in defense of the capital in the War of 1812 came from this house, the Sewall-Gallatin-Belmont House, which is still standing on Maryland Avenue NE, a block from the Capitol. Albert Gallatin, Secretary of the Treasury under Jefferson and Madison, lived in the house during most of his thirteen years in office. The shots were fired as Ross and his aides approached the house. Michael Shiner, a Washington slave, recorded the event in his diary:

> "Master left a colored man and me sleve with a olde lady by the name of Mrs. Ried on Capitol Hill and as sone as got sight of the British army raising that hill they looked like flames of fier all red coats and the staks of their guns painted with red vermelion and iron work shimered like a Spanish dollar. . . . The British army still continued ther march on toward the Capitol ontill they got against a large brick house on Capitol Hill fronting Maryland. . . . This house now sets to the Northe east of the United States Senate and as the British army approach that house under the command of General Ross and his aides, his horse wher shot from under him and in a twinkle of the eye the house wher sorounded by the British army and search all through upstairs and downstairs . . . but no man whar found. . . . They put a globe match to the house and then stood oft a sertin distance . . . and those rockets burst until they came to the explosion part they made the rafters fly East and West."

This British rendering of the attack on Washington appeared in October 1814. As Richard Rush recalled:

"I have, indeed, to this hour, the vivid impression upon my eye of columns of flame and smoke ascending throughout the night of the 24th of August from the Capitol, President's house, and other public edifices, as the whole were on fire, some burning slowly, others with bursts of flame and sparks mounting high up in the dark horizon."

115

At right, the Capitol in flames. Margaret Bayard Smith described the manner in which the British set the Capitol and other buildings on fire:

"50 men, sailors and marines, were marched by an officer, silently thro' the avenue, each carrying a long pole to which was fixed a ball about the circumference of a large plate,— when arrived at the building, each man was station'd at a window, with his pole and machine of wild-fire against it, at the word of command, at the same instant the windows were broken and this wild-fire thrown in, so that an instantaneous conflagration took place and the whole building was wrapt in flames and smoke. The spectators stood in awful silence, the city was light and the heavens redden'd with the blaze!"

Below, the ruins of the Capitol and the White House. Margaret Bayard Smith reported that these two, of all the public buildings, were the most thoroughly destroyed. "Those beautiful pillars in that Representatives Hall were crack'd and broken, the roof, that noble dome, painted and carved with such beauty and skill, lay in ashes in the cellars beneath the smouldering ruins." Their home gutted, the President and Mrs. Madison moved into nearby Octagon House, where, on February 17, 1815, the President signed the Treaty of Ghent, which ended hostilities.

The destruction went on through the night and into the morning of August 25. That day, however, a great storm blew up, moderating the fires and driving the invaders from the city. Mary Ingle Campbell, then a girl of thirteen, later recalled (for the Columbia Historical Society):

"I well remember the terrific tornado which drove the enemy in haste to their ships, from which they were in dread of being cut off . . . The sky changed from the peculiar leaden hue portending a wind storm, into almost midnight blackness. Then came the crash and glare of incessant thunder and lightning, and the wild beating of the rain . . . At last, however, the storm slowly died away . . . thanks to the heavy rain which had fallen [the flames], were kept from spreading over the entire city . . . Later we encountered a group of British officers taking a last drink from the old pump. 'Great God, Madam!' said Admiral Cockburn, 'is this the kind of storm to which you are accustomed in this infernal country?' 'No, sir,' was the reply; 'this is a special interposition of Providence to drive our enemies from our city'. 'Not so, Madam', he answered; 'it is rather to aid them in the destruction of your city.' With this parting shot the 'Red Coats' galloped off and disappeared forever from the Nation's Capital."

Amid the destruction, the Patent Office, with its hundreds of models, was saved—thanks to the heroism of Dr. Thornton. Standing on the steps of the building, he persuaded the British officer (as he later wrote in *The Intelligencer*) that "to burn what would be useful to all mankind, would be as barbarous as formerly to burn the Alexandrian Library, for which the Turks have since been condemned by all enlightened nations."

When the war ended, rebuilding the city's coastal defenses became the first order of business. Fort Washington, below Alexandria, which had fallen to Admiral Cockburn without a shot being fired from its batteries, was ordered rebuilt and refortified. The job fell to Pierre L'Enfant. But he failed to produce the plan for the fort on time and was fired. It was a job he could ill afford to lose. Having earlier refused as inadequate the compensation offered by the government for his work on the plan of the Federal City, he was living in severely reduced circumstances. His later years were spent in poverty. Befriended by William Dudley Digges of Green Hill (now Chillum), he lived out his days as the guest of Digges and his family. In 1825 he died and was buried at Green Hill. The inventory of his personal belongings totaled three watches, one compass, two pocket compasses and a small collection of surveying instruments, books and maps, all valued at $45. Not until the present century did he begin to receive his due. Today L'Enfant's name is heaped with honors, and his grave, removed to the brow of the hill at Arlington, overlooks the city of his vision.

Fort Washington

Kiplinger, Washington Collection

Shabby country houses and dusty roads surround the Capitol in a detail (above) from an 1844 landscape by William McLeod. The English porcelain plate (opposite), made between 1838 and 1845, is decorated with a view of the White House as seen from Tiber Creek. John Quincy Adams, for one, much enjoyed having the creek so near his official residence. According to Benjamin Ogle Tayloe, Adams once told a visiting Englishman, a Mr. Featherstonehaugh, that after bathing in the Potomac one day

"He discovered that his clothes had disappeared, owing to the rise of the tide. 'What did you do?' inquired Mr. Featherstonehaugh. 'I walked along the shore,' said Mr. Adams, 'until I met a boy, whom I dispatched to the house with a message to Mrs. Adams, and after some delay he returned with another suit of clothes.'

"Mr. Featherstonehaugh left the Executive Mansion with a clearer idea of Republican simplicity than he had ever had before."

118

3 A Mingling of Great and Small Concerns (1814–1860)

"A great[er] benefit could not have accrued to this city than the destruction of its principal buildings by the British. It has now acquired the confidence of its own inhabitants in its permanence, and everybody who could save a little money, is now employing it in building himself a house."

—Benjamin Henry Latrobe, 1816

Henry Francis du Pont Winterthur Museum

From the smoking ruins of Washington, 1814, came the questions editorial writers would continue to ask throughout the nation's first century: "Had the Potomac been a bad choice for the site of the Federal City? Shouldn't the capital be moved to a site with a better harbor, less swamp fever, more conveniences, a place free of slavery, closer to the developing West, a city with more cosmopolitan airs?" The answer was always "no."

After 1814, local businessmen quickly financed a brick capitol to serve as the seat of government; architect and engineer Benjamin Henry Latrobe repaired the one that had been burned by the British. Although the Jacksonian change of command brought down many personal power networks, the city flourished under the new elite: Marylanders and Virginians, as well as newer arrivals from Kentucky, Tennessee, Georgia and the West. Southern by sentiment, the city was enriched by the presence of New Englanders, the Diplomatic Corps and by a constant trickle of visitors who were curious to observe the new Jacksonian Democracy at work.

Washington has been from the first a kind of showcase city. Abolitionists, temperance advocates, zealots and reformers of every stripe made their mark here. The District was the first place where the domestic slave trade was abolished by federal legislation, the first place where slaves were emancipated, the only place where slave owners were recompensed by the government.

Changing times dealt harshly with George Washington's vision of the capital as a center of trade and industry. By 1830, the Chesapeake and Ohio Canal, which Washington had envisioned as the primary route to the riches of the West, was open for business; but it was the Baltimore and Ohio Railroad that grew rich off Virginia coal, the Cumberland Gap on the Tennessee–Kentucky border that opened passage through the mountains for the settlers and the Erie Canal that provided Atlantic Coast merchants with access to the Western waters. Alexandria's efforts to be part of the canal system brought on fiscal disorder. The port voted to rejoin Virginia in 1846, after more than half a century of decline as Alexandria, D.C.

119

White House Collection

Columbia Historical Society

"The city . . . must necessarily become one day or other a great place. A few hundred Years hence some historians may notice the labors of Yourself and perhaps mine; with a skim of praise qualified by an apology for us, in these words, 'considering the infancy of the arts and of the empire.' This is all we have to hope or expect."

—Benjamin Henry Latrobe, 1810

To Benjamin Henry Latrobe fell much of the work of rebuilding the capital city after the War of 1812. Seen here in a portrait by Charles Willson Peale, Latrobe was British-born but had emigrated to America in 1788, when he was twenty-four. In Philadelphia he had engineered the city's water supply system.

Latrobe came to Washington in 1803, when Thomas Jefferson appointed him a surveyor of public buildings. His early work in the Federal City included designing the Navy Yard and adding the south wing to the Capitol Building. Later he lost his fortune in a Hudson River steamboat scheme with Robert Fulton. But the task of rebuilding Washington after the War of 1812 brought him many lucrative commissions.

Latrobe designed the country house below in 1816 for Robert Brent. Brentwood, as the house was called, stood a mile and a half north of the Capitol at what is now 5th Street and Florida Avenue. It was demolished in 1917, but that part of the city is still called by its name.

"Several very considerable dwelling houses are under my direction," Latrobe wrote in 1816; "and one especially for General Van Ness is the largest private house I have designed." The owner, General John Peter Van Ness, a member of Congress from New York, married Marcia Burns, the Washington heiress (see page 58).

The Van Ness mansion is seen in Walter Paris' 1893 painting above and amid its grounds and outbuildings in the watercolor at bottom right, which A. C. Harkness painted in 1888, just after completion of the Washington Monument. (The turreted coach house at far right in the watercolor still stands at E Street, beside Constitution Hall.)

In its day, the Van Ness mansion was considered one of the city's great sights. In 1830 Jonathan Elliot described the Van Ness estate:

"In the plan of the City, this beautiful Square, containing about six acres of ground, was retained by the proprietors. . . . It is handsomely situated at the junction of the classical Tiber and the majestic Potomac. . . . [The Van Ness family improved the square] in the best modern taste, both as to buildings and [to] grounds—the latter of which, in addition to their lofty, dignified paternal trees, are abundantly supplied with the best native and foreign fruits, including figs and grapes, and adorned with a great variety of ornamental shrubs and plants, hedges, quincunxes, gravel walks, vines, bowers, etc. . . . The spacious Mansion itself . . . built in a style of the finest architecture, near the President's House, is probably not excelled by any private building in this country. The entrance into this walled square is through an iron gate between two lodges at the north east angle, fronting on the street and the President's Square. Thence there is a winding carriage way, skirted by ornamental trees, shrubbery and flowers, ascending an artificial mound at the north front of the house, and passing under an elegant, projecting stone portico at the door. This portico is the first of the kind, if not the only one, excepting that recently erected at the President's House, in the United States."

But the pleasures to be found at the Van Ness house were more than scenic. As Washington Irving wrote during an 1811 visit: "I am delightfully moored 'head and stern' in the family of John P. Van Ness . . . an old friend of mine. . . . Mrs. Van Ness is a pretty and pleasant little woman, and quite gay; then there are two pretty girls likewise . . . you see I am in clover—happy dog!"

Fine Arts Commission, photo number 66-G-15F-6 in the National Archives

The Washington Canal, shown in this detail of an 1800 rendering of L'Enfant's plan of the city, incorporated two streams that have long since disappeared. Tiber Creek, whose main branch rose in the Soldier's Home grounds near 3rd Street and meandered along present-day Constitution Avenue, was straightened out so that the canal ran in a direct line from the Ellipse to the base of the Capitol. The canal then bent south and east along what is still Canal Street. South of the Capitol the canal split in two. One fork followed St. James Creek (which once bisected present-day Fort McNair). The other fork entered the Anacostia near the Navy Yard.

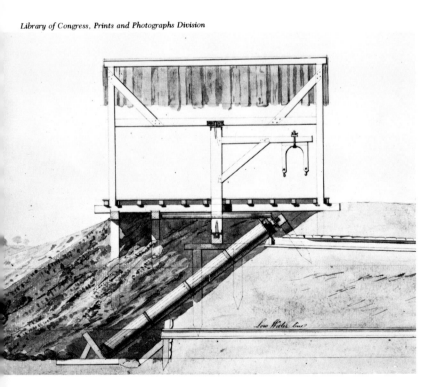

"Should this canal be finished, Washington need not envy London its Thames, nor New York its North River."

—Thomas Law, 1807

The Van Ness house was not Latrobe's first work in the boggy lowland along Constitution Avenue. In 1810 he began construction of the Washington Canal, which had been planned by L'Enfant in 1791 and which appears on the city's earliest maps. As Latrobe wrote early in 1810: "We are going this Summer to cut a Canal from the Potowmac thro' the heart of our city to the Harbor or Eastern Branch."

By 1815 the advantages of the canal were beginning to claim attention. As *The National Intelligencer* reported in that year: "Marble, stone, etc., are now landed at the foot of the Capitol, which otherwise must have been hauled at a great expense from four times the distance. The citizens can now land everything near their doors with considerable reduction of expense, trouble and time." One writer noted that Thomas Law, the canal's chief promoter, was planning to run packet boats between the Tiber and the Navy Yard: "a conveyance which may be rendered more economical and comfortable than the hackney coach."

The canal, however, was only navigable for boats of narrow beam and shallow draft. By 1826 Washington merchants and tradesmen were complaining that unless it was widened and deepened it would constitute "an insurmountable impediment to the commercial prosperity of the City of Washington." Even without being widened the canal required frequent dredging, and the canal company's profits were not sufficient to offset the maintenance costs. Traffic steadily declined. Eventually the canal was condemned as an eyesore and a health hazard. In the early 1870s it was covered over. Today almost all that remains is the lock house at 17th Street and Constitution Avenue—and the name of Canal Street.

Latrobe's meticulous drawing (left) shows in cross section the mechanical details of the lock at the entrance to the canal. The angled tube contains an Archimedes' screw, which was used to raise and lower the level of the water in the lock.

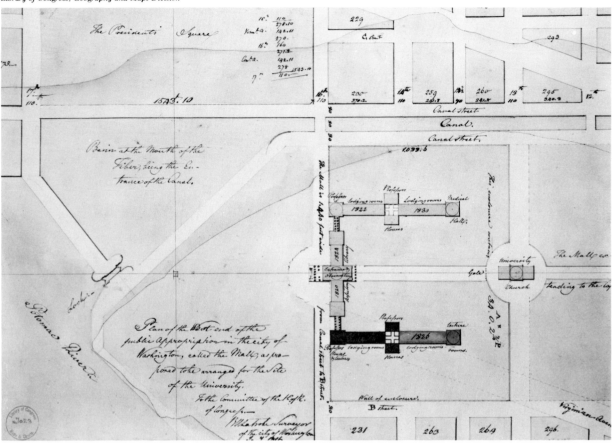

"Plan of the West end of the public appropriation in the City of Washington, called the Malle, as proposed to be arranged for the cite of the University. To the Committee of the H. of R. of Congress— B. H. Latrobe Surveyor of the City of Washington Jan. 4, 1816."

According to Latrobe's plan, a national university was to be constructed along the banks of the ill-fated Washington Canal, on what later became the site of the Washington Monument. The university was to be funded by the canal stock left to that purpose in George Washington's will. Although the plan never came to fruition in Washington, it does bear a remarkable similarity to the University of Virginia, which was established several years later. Before the university could be built the stock had become worthless. Like the feasibility of canals, the idea of a national university was one of the recurring themes in George Washington's correspondence. As he wrote in March 1795:

"It is with indescribable regret that I have seen the youth of the United States migrating to foreign countries, in order to acquire the higher branches of erudition and to obtain a knowledge of the sciences. —Altho' it would be injustice to many to pronounce the certainty of their imbibing maxims not congenial with republicanism it must nevertheless be admitted that a serious danger is encountered by sending abroad among other political systems those, who have not well learned the value of their own. The time is therefore come when a plan to universal education ought to be adopted. . . ."

This sketch by Seth Eastman shows a view of the Washington Canal as it appeared in the 1840s and 1850s.

"La Fayette Square was society."

—Henry Adams, 1906

This aerial view, drawn about 1845 for a proposed remodeling of the White House grounds, shows Lafayette Square, or the President's Square, as it was called prior to Lafayette's visit in 1824. The President's House, which dominated the square, was the only important structure in the vicinity until the building of St. John's Episcopal Church (below) in 1816 and the Decatur House in 1818. According to Christian Hines, the Pearce family, who were the proprietors of the land, had a farmhouse and barn near the northeast corner (upper right in the aerial view) as late as 1800. A graveyard was "situated on the north side of Pennsylvania Avenue, opposite the President's House, between the southwest corner and the south gate of Lafayette Square. This yard belonged originally to the Pearce family. . . . There was an apple orchard attached which covered nearly the whole of the square."

In the watercolor (above) drawn by the Baroness Hyde de Neuville in 1820, the White House (as the President's House came to be called sometime before the War of 1812) is seen as it looked from the square. It is flanked by the Departments of (from left) State, Treasury, War, and Navy.

St. John's was built across the square from the White House shortly after the War of 1812. Benjamin Latrobe, who designed the church and was its first organist, was justly proud of his creation. "I have just completed a church that made many Washingtonians religious who had not been religious before," he wrote to his son in 1816. In Latrobe's sketch the White House, which is seen across the square, still shows the effects of the 1814 fire. President Madison, offered his choice of pews in the new church, asked the church committee to choose for him. The committeemen selected Pew 28, which has since been known as the President's Pew and has been used at some service by every Chief Executive.

St. John's Church, Lafayette Square

Commodore Stephen Decatur, the American naval hero whose portrait appears on an English mug, used the prize money he had won in his victories over the Barbary pirates and the British in the War of 1812 to build the first private house on the President's Square (seen at left). Benjamin Latrobe, who designed the house, wrote in April 1818 that he had been seeing Commodore Decatur "often & have been very busily engaged for him. In fact I have hardly set foot out of the room where my drawing instruments are collected." Decatur House, later adorned with Victorian embellishments, was afterward restored using Latrobe's original sketches, including the drawing (below) for the entrance hall. Below (left), restored entrance hall.

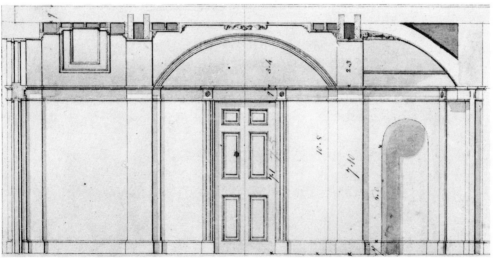

Decatur's house was hardly finished before he was killed on the dueling ground at Bladensburg (above). His challenger, Commodore James Barron, had blamed Decatur for damaging his career and reputation. "Mourn Columbia! for one of thy brightest stars is set!" read the eulogy in *The National Intelligencer* on March 22, 1820, the day of Decatur's death.

Bladensburg's "Valley of Chance," the scene of more than fifty duels, was described in *Morrison's Guide* of 1855 as being

> "within a mile and a half of Bladensburg. . . . It is enclosed by two hills, at the base of which runs a small and reedy brook. To the east the hills sweep round a little, and conceal the parties from the Baltimore and Washington turnpike road. . . . The District line runs through this valley, and the parties from the District of Columbia and Virginia pass over the line into Maryland and thus evade the laws of their own territories."

Decatur's young widow, Susan, whose portrait is attributed to Gilbert Stuart, lived in their house briefly after his death, but financial difficulties soon forced her to find more modest accommodations. Offering to sell the family china and silver, she wrote to Andrew Jackson: "I am literally without a dollar to send to market, and am living upon the patience and kindness of my Butcher and Baker." She was a romantic and legendary figure in Georgetown until her death in 1860.

Privately owned; National Trust for Historic Preservation photograph

127

The F Street House (above) was, for a time, the home of the Baroness Hyde de Neuville. The wife of the French minister, the Baroness was a talented amateur artist. Her watercolors provide rare visual records of early Washington between 1816 and 1822. Living first on F Street and later in the Decatur House, she and her husband entertained often. Margaret Bayard Smith noted in her diary that the Baroness and her husband "have company I believe almost every day to dinner, or of an evening. Always on Saturday,—we have a general invitation for that evening." Benjamin Ogle Tayloe wrote of the Baroness that she "enjoyed making others happy. On receiving her guests, she used to say, 'I am charming to see you!' "

Abby Aldrich Rockefeller Folk Art Collection

In the watercolor (left) the Baroness depicted a "Danse Militaire des Sauvages," which was staged on November 29, 1821, when various Indian tribes were visiting President James Monroe. The President and three escorts have been faintly penciled in in the background.

The watercolor (right) previously unpublished, is identified by the Baroness as "Wash. F Street Maison de Mlle N. 17 Septembre 1821 last night in Mr. Forest's house." The Forest house was on the southeast corner of 14th and F Street.

The view below is what the Baroness saw looking north from the window of her F Street house. The building at left housed the State Department. In the foreground is the Bank Metropol. The oldest extant commercial building in downtown Washington, it has served various functions. In its earliest years it was Rhodes Tavern, and in 1801 it was the meeting place for the Orphan's Court. It subsequently became the Indian King Tavern and then Mrs. Suter's boardinghouse, during whose tenure in 1814 part of the building became the Bank of the Metropolis (now the National Metropolitan Bank). It was also an early home of Riggs Bank and the Press Club. It is still recognizable on the northeast corner of 15th and F.

From Decatur House, which the Baroness and her husband occupied after Susan Decatur was forced to move to smaller quarters, the Baroness looked out upon the newly remodeled St. John's Church, which she sketched in this watercolor of 1822. Latrobe's son noted that the church had been "really a beautiful little thing in its day, before some dull fellow . . . stuck on a stupid, nondescript portico and an abominable pretext for a tower." (Actually the portico followed a Latrobe design.) The steeple bell, given by President Monroe, was cast from a British cannon. Rung to announce services, to celebrate days of thanksgiving and to toll a President's death, the bell once also sounded fire alarms.

To the right of the church, on H Street, stands the Cutts-Madison House. Built in 1820, it came to the widowed Dolley Madison in payment for a debt owed her late husband by her brother-in-law, Congressman Richard Cutts. Although in constant financial trouble because of her son's gambling, she was described by Tayloe as ". . . a remarkable woman, had been very handsome, was graceful and gracious. Her bonhomie could not be surpassed."

Benjamin Ogle Tayloe, seen at left in a portrait attributed to Thomas Sully, built his house (opposite, top) just to the south of Dolley Madison's. The son of John Tayloe, builder of The Octagon, Benjamin Ogle Tayloe kept a diary that records thirty years of the Lafayette Square neighborhood.

130

Benjamin Ogle Tayloe's house (right), though altered, still stands today on Lafayette Square, as do the Decatur and Madison houses. Here, wrote Sarah E. Vedder (another chronicler of the neighborhood), Mrs. Tayloe "died in the bath, one day, after eating a hearty dinner." Next door—two doors down from Dolley Madison's house, toward Pennsylvania Avenue—was what Sarah Vedder called

"the 'unlucky' house, exactly like the Tayloe house, but it had a bad reputation—no one prospered who lived in that house. In after years, in front, under the beautiful trees, P. Barton Key was shot. In the house Hon. William Seward was attacked, and where lately James G. Blaine lived. Had he been superstitious as I, he never would have purchased it, and not anyone could persuade me to attend the theatre [the Belasco] erected thereon."

Philip Barton Key, son of Francis Scott Key, was killed by Representative Daniel Sickles over Key's liaison with Mrs. Sickles. The engraving below shows the wounded Key being carried from the street. In the celebrated trial that followed the shooting, the jealous husband was acquitted on the grounds of "temporary aberration of mind."

According to Sarah Vedder, the houses on this block had gardens enclosed by "high brick walls, the tops finished with broken glass. Many walls in the city were finished in the same manner. It gave the place an awful look."

131

Such Lafayette Square residents as Andrew Jackson, Henry Clay and Daniel Webster made the neighborhood a center of national political power. Jackson (left, in a life study by Thomas Sully) was described by another neighbor, Benjamin Ogle Tayloe, as being "decided and unwavering, firm in friendship, and unforgiving in hatred." Jackson's arch enemy, Henry Clay of Kentucky (at the right, in a portrait by Charles Bird King), lived just across the square from the President's House during the years he and his family occupied Decatur House. Jackson is said to have had two regrets in his long, full life: he had not been able to shoot Henry Clay nor hang John Calhoun.

Daniel Webster of Massachusetts, seen below on the floor of the Senate delivering his famous defense of Clay's Compromise of 1850, lived on the north side of the square, in the house seen on the opposite page (at top). Webster's long career in Washington, like Clay's, included service as a Representative, a Senator, a Secretary of State and an unsuccessful candidate for the Presidency. His support of Clay's Compromise ("I speak today for the preservation of the Union! Hear me for my cause!") insured its passage. A provision of the Compromise outlawed the slave trade in the District of Columbia.

This view of the north side of Lafayette Square shows Daniel Webster's house as it looked during the early 1850s, after it had been enlarged by William W. Corcoran. Living among the luminaries on the square, President Tyler's daughter-in-law, who acted as White House hostess, found it difficult at times to "appreciate the blessing." As she wrote in 1841, "when you meet them in every-day life, you forget that they are great men at all, and just find them the most charming companions in the world, talking the most delightful nonsense, especially Mr. Webster, who entertains me with the most charming gossip."

Directly east of St. John's Church on Lafayette Square stands the Ashburton House, now the Parish House. It was the site of the signing of the Webster–Ashburton Treaty in 1842, which established the boundary between the United States and Canada.

The house, built in 1836 by Matthew St. Clair Clark, former Clerk of the House of Representatives, was later sold to Joseph Gales, editor of *The National Intelligencer*. In 1842 it was selected by Daniel Webster, then Secretary of State, as a residence for Alexander Baring, Lord Ashburton, the British Minister. Ashburton's arrival at the house in April 1842 with three secretaries, four servants, his own horses, carriages and great quantities of luggage created a "delightful stir," and the season which followed "was one of unparalleled gayety in the history of the first half century of Washington life. Balls, parties, receptions, and dinners succeeded one another in bewildering rapidity." Both Ashburton and Daniel Webster set great store by an excellent table as one means of smoothing out difficult negotiations.

Blair House —

Theodore Hanoss

Blair House, near the President's Square, was built by Surgeon General Joseph Lovell in 1824. In 1836, when it was for sale, the house was described in an advertisement as having "every convenience for a family in and about it; a well of excellent water in the yard, brick stable and carriage house adjoining the alley; flower and fruit garden tastefully laid out and highly cultivated." It was bought by Francis Preston Blair, right, who had come to Washington from Kentucky at the request of Andrew Jackson to found *The Globe*, which became the voice of the Jackson Administration. Later, in the year of his death, Jackson wrote to Blair: "live or die I am your friend (and never deserted one for policy), and leave my papers and reputation in your keeping. As far as justice is due to my fame, I know you will shield it." Washington descendants believe Jackson gave his portrait (page 132) to Francis Preston Blair at this time, when he appointed him his literary executor. The portrait is still in the family.

Owned by a Washington descendant

"Not a soul intruded upon the privacy of the visit to the tomb. . . . Not a murmur was heard, save the strains of solemn music and the deep and measured sound of artillery, which awoke the echoes around the hallowed heights of Mount Vernon." So wrote George Washington Parke Custis of Lafayette's visit in 1824 to the tomb of his old comrade-in-arms, George Washington. The visit, commemorated in this lithograph, took place during Lafayette's "triumphal return" to America—a tour that lasted for over a year and occasioned the renaming of the President's Square in his honor.

From about the time of Lafayette's visit onward for perhaps a century, the square was the city's center of social and political life. Just as Decatur House had been the first fashionable private residence on the square, it again led the way to the square's present-day style. Mrs. Truxton Beale, who came to Decatur House in 1912, removed the additions made after her father-in-law bought it in 1872. She meticulously restored it. Through her bequest it became in 1956 the headquarters of the National Trust for Historic Preservation, thereby providing an impetus for the entire restoration and rebuilding of Lafayette Square. Today all around the square the buildings serve various public uses.

Kiplinger Washington Collection

"*Below reposes the city of Georgetown with its spires.*"

—Morrison's *Stranger's Guide*, 1844

The prosperous port of Georgetown exerted a strong pull on the citizens of Washington. Settled for fifty years before the government moved to the Federal City, Georgetown offered the best inns, the best shops and some of the best schools in the area. When Baron von Humboldt visited the capital Jefferson suggested that he and his party would have more convenient access to the White House if they would quit their lodgings at Stelle's Hotel on Capitol Hill and move to Georgetown. While

Library of Congress, Prints and Photographs Division

Georgetown is seen at left in an 1853 view from Observatory Hill in Foggy Bottom. The watercolor seen below, a sketch by James Heriot, shows the bridge over Rock Creek as it appeared in 1815. The succession of bridges that were built on the site provided the vital link between Georgetown and the Federal City. Frequently washed away, they were quickly rebuilt, for Washingtonians demanded ready access to the amenities of Georgetown. The importance of the bridge was recognized in 1788, when the construction commissioners advertised that bids would be welcome for a new bridge: "As this is a building of some consequence it is expected that no person will apply but those who are well qualified to execute the work in the neatest manner and to give ample security of the performance."

Sturdy as a bridge might be, crossing to Georgetown could still be a precarious business. J. Holdsworth Gordon of Georgetown wrote that he remembered

> "the terrible stone battles that used to take place between the Washington, or 'City Pigs' as we used to call them, and the Georgetown boys. No Georgetown boy dared to venture to Washington unless in company with a strong body guard of his fellow townsmen, and woe to the 'City Pig' that came to our town without a similar escort. I have seen men and boys, white and colored, fighting like savages. The Georgetown boys would go in swimming in Rock Creek at a place called 'The Willows', at or near the old ruins then known as 'The Paper Mill'. While in the water a sudden descent would be made upon them by the city roughs, and the only thing to do was to run for it. I have often seen half naked men and boys rushing through West Street, with garments in one hand and rocks in the other, fighting, charging and yelling. At times the utmost brutality was shown and many serious injuries inflicted."

The New-York Historical Society

shops failed in the Federal City they flourished in Georgetown. Mercantile fortunes were made there long after the river commerce of the port had begun its decline. Washington children came to school in Georgetown, and there was a brisk trade in personal services between the city and the town. It may well be that Washington's western-oriented prosperity derives from the city's early leaning toward its thriving neighboring port town on the other side of Rock Creek.

137

"Mr. McLeod could stand in front of the first row and, with one sweep of his 'hickory' . . . could wrap it around a boy or girl sitting on the last, or highest, seat. There was no confusion in that school."

—Sarah E. Vedder, *Reminiscences, 1830–1909*

One of the many kinds of education offered in Georgetown was the Lancaster School, which used an approach developed by an English Quaker. The emphasis was on having the pupils instruct each other, as in the illustration above from a Georgetown publication of 1812. In this way scores of children could be taught on one teacher's salary. The 1812 booklet offered this suggestion to Lancastrian instructors:

"Few punishments are so effectual as confinement after school hours. It is, however, attended with one unpleasant circumstance. In order to confine the bad boys in the school-room, after school hours, it is often needful that the master, or some proper substitute for him, should confine himself in school, to keep them in order. This inconvenience may be avoided by tying them to the desks, or putting them in logs, &c. in such a manner that they cannot loose themselves."

Georgetown's Lancaster School operated for thirty-two years, at 3126 O Street, in a building that still stands. There were also Lancaster schools in Alexandria and Washington.

Miss Lydia English's Seminary was in this house at 3017 N Street at one time, and for many years at 30th Street, a block away, in the building now called the Colonial Apartments.

138

The comely muse seen at the right adorned a certificate issued to a first-grade student at Miss Lydia English's Female Seminary. The Seminary Building, still standing on N Street, is now a private house. Mrs. John M. Binckley, who traveled to the seminary from her home in Washington, wrote:

> "In very bad weather we went in a carriage . . . but on good days we thought nothing of the walk, nor did anyone else. Walking was almost the only way to get anywhere in those days. Even where there were carriages the children of the family were not expected to make any very general use of them. The mud was awful. Cows roamed the streets at will, and a great many people felt quite unashamed of keeping a pig or so where their grounds allowed it."

The Georgetown Seminary (below) "had a great reputation," according to Sarah Vedder. Its students came from every state in the Union and from Canada. One of the students, Mrs Vedder wrote, was

> "Miss Harriet Williams, who lived in Georgetown and who . . . married Count De Bodisco, the Russian minister. . . .
> "The Williams were not in very good circumstances, the father being a hatter, having his establishment on Bridge street, near High. His daughters attended the school, and one day, as the minister was driving by the seminary at noon, as he often did,

the young ladies were being dismissed. . . . He rode in an open barouche, drawn by four white horses, two postillions in livery behind, two drivers in front, Bodisco sitting on the back seat. They were an imposing sight, moving slowly along to catch a good view of the girls. Miss Williams, full of fun, said, so I have heard, 'Girls, shall I stop the Russians?' and immediately stepped into the street, in front of the horses and stooped down to tie her shoe. All were astonished at the action, but as she looked up, so full of mischief, the minister was captivated. Not many months after they were married."

"Evermay" (above) is located at 1623 28th Street NW. It was built in 1801 for Samuel Davidson, whose account books name Nicholas King as responsible for its "surveying, leveling, designing, and planning."

"The houses of Georgetown, chiefly of brick, have a neat appearance. Several were built before the streets were formed, which gave rise to an observation from a French lady, that Georgetown had houses without streets, and Washington, streets without houses. . . . The Bank is a neat building. The Churches, under the direction of trustees, are without ornament."

Most of the imposing Georgetown houses fall into two general catagories: a line of prosperous houses along the N Street area (many with property stretching down to their own wharves) and, at the brow of the hill around R Street, "a ring of pretty country seats." Cox's Row, one of the town's most elegant row of houses, was situated on the northeast corner of N and 34th streets. Colonel John Cox built these houses in 1805, and, as mayor of Georgetown (1823 to 1845), he here entertained Lafayette during the hero's visit to the town. The house on the corner belonged to Commodore Charles Morris, naval hero at Tripoli.

140

Red Hill, a favorite picnic place, was sketched by Georgetown artist William R. Dougal, who owned the house at R Street and Wisconsin Avenue, across from the library. Formerly the site of Mt. Alto Hospital, the property was acquired by the Soviet government in the 1970s for its embassy.

Francis Scott Key, Georgetown lawyer, three times U.S. Attorney for the District of Columbia, the affectionate father of eight children and the author of "The Star-Spangled Banner," lived in the Georgetown house seen below. The following excerpts are from a letter dictated to Key by his small daughter, who addressed it to a sister:

> "Papa rides on horseback to Court every day after breakfast, and sometimes he takes me and Elly to market, and there we get cherries and raspberries and dewberries and Charles Henry calls them all strawberries . . . . Mama has got a Jackson hat, and when she goes to Church she wears it sometimes. It is a beautiful one. Nobody wears it but Mama—it is brown. Mother has been making currant jelly and jam, and last night she had company at supper and she had cake and whistleberries and apples."

The Key-family house, which stood just west of the Key Bridge, was torn down in 1949, when the Whitehurst Freeway was built. When it was demolished there were plans and promises to rebuild it, at the estimated cost then of $65,000. Photographs and measured drawings were taken, and parts of the house were removed to storage.

Looking down the Potomac R.

Among the foremost craftsmen of Georgetown was cabinetmaker William King (left). Born in Ireland in 1771, King came to Baltimore with his parents in 1774 and was later apprenticed to cabinetmaker John Shaw of Annapolis. King started his own business in Georgetown in 1795, in a shop on the west side of Jefferson Street, where he continued until his death in 1854. This portrait, painted for his seventieth birthday, shows King seated in one of his own chairs. President Monroe bought two dozen of the chairs for the East Room of the President's House. One of them is still in the White House today. The portrait and several pieces of furniture made by King, among them another "White House chair," are owned by King descendants in Washington.

The small trunk above bears the label of "John Lutz, Saddle, Trunk, and Harness Maker, High-Street, Georgetown, D.C.—1838."

The breakfront (left) was made by King for his own house in Georgetown. He also made coffins and began an undertaking business in 1795. One of King's "Mortality Books," in which he listed deaths in the area between 1795 and 1832, lies on the desk. It is open to pages for 1796–99 and lists such familiar names as Clagett, Lowndes, Worthington, Balch, Holmead, Beall, Burns, Duncanson, Deakins. Epidemics forced King to work overtime on coffins.

142

The inns and private houses of Georgetown were gathering places for the most prominent citizens and visitors of the District. The building above was one such popular rendezvous. A Masonic Lodge from 1810 to 1840, it still stands today along the canal towpath at Thomas Jefferson Street NW. In 1830 James Greer sold Belfast Liquors and Beer on its lower floor. Francis Baily, a visitor to Georgetown in 1796, noted that "The Federal Arms, where we put up, is the best, though the dearest tavern in Georgetown. It cost us, whilst we were there, for dinner, supper, breakfast, luncheon, and horses, four dollars each." The sketch below is identified as "A party in Georgetown at Mrs. Peters Tudor Place. 1840 by Mr. Glass." The tea service (right) is owned by Washington descendants of John Laird, who ordered it for his N Street house, known today as the Laird-Dunlop house. The silversmith, Charles Burnett, was one of several who moved his shop from Alexandria to Georgetown in about 1800. There were some 65 silversmiths in the area from 1740 to 1840.

"I now ascended a hill that led to the Great Falls, *and on a sudden my steps were suspended by the conflict of elements, the strife of nature. I beheld the course of a large river abruptly obstructed by rocks, over which it was breaking with a tremendous roar; while the foam of the water seemed ascending to the clouds, and the shores that confined it to tremble at the convolution."*

—John Davis of Salisbury, 1801

144

It is no accident that Washington is situated so near the imposing natural phenomenon of Great Falls. The site of the capital—like that of Georgetown before it—was chosen precisely for its proximity to the falls. As an East Coast river with headwaters rising close to the Mississippi watershed, the Potomac offered access to the developing interior. Georgetown's early prosperity stemmed from its unique position as the tobacco inspection station closest to the Potomac headwaters. It is still the last port to which a ship can sail from Chesapeake Bay.

Efforts to reach past the fall line began in the middle of the eighteenth century and promised to increase Georgetown's importance as a center of commerce. The chartering of the Ohio Company in 1749 was a move in that direction. So was the opening, in 1785, of the Potomac Canal, which carried river traffic around Great Falls on the Virginia side (where the ruined locks can still be seen) and Little Falls on the Maryland side. With the opening of the canal George Washington's passionate efforts on behalf of the area's commercial development began to bear fruit. As his secretary, Tobias Lear, wrote in 1793:

"Early in life General Washington contemplated the opening of this river, from tide-water to its source, so as to make it navigable for such vessels as were suitable for carrying the produce of the country to the shipping ports below . . . but the period for undertaking a work of such magnitude

had not yet arrived. The country was then but sparsely inhabited—Canals and Locks but little understood, especially in America; and but few men of property were willing to engage in an undertaking, the cost of which they could not clearly calculate, and the profits of which were to many doubtful. General Washington, however, kept the object steadily in view, waiting until time and circumstances should enable him to bring it forward, with a prospect of success. The war with Great-Britain took place about the time when the importance of this object began to be understood, and a willingness to embark in it began to appear among men of property. . . . In 1784 a company was formed for the purpose of removing the obstructions and opening the navigation of the River from its source down to tide-water.

"The principal work in completing the above mentioned navigation, is at the Great Falls, fourteen miles above the City of Washington—at the Little Falls, four miles above the said City, and in clearing the river between these two Falls. At the Great Falls, the water falls 72 feet in one mile and a half—and at the Little Falls 36 feet 8 inches in about two miles. At the former there will be six, and at the latter, three locks. . . . This will finish the navigation of the main river, from Cumberland down to tide-water, and enable the Company to receive the reward of their expence and labor. Boats, carrying from one hundred and fifty to two hundred barrels of flour, already pass from Cumberland to the Great Falls; and many thousand barrels of flour have actually been brought in boats to the latter place during the present year."

The Great Falls of the Potomac are seen in the 1802 engraving opposite. The view of the Little Falls (right) was painted in 1830 by Richard Redin of Georgetown.

Georgetown Public Library, Peabody Room

145

The Chesapeake and Ohio Canal was to be "a conquest over physical nature such as has never yet been achieved by man," declared President John Quincy Adams as he turned the first shovelful of earth on July 4, 1828. "The wonders of the ancient world, the Pyramids of Egypt, the Colossus of Rhodes, the Temple of Ephesus, the Mausoleum of Artemisia, the Wall of China, sink into insignificance before it."

While the canal never lived up to the high expectations of its promoters, it did revive Georgetown's lagging port life. As a shallow-water port, Georgetown had suffered when deep-draft vessels began being built for the ocean trade at the end of the eighteenth century. The canal, though it was a long time in building, attracted fresh capital and a new population to Georgetown. Canal stock went through Georgetown banks. Canal laborers debarked at the port, lived nearby and caroused in Georgetown grog shops.

By 1850 the canal stretched to Cumberland: 184 miles, with 74 locks. Coal was the chief cargo carried downstream by the canal barges. Other cargo included flour, wheat, corn, lumber, stone and cord wood. Tobacco, the crop on which Georgetown had been founded but which had been diminishing in commercial importance ever since the Revolution, is not even mentioned in the canal company's annual reports.

The C & O Canal never became the key to western prosperity and westward migrations. By a nice twist of fate, the same day that ground was broken for the canal, Charles Carroll of Carrollton turned the first spadeful for America's first railroad, the Baltimore and Ohio—which doomed the canal to failure. The canal could never compete with the efficiency of the railroad. Nor was the company able to develop sufficient trade for the upstream journey. There were also problems with winter ice, summer droughts and spring floods. Commerce continued to dwindle. After a 1924 flood it ceased entirely. The Georgetown-to-Cumberland stretch of the canal is today maintained by the National Park Service as a recreational and scenic resource.

The *Ludlow Patton*, a steam-driven canal barge, is seen in this 1875 view of the canal from just above the Aqueduct. Beyond lies Georgetown harbor, with the Capitol in the distance. The usual canal journey between Georgetown and Cumberland took ten days upstream, three days down. The record was sixty-two hours. Steam-driven boats, which were briefly permitted to use the canal, had to be banned because the wash damaged the banks.

From Boyd's Washington and Georgetown Directory, *1886*

Georgetown teemed with blacksmiths, with boat builders, teamsters, wharf workers and their families—all part of the community supporting the canal and its commerce. Millers, too, played an important new role in the life of the port town, for wheat had replaced tobacco as Georgetown's primary cash crop. (One resident recalled standing on the brow of the hill at R Street and Wisconsin Avenue and seeing wheatfields stretching as far north of Georgetown as the eye could see.) Mills, run by waterpower generated at the canal locks, lined the Georgetown waterfront, and some of them still survive, although powered now by other sources. The Bomford Mill (later the Pioneer Flour Mills) at Potomac Street between Canal and K was first built in 1832 as a flour mill. By 1847 Colonel Bomford had converted it into a cotton mill, but that operation failed. Many early waterfront commercial buildings were rebuilt as offices, shops and restaurants in the 1970s.

Georgetown Public Library, Peabody Room

148

A typical canal boat carried fresh teams of horses or mules in its forward shelter and a "hayhouse" amidships; the captain and his family or crew were housed in an aft cabin. Small children raised on canal boats had to be tethered for safety.

149

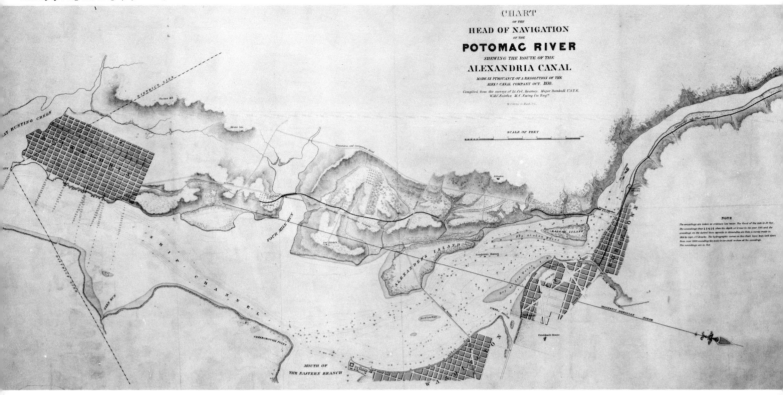

CHART
OF THE
HEAD OF NAVIGATION
OF THE
POTOMAC RIVER
SHEWING THE ROUTE OF THE
ALEXANDRIA CANAL

The Aqueduct Bridge and the Alexandria Canal, seen here in an 1841 chart, permitted barge captains to bypass the port of Georgetown and deliver their cargo directly to the deep-water port of Alexandria. The bridge, sometimes called the "water-trough bridge," carried the barges high above the Potomac, crossing upriver from present Key Bridge. Piles that supported the aqueduct are still visible next to Key Bridge.

The 1845 plan of Alexandria (opposite) shows the Alexandria Canal flowing into the river just to the right of the town's grid of streets. Alexandria's street names reflect popular causes: Wolfe, for that general's victory over Montcalme at Quebec; Pitt and (the bishop of) St. Asaph, for their championing of the American cause in Parliament; Payne, Patrick Henry, (la)Fayette and, of course, Franklin, Washington and Jefferson, for their contributions to the winning of American independence. King, Prince, Duke, Queen and Princess reflect early Royalist feeling. Fairfax and West (the family that rivaled the Alexanders as major property holders) recall the town's early landowners.

The woodcut (left), the earliest known view of Alexandria, was done in the 1830s by Louis Miller. Published in an antislavery tract (see page 171), it shows a slave ship receiving a cargo of slaves for shipment to Southern ports.

150

In Alexandria, D. C.

Fine houses and churches and a brisk trade in such luxuries as silver and elegant cabinetwork attest to Alexandria's prosperity as a port town, though like all Tidewater shipping points its growth was checked by the American Revolution. Its harbor was better favored than that of Georgetown, but of the two major towns within the District of Columbia the Virginia port fared less well. Unlike Georgetown, it was too far from Washington to benefit from the growth of the Federal City. George Washington, seeking perhaps to silence criticism of his role in placing the seat of government so near his own vast land-holdings, had insisted that no federal building take place on the Virginia side of the District. Alexandria, too close to Washington to thrive independently, was thus forbidden the federal offices that might have brought it prosperity. It also suffered its own special trials: yellow fever in 1803, trade blockades prior to and during the War of 1812, cholera in 1832 and fires in 1810 and 1824. Alexandria's importance as a slave-trading center also drove a wedge between it and the rest of the District.

The last straw, the end of Alexandria as part of the District of Columbia, was the heavy debt laid on the town by the canal system. The Virginia link of the canal, built to secure the Cumberland coal trade for Alexandria, proved to be too great a financial burden for the port town to bear. When Congress failed to provide fiscal relief, Alexandria turned to the Virginia legislature for help. To facilitate matters, Congress offered to retrocede all Virginia lands in the District to Virginia. The residents voted their consent, and in 1846 Alexandria ceased to be part of the District. Mrs. William Thornton noted that Alexandrians celebrated with "Great rejoicing and cannon firing."

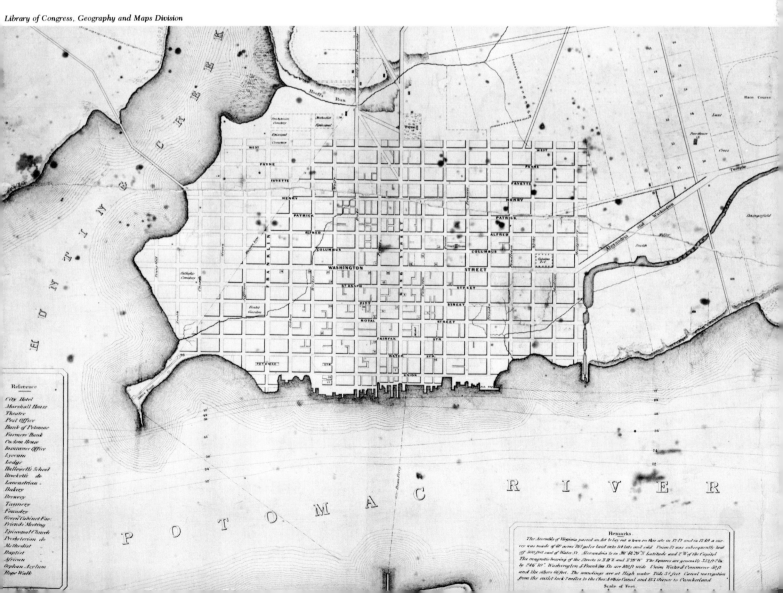

This bird's-eye view of Alexandria, dated 1862, looks south along Washington Street. The cotton factory on the east (left) side of the street—the building with the cupola—has long since been transformed into an apartment building, with an ornate columned portico disguising its humble origins. (The portico was built for use in a reviewing stand for one of Franklin Roosevelt's inaugurals.) Behind the building are two houses associated with the Lee family, both now museums. The old flour mill (left), sketched by William Newton in 1870, was one of many mills in the Alexandria area. Here, as in Georgetown, grain had superseded tobacco as the major cash crop. Brought by wagon from the nearby farms or by canal barge from the fields farther upriver, the grain was ground to flour in Alexandria mills, baked into bread in Alexandria ovens and shipped out to distant markets from Alexandria wharves.

This former Alexandria slave market, being guarded by Union soldiers, was photographed by Mathew Brady. Describing the slave trade that flourished in Alexandria before the Civil War, the *Alexandria Gazette* reported in June 1827:

> "Scarcely a week passes without some of these wretched creatures being driven through our streets. After having been confined and sometimes manacled in a loathsome prison, they are turned out in public view to take their departure for the South. The children and some of the women are generally crowded into a cart or wagon, while others follow on foot, not infrequently handcuffed or chained together."

Collection of William F. Smith

REMOVAL.

BENJAMIN WOOD,

COMB MANUFACTURER,

HAS JUST RECEIVED

In addition to his former assortment, a handsome selection of FANCY ARTICLES; consisting of

Tortoise-shell,
Mock,   } *COMBS.*
And Ivory

ALSO,
LOOKING GLASSES,

In gilt, curled maple, & mahogany frames; cloth and hair brushes, fancy baskets, &c.
may 29   2w

Pickled Oysters.

THE subscriber has for sale *PICKLED OYSTERS* of the first quality They are pronounced by good judges, to be superior to any in the market   Persons can be supplied by the jar or smaller quantity.
                        D. BARCROFT,
                        opposite the old Market,
may 27

WILL'M A. WILLIAMS,

GOLD & SILVER-SMITH,

Clock & Watch Maker,

Has removed his shop to King-street, between Royal and Fairfax-streets, (south side,) where he is prepared to execute all orders in the above lines in the best and most expeditious manner, and on the most reasonable terms.   He has on hand and intends keeping, a handsome assortment of

Jewelry, Silver and Plated

Ware, &c. &c.

ALSO, 1 case elegant
BRITTANNIA WARE.

may 29   2w

Board of Health...May 21.

Ordered, That the members of the Board of Health, each in his particular district, undertake to scrutinize the various portions of the town, for the discovery and removal of nuisances according to the following arrangement;

Daniel Wright, east of Royal, and south of Prince street

William A. Williams' Notice of Removal in 1823 and the Picture of his new Quarters.

William A. Williams, "Gold & Silversmith, Clock & Watch Maker," published the notice (opposite) in 1823, informing his customers that he had moved to new quarters on King Street in Alexandria, next door to Benjamin Wood's comb factory. Examples of Alexandria silver include a "coffin-cornered" ladle (above) and a spectacle case (below), engraved with the name of the owner and "Alexandria D.C." Jugs like those at right were made through the nineteenth century for local merchants by the Alexandria firm of B.C. Milburn.

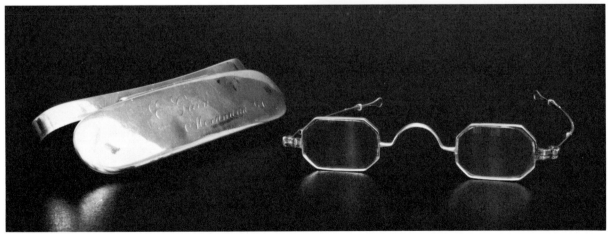

Captain's Row, on Prince Street leading to the waterfront (below), housed many early sea captains. The cobblestones are said to have been brought over as ballast on ships and laid by Hessian mercenaries during the Revolutionary War. The block has been carefully restored. The Green Factory Steam Furniture Works (left) was established in Alexandria in 1823. In 1877 it was advertising: "Chamber, Hall, Parlor, Dining Room, School and Church Furniture, Wholesale and Retail," as well as "Handrails, Newells, Balusters, Bracketts, Bed-posts, Table-legs, Fancy Turnings, Sawing, Carving and Molding, Woven wire and other springs, Hair moss, Sponge and shuck mattresses, Cabinet and upholsterer's materials."

Both: Collection of William F. Smith

These twin houses on Oronoco Street—the Hallowell School (on the left) and Robert E. Lee's boyhood home (on the right)—were built between 1793 and 1795. Robert Edward Lee, a son of Light-Horse Harry Lee, came to live in Alexandria after his birthplace, Stratford Hall, was inherited by his elder half brother. Next door to the house on Oronoco Street, at the school run by Quaker Benjamin Hallowell, Lee prepared for West Point.

Virginia Theological Seminary, Alexandria

The Virginia Theological Seminary (above), which was founded in Alexandria in 1823 but later moved to the hills outside the city. Next to it was the Episcopal High School (right), founded in 1839 on Seminary (or "Holy") Hill.

Old Churches, Ministers and Families of Virginia *by Bishop Meade, Philadelphia, 1857*

"Facilities for reaching [Alexandria] are afforded by the steamboats which ply at almost every hour of the day, and also by a bridge across the Potomac, and an excellent turnpike. The strikingly beautiful features of the intervening country—the graceful outline of the Virginia hills, confronted by those of Maryland—the broad and majestic expanse of the Potomac, (whose name, we have been told signifies in the Indian language, 'the River of Swans,' and might seem descriptive of its characteristic grandeur and stateliness)—all these conspire to render an excursion to Alexandria one of the most agreeable incidents which can await the sojourner in Washington."

—Morrison's *Stranger's Guide*, 1844

Washington's first bridges and ferries, like many of the city's early roads, were built with private funds and their operations paid for with tolls. The first bridge across the Potomac, Chain Bridge, at the Little Falls above Georgetown (page 83), was built in 1797. Potomac (or Long) Bridge, which opened in 1809, is visible on the right-hand side of the panorama above: an 1838 view of the capital city from Arlington, Virginia. Drawbridges on either end of Potomac Bridge allowed boats to pass through. One of the draw spans is seen in Seth Eastman's 1850 sketch (left).

Like Chain Bridge, the Potomac Bridge was repeatedly washed away by ice and floods and repeatedly rebuilt. According to an 1836 guidebook:

> *"The Potomac Bridge,* crossing the river at Washington, has just been reconstructed by the Government, and rendered henceforth a *free* bridge. It is about a mile in length, the other parts being across the shallow portions of the river, are permanent embankments. This great work was completed in a little more than one year, for the comparatively small sum of 120,000 dollars."

The advent of the steamboat made the journey between Virginia and Washington easier and quicker than it had been. By 1839, when August Köllner painted this view of a Washington wharf, steamboats were well established on the Potomac. Initially, however, the public had greeted the new contraptions with some trepidation—as is evident in the following 1817 advertisement in *The National Intelligencer:*

> "This new and beautiful Steam Boat is now fitted up in the most complete and efficient manner, for the accommodation of passengers, and will commence running from my wharf (mouth of Tiber Creek) to Alexandria on Sunday next, and continue to run regularly every day; leaving this place at 9 o'clock A.M., and Alexandria at 4 o'clock P.M. She will be commanded by a careful man, well qualified, who will pay every attention to the comfort of the passengers, and take particular care of all freight that may be committed to his charge.
>
> "The Experiment runs remarkably fast, and as to the general apprehension from the busting of boilers any person (acquainted with the nature of them) can be satisfied in a moment, that these boilers are so constructed (with safety valves) as to prevent a possibility of injury from them, or any other part of the machinery.
>
> "It is hoped that the citizens of Washington and Alexandria will give ample encouragement to this useful and pleasant mode of communication between the two places, otherwise she will be sent from this District, when they will, no doubt, regret the loss of this most desirable convenience to the great body of our city."

Library of Congress, Prints and Photographs Division

159

NOTICE.—The steamboat Jo EPH JOHNSON will, on and after Sunday, the 12th March, commence running between Alexandria and Washington, and run as follows, viz:

Leave Alexandria at 9 and 11 o'clock, A. M.
Do.   do.   2   4   do.   P. M.
Do. Washington 10   12   do.   A. M.
Do.   do.   3   5   do.   P. M.

JOSEPH JOHNSON,

March 14—1w   Master.

Martin Luther King Library, Washingtoniana Collection

Collection of William F. Smith

"Omnibuses are running every hour in the day between Washington and Georgetown; distance about two miles. And when the navigation is not prevented by ice, steamboats are hourly passing between Washington and Alexandria, about five miles; fare to either place only twelve and a half cents."

—A guidebook, 1836

Horses and mules provided the only overland rapid transit prior to the mid-1830s, when the railroads came. Omnibuses like the 1830 one shown (left) ran from Georgetown to the Navy Yard and between the wharves and L Street. They seated twelve and were known as "seagoing hacks" because the streets were so often awash with mud. The advertisement for steamboat transportation appeared in *The Globe* in 1836. The Phoenix Line, whose letterhead appears below, offered transportation between Baltimore and Washington in the 1830s.

In an interview reported in the Washington *Evening Star* on August 15, 1896, Charles Elliott, a noted stagecoachman on the Richmond-to-Washington run, gave this description of how travelers amused themselves on long journeys by stagecoach:

"You see, a pack of cards or two, and two or three bottles of good whiskey or brandy made the time go faster than the horses. As soon as the stage bowled away from Lexington, which was generally at night, they would take a drink or two, tell some yarns and then go to sleep. Next morning they would stop a good while at breakfast, dress, stretch their limbs, enjoy the company of some gentlemen in the neighborhood where the stop was made, and sometimes go a hunting and let the stage go on and wait for the stage the next day.

"They never traveled at night after the first night. They would set up all night at the hotel drinking and playing cards, get into the coach after an early breakfast next mornin' and sleep all day, except when they stopped at the wayside house for dinner. If they were awake a little while after dinner, they had a sociable game and several drinks in the stage and then went to sleep again.

"Every night after supper at the taverns where we stopped they would have a royal good time. A royal blue time, they called it, for, you see, they knowed nothing about painting the town red. So they come on until they get to Fredericksburg, where they cleaned themselves up, took a bath, and come into Washington fresh as kids.

"That's the way they did it, sir. These kind of men never knew what a tiresome hour was in the old stage coach. It was the best of travel for gentlemen that they ever knowed. Why sir, every one of them were sorry when the stages stopped carrying them through the country. If horses could have draw'd as fast as steam they'd have been going in the stages yit."

Phœnix Line for Washington.

160

Tiber creek.
North east of the Capitol. Was

"On the 25 day august 1835 on Tuesday the Cars started the first time from Washington to Baltimore and a hold parsel people went and the councilmen and alldermen went free passage to Baltimore and back," reported Michael Shiner. In Köllner's 1839 drawing (above) the train is seen crossing Tiber Creek, a few blocks from the Capitol. An 1836 guidebook reported that "the hitherto tedious journey" between Baltimore and Washington—a distance of thirty seven miles—was accomplished by train in two and a half hours. As a safety precaution, early trains stopped their engines on the outskirts of the city and were drawn into town by horses. Their terminus was the B&O depot (seen at right), Washington's first railroad station and one of the first in the country. It was on the northwest corner of Second Street and Pennsylvania Avenue NW. In 1852 a second B & O station was built at New Jersey Avenue and C Street, where it stood for fifty-five years.

After his first train ride, Washington mayor Joseph Gales declared that "for celerity of transportation of persons, the Rail-Road possesses advantages over every other mode." He predicted that "wherever the cost of a Rail-Road can be borne, it will supersede all other modes of travelling." In an article for the Baltimore *Patriot* Gales described his trip:

> "We experienced in a very slight degree the jarring which we have heard spoken of in the motion of the cars, or the other inconveniences which we had apprehended. It will require care, to be sure, to guard against accidents in this mode of conveyance; but that will be the case with every description of rapid locomotion. For ourselves, we met with no accident of any sort; nor had any just reason to apprehend any, during our jaunt. One of the cows, indeed, which we overtook strolling or grazing along the edge of the road, cast a suspicious glance with a momentary alarm, lest she should attempt to cross our path; but, luckily, she forthwith took a direction *from* the road instead of crossing it, and we were let off for the fright."

161

The Capitol (above) as it looked after it had been completed by Charles Bulfinch, in a wood engraving printed in gouache, which was probably produced in Alsace as a wallpaper design. Bulfinch, often referred to as "the First American Architect," came to Washington in 1818 and succeeded Latrobe as Architect of the Capitol. He completed the dome and rotunda by about 1825, nearly forty years after Dr. William Thornton's design had been accepted. The result, however, was impressive, even to the critical eye of Frances Trollope. Viewing the Capitol in 1827, she was "struck with admiration and surprise. None of us, I believe, expected to see so imposing a structure on that side of the Atlantic. I am ill at describing buildings, but the beauty and majesty of the American capitol might defy an abler pen than mine to do it justice. It stands so finely too, high, and alone." Today the only visible remains of Bulfinch's Capitol are the small domes above the original Senate and House chambers. His gatehouses have been moved to Constitution Avenue at 15th and 17th streets; some gateposts are nearby.

The interior view of the House of Representatives (right) was painted by Samuel F. B. Morse in 1821–22, when the Capitol was still under construction. The painting includes portraits of some seventy Congressmen, as well as those of the Supreme Court Justices (on the dais at left, rear). In 1821 Morse wrote to his wife:

> "I receive every possible facility from all about the Capitol. The door-keeper, a venerable man, has offered to light the great chandelier expressly for me to take my sketches in the evening for two hours together, for I shall have it a candle-light effect, when the room already very splendid will appear ten times more so."

162

"The proper way to have built the Capitol was to have offered an adequate sum to the most eminent architect in any of the European cities, to furnish the design and working drawings, also a person of his own choice to superintend the work. In that case the Capitol would have been long ago completed and for half the sum that has been expended on the present wreck."

  —English architect George Hadfield, in his 1820 report on the Capitol

The old City Hotel, afterward famous as the Willard (above), was located at 14th Street and Pennsylvania Avenue, just down the avenue from the White House (which is on the left in the engraving). Despairing of the hotel's rundown condition, its owner, Benjamin Ogle Tayloe, hired as manager the young steward of a Hudson River steamer. The steward, Henry Willard, came to Washington in 1847. First leasing the hotel from Mr. Tayloe, he soon afterward purchased it and gave it his own name. He and his brothers, who joined him, became legends as Washington hotelkeepers.

"Hotel-keeping was very different in those days from what it is now [Willard's son recalled]; almost every morning at three o'clock, my father would be called to go down to Centre Market to buy provisions and supplies for the hotel; then at meal hours, especially at dinner, he did the carving, and in this way no waste occurred. Everyone was interested and worked."

Willard's attention to the details of running his hotel were also noted by his wife, Sarah Bradley Willard. Writing to her grandfather in 1857, she said: "We are all very busy now making carpets. Henry cuts and plans everything, and then we all sew as fast as possible." Willard's careful management paid off. His hotel quickly became one of the city's principal hostelries, along with The National, the Ebbitt House and Brown's.

"The hotel in which we live is a long row of small houses fronting on the street, and opening at the back upon a common yard, in which hangs a great triangle. Whenever a servant is wanted, somebody beats on this triangle from one stroke up to seven, according to the number of the house in which his presence is required; and as all the servants are always being wanted, and none of them ever come, this enlivening engine is in full performance the whole day through. Clothes are drying in the same yard; female slaves, with cotton handkerchiefs twisted round their heads, are running to and fro on the hotel business; black waiters cross and recross with dishes in their hands; two great dogs are playing upon a mound of loose bricks in the centre of the little square; a pig is turning up his stomach to the sun, and grunting 'that's comfortable'; and neither the men, nor the women, nor the dogs, nor the pig, nor any created creature, takes the smallest notice of the triangle, which is tingling madly all the time."

—Charles Dickens, *American Notes,* 1842

164

Brown's Indian Queen Hotel, shown here at the head of a customer's bill of 1828, stood on the north side of Pennsylvania Avenue between 6th and 7th streets, conveniently near the Stage and Steamboat Office. A hotel since 1804, it had been the Indian Queen since 1810. It often provided lodgings for Indian chiefs who came to Washington to negotiate with the President.

The Indians below, each wearing a Presidential medal around his neck, were among twenty-five chiefs who visited Washington in 1821. At the urging of the Superintendent of Indian Trade, Charles Bird King was commissioned to paint the portraits of all twenty-five. The chiefs shown here are Monchousia, or White Plume (left), of the Kanza tribe; Petalesharro, or Generous Chief (right), a Pawnee; and Sharitarish, or Wicked Chief (center), also a Pawnee. Of King's Indian portraits the English traveler Frances Trollope observed in 1827 that they were

"inexpressibly engaging, and the more touching, perhaps, because at the moment we were looking at them, those very hearts which lent the eyes such meek and friendly softness, were wrung by a base, cruel and most oppressive act of their *great father*.

"We were at Washington at the time that the measure for chasing the last of several tribes of Indians from their forest homes, was canvassed in Congress, and finally decided upon by the *fiat* of the President [Jackson] . . . . It is impossible for any mind of common honesty not to be revolted by the contradictions in [Americans'] principle and practice. . . . you will see them with one hand hoisting the cap of liberty, and with the other flogging their slaves. You will see them one hour lecturing their mob on the indefeasible rights of man, and the next driving from their homes the children of the soil, whom they have bound themselves to protect by the most solemn treaties."

The Old Print Shop, New York

All: White House Collection

"There were a great variety of manufactured articles . . ."

—James K. Polk, *Diary* (May 21, 1846)

Peter Force (left) was distinguished as a collector of books and documents of American history (whose collection became an important addition to the Library of Congress) and as the editor and printer of the *National Journal*. It is one mark of the importance of the press in early Washington that he, like Gales and Seaton of *The National Intelligencer*, was also elected a mayor of the city (1836 to 1840).

The printing industry was a major source of employment in Washington. Its role in the city's economy became even more significant when the Government Printing Office—one of the largest plants in the world—began operations in 1852. A glimpse of Force's printing business is found in a letter that a North Carolina Congressman, John Heritage Bryan, wrote to his wife in 1828:

"It is such a wearisome drudgery to prepare a speech, to wait with feverish anxiety for an opportunity to deliver it, and then to prepare it for the press, and superintend its publication . . . . I was kept up last night 'til near midnight waiting for the proof sheets. I waited for them with great impatience, and then went to the office through the rain to correct them. After all there are several errors.

"I really pity the poor journeymen whom I saw at work at Force's office. They were employed in a heated atmosphere setting types. They sit up night after night nearly all night long and sleep in the day—the poor creatures strain their eyes in arranging the small type by a bad light and altogether they look very wan and meagre."

Efforts to stimulate Washington's trade and maufacturing included holding the Mechanics Exhibition shown in this 1830s engraving. One such exhibit is described in President James K. Polk's *Diary:*

"I visited the fair accompanied by the Mayor and committee and the ladies of my family. There were a great variety of manufactured articles collected in a very large temporary building erected for the occasion by the manufacturers. I was informed that the building alone cost over $6,000, and that as soon as the fair was over would be taken down. The specimens of manufacture exhibited are highly creditable to the genius and skill of our countrymen."

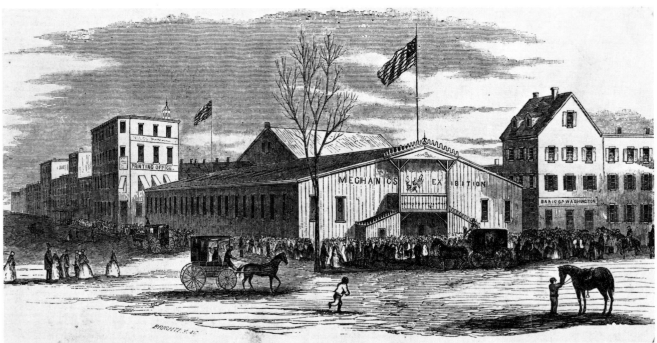

The Washington Directory *of 1822 included this "Occupational Breakdown of Listed Heads of Household":*

5 Adjutant General's Office
5 Apothecary
2 Auctioneers
69 Auditor's Office
17 Attorney at Law
2 Architects
1 Architect of the Capitol
9 Bakers
4 Barbers
2 Barkeepers
2 Bell Hangers
1 Billiard Table
3 Black and White Smiths
39 Blacksmiths
4 Blockmakers
31 Boarding Houses
4 Boatmen
5 Bookbinders
3 Booksellers
1 Brewer
37 Bricklayers
5 Brickmakers
1 Brushmaker
23 Butchers
9 Cabinetmakers
1 Capt. of Steamboat *Dandy*
1 Capt. of Steamboat *Washington*
140 Carpenters
2 Carriers
16 Carters
3 Carvers
1 Chairmaker
1 China and Glass Store
1 Cloth Manufacturer
10 Coach Makers
1 Coal Merchant

1 Cobbler
3 Commission Merchants
22 Comptroller's Office
7 Confectioners
2 Cooks
1 Coppersmith
1 Currier
1 Dairyman
2 Dancing Masters
3 Dentists
13 Doctors
3 Dressmakers
1 Druggist
23 Dry Goods Stores
3 Fancy Stores
1 Farrier
2 Farmers
2 Filers
1 Fowler
12 Gardeners
2 Gilders
5 Glass Blowers
4 Gunsmiths
103 Grocers
3 Hack Drivers
5 Hairdressers
4 Hardware Merchants
2 Hat and Shoe Stores
9 Hat Stores
1 Huckster
1 Intelligence Officer
1 Jailor
1 Ladies Fancy Wareroom
24 Land Offices
1 Leather Merchant
1 Librarian
5 Livery Stables

7 Lottery and Exchange Brokers
5 Lumber Merchants
3 Lumberyards
1 Mathematician
2 Marine Band
25 Marine Barracks
6 Messengers
2 Millwrights
16 Ministers
8 Milliners
12 Navy Department
9 Navy Yard
1 Nurse
2 Notary Public
3 Ordnance Department
1 Organ Builder
6 Oyster House
12 Painters
1 Paperhanger
3 Patent Office
4 Pension Bureau
13 Plasterers (Ornamental)
8 Porter Cellar
1 Portrait Painter
31 Post Office
26 Printers
3 Printers and Engravers
10 Professors
1 Publisher
3 Pumpmakers
22 Register's Office
2 Ropemakers
4 Saddlers
4 Scavengers
6 School Masters and School Mistresses

1 Seedsman
47 Shoemakers
2 Shoe Stores
2 Sign Painters
3 Silversmiths
1 Soap and Candle Manufacturer
13 State Department
3 Steam Mill
27 Stone Cutters
3 Stone Masons
2 Stone Quarriers
6 Subsistence Office
17 Tailors
1 Tallow Chandler
1 Tanner and Currier
33 Tavernkeepers
3 Teachers and Tutors
7 Tinmen
3 Tobacconists
1 Topographical Engineer
25 Treasury Department
4 Turners
1 Umbrella Maker
3 Upholsters
2 Waiters
29 War Department
2 Watchmakers
2 Watchmakers and Jewellers
2 Weavers
4 Wheelwrights
1 Whitewasher
103 Widows
1 Wine Merchant
2 Wood Corders
2 Wood Merchants

The following list from The Washington Directory, 1822, *shows the occupations of "Colored Heads of Household":*

4 Barbers
2 Blacksmiths
1 Bricklayer
3 Carpenters
1 Carter
1 Cobler
1 Cook
1 Hackman
2 Hairdressers

1 Huckster
12 Laborers
1 Livery Stable
4 Messengers
1 Messenger (Assistant) General Post Office
1 Messenger (Assistant) Navy Department
1 Nurse

5 Oyster Houses
1 Paster
1 Plasterer
2 Sawyers
1 Sexton
1 Shoemaker
1 Sweepmaster
1 Tailor
2 Waiters

1 Whitewasher
1 Widow
7 Women, no listing
8 Men, no listing

For industry and for sport, the Potomac and its tributaries were among Washington's most valuable resources—as the city's founders knew they would be. In early Washington, remembered Christian Hines, "large flocks of wild ducks could be seen on the Potomac. They would even come as near Georgetown as Mason's Island, and up the Tiber . . . . almost to . . . . the center market. They would approach so near the shore that people used to throw stones at them. Even I used to try my hand at it, but never succeeded at killing any that way." In the engraving below, which illustrated Morrison's *Stranger's Guide* of 1845, fishermen are seen hauling in their nets at Giesborough, the point of land at the mouth of the Anacostia, opposite the Military Arsenal. (The Capitol Building is just visible on the horizon, at the center of the picture.) Morrison noted that "Millions of Herrings, and immense numbers of Shad, are annually caught, packed up in barrels, and thence distributed to every region of the

United States. The fisheries commence in the spring, and usually last from four to six weeks."

Up the Anacostia from Giesborough was the Washington Navy Yard (just visible above the peak of the fisherman's cottage). Here, as early as 1806, more than 200 men were employed in building, outfitting and repairing ships. It remained a major Washington employer through World War II. About the middle of the nineteenth century, work at the Navy Yard began to center on the development and manufacture of heavy ordnance, and the name was officially changed to the Naval Gun Factory. During World War I the emphasis shifted again, with manufacturing ranging from huge gears for drawbridges and canal locks to precision optical instruments. Techniques for building rockets were developed here during World War II. Until the days of the airplane the Navy Yard also served as a ceremonial Gateway to the City for arriving dignitaries.

Morrison's Stranger's Guide, 1852

Another prominent shipbuilding concern was Easby's Shipyard on the Potomac in Foggy Bottom west of the Naval Observatory. This 1850 watercolor was painted by Montgomery Meigs.

"Most Awful and Most Lamentable Catastrophe!" read the headline in *The National Intelligencer* the day after a gun exploded aboard the *U.S.S. Princeton* during a gala inspection cruise. As the paper reported in its issue of February 29, 1844, the accident occurred

"yesterday afternoon, whilst [the *Princeton* was] under way, in the river Potomac, fourteen or fifteen miles below this city.

"Guests to full four hundred of Commander Stockton, men and women, were on board. The ship went below Fort Washington. To entertain the guests and at the same time to exhibit the capacity of a formidable gun (carrying a ball of 225 pounds) it was fired several times. On the return and at a time when all the women and most of the men were in other parts of the ship—the time of a sumptuous repast—to the request that the gun be fired the Commander gave consent. The gun burst. The commander was stunned to the extent he did not recover for some days. Seventeen seamen were wounded and if any were killed it is not mentioned. Five distinguished men were killed: Abel P. Upshur, Secretary of State; Thomas W. Gilmer, Secretary of the Navy; Captain Beverly W. Kennon, Chief of the Bureau of Construction and Equipment of the Navy; Virgil Maxcy, Charge d'Affairs of the United States in Belgium; David Gardiner, Ex-Senator of New York.

"From the ship the next morning the bodies were transferred to the east room of the President's Mansion and lay in State at the Mansion. . . . The procession was impressive. Twelve men of honorable distinction preceded each hearse. The bodies were placed in the vault of the Congressional burying ground."

"In no part of the earth—not even excepting the rivers on the Coast of Africa, was there so great, so infamous a slave market, as in the metropolis, in the seat of government of this nation which prides itself on freedom."

—John Randolph of Roanoke

Born a slave, Alethia Browning Tanner is said to have sold vegetables to Thomas Jefferson at a small produce stall near the President's Square. She bought her own freedom in 1810 and later bought the freedom of several relatives. Blacks could be free if descended from a free mother or emancipated by will or deed. Sometimes they earned money by special tasks or by producing or growing something they could sell. Freed blacks often bought a kinsman or wife out of slavery, which is one reason why blacks appear occasionally as slave-owners on District rolls. To certify their freedom they were given Freedom Papers which had to be produced on demand and were very specific in their description of the holder. Papers issued in 1853 to a slave of Dolley Madison by the Circuit Court of the District read: "bearer hereof Catherine Taylor, a dark mulatto woman, stout and well made about 32 years of age 5 feet 4 another ¼ inch high round oval face forehead high with good features having 2 small scars on the back of the right hand occasioned by her hand being or having been broke." Alethia Tanner was the first woman on the Roll of Members of the Union Bethel AME Church, now the Metropolitan AME Church on M Street near 15th (see page 318). She owned land and a store at 14th and H streets, which she left to her nephews. Later one of the nephews realized $100,000 for this property.

As the capital of a nation founded on the principles of freedom and equality, Washington had long been notorious as the center of the slave trade. Foreign visitors enjoyed criticizing America's pretensions to social justice; and Washingtonians, too, raised their voices against slavery. In the District, two abolitionist societies were formed in the 1820s. More than a thousand local citizens signed a petition in 1828 urging Congress to end the slave trade. Efforts were also undertaken to help resettle American blacks in Africa. The African Education Society was formed by whites in 1829 to give "persons of color destined to Africa" an education "in letters, Agriculture, and Mechanic Arts."

Generally, freedmen in the area resisted these resettlement efforts. In 1831, at a meeting at the African Methodist Episcopal Church, Washington freedmen proclaimed "the soil that gave us birth is our only true and veritable home." Meanwhile, as a 1972 study by historian Letitia Woods Brown has shown, the proportion of freedmen to slaves in the District's black population grew steadily: from 19 percent in 1800 to 78 percent in 1860. By then, the slave trade—though not slavery itself—had been outlawed in the District under the terms of the Compromise of 1850.

The broadside opposite, published in New York in 1836 by the American Anti-Slavery Society, demands an end to slavery in the District of Columbia. It begins by citing the Bible's denunciation of "the Oppressor," then quotes the Declaration of Independence and the Constitution on liberty and equality and the constitutions of the states on freedom of the press. It then outlines the legal grounds on which the Federal government could abolish slavery in the District and gives evidence of how public prisons, public officers and public funds were being used to perpetuate slavery. The names at the bottom are those of 163 Congressmen who had voted not to interfere with slavery in D.C. (against 47 who voted for abolition).

SLAVE MARKET OF AMERICA.

THE WORD OF GOD.

"ALL THINGS WHATSOEVER YE WOULD THAT MEN SHOULD DO TO YOU, DO YE EVEN SO TO THEM, FOR THIS IS THE LAW AND THE PROPHETS."

"AND THEY SIGHED BY REASON OF THE BONDAGE, AND THEY CRIED, AND THEIR CRY CAME UP UNTO GOD BY REASON OF THE BONDAGE, AND GOD HEARD THEIR GROANING."

"THUS SAITH THE LORD, EXECUTE JUDGMENT IN THE MORNING, AND DELIVER HIM THAT IS SPOILED OUT OF THE HANDS OF THE OPPRESSOR, LEST MY FURY GO OUT LIKE FIRE AND BURN THAT NONE CAN QUENCH IT, BECAUSE OF THE EVIL OF YOUR DOINGS."

THE DECLARATION OF AMERICAN INDEPENDENCE.

"WE HOLD THESE TRUTHS TO BE SELF-EVIDENT:—THAT ALL MEN ARE CREATED EQUAL; THAT THEY ARE ENDOWED BY THEIR CREATOR WITH CERTAIN UNALIENABLE RIGHTS; THAT AMONG THESE ARE LIFE, LIBERTY, AND THE PURSUIT OF HAPPINESS."

THE CONSTITUTION OF THE UNITED STATES.

"THE CITIZENS OF EACH STATE SHALL BE ENTITLED TO ALL THE PRIVILEGES AND IMMUNITIES OF CITIZENS OF THE SEVERAL STATES." Article 4. Section 2.

"CONGRESS SHALL MAKE NO LAW ABRIDGING THE FREEDOM OF SPEECH, OR OF THE PRESS, OR OF THE RIGHT OF THE PEOPLE PEACEABLY TO ASSEMBLE, AND TO PETITION THE GOVERNMENT FOR A REDRESS OF GRIEVANCES."—Article 1. Amendment.

"CONGRESS SHALL HAVE POWER TO EXERCISE EXCLUSIVE LEGISLATION, IN ALL CASES WHATSOEVER, OVER SUCH DISTRICT (NOT EXCEEDING TEN MILES SQUARE) AS MAY, BY CESSION OF PARTICULAR STATES AND THE ACCEPTANCE OF CONGRESS, BECOME THE SEAT OF GOVERNMENT OF THE UNITED STATES."—Article 1. Section 8.

CONSTITUTIONS OF THE STATES.

"EVERY CITIZEN MAY FREELY SPEAK, WRITE, AND PUBLISH HIS SENTIMENTS ON ALL SUBJECTS, BEING RESPONSIBLE FOR THE ABUSE OF THAT LIBERTY." Constitutions of Maine, Connecticut, New York, Pennsylvania, Delaware, Ohio, Indiana, Illinois, Tennessee, Louisiana, Alabama, Mississippi, and Missouri.

"THE FREEDOM OF THE PRESS IS ONE OF THE GREAT BULWARKS OF LIBERTY, AND THEREFORE OUGHT NEVER TO BE RESTRAINED."—North Carolina.

"THE LIBERTY OF THE PRESS OUGHT TO BE INVIOLABLY PRESERVED."—Maryland.

"THE FREEDOM OF THE PRESS IS ONE OF THE GREAT BULWARKS OF LIBERTY, AND CAN NEVER BE RESTRAINED BUT BY DESPOTIC GOVERNMENTS."—Virginia. Other States nearly the same.

DISTRICT OF COLUMBIA.

"THE LAND OF THE FREE."   THE RESIDENCE OF 7000 SLAVES   "THE HOME OF THE OPPRESSED."

READING OF THE DECLARATION OF INDEPENDENCE.

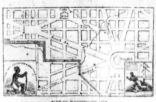

PART OF WASHINGTON CITY.

CAPITOL OF THE UNITED STATES.

RIGHT TO INTERFERE.

PUBLIC PRISONS IN THE DISTRICT.

Built by Congress with $15,000 of the People's money, perverted from the purposes for which they were built, and used by Slaveholders for the confinement of refractory Slaves, by licensed Slave-dealers as depots for their victims, and by kidnappers for the imprisonment of Free Americans, seized and sold to pay their jail fees.

JAIL IN ALEXANDRIA.

FACTS.

VIEW OF THE INTERIOR OF THE JAIL IN WASHINGTON.—FANNY JACKSON.

FACTS.

JAIL IN WASHINGTON.—SALE OF A FREE CITIZEN TO PAY JAIL FEES.

FACTS.

PRIVATE PRISONS IN THE DISTRICT, LICENSED AS SOURCES OF PUBLIC REVENUE.

"For a license to trade or traffic in slaves for profit, whether as agent or otherwise, four hundred dollars;"—the Register to "deposit all monies received from taxes imposed by this act to the credit of the Canal Fund." approved July 2d, 1831. City Laws, p. 249.

SLAVE HOUSE OF J. W. NEAL & CO.

VIEW OF A SECTION OF ALEXANDRIA, WITH A SLAVE SHIP RECEIVING HER CARGO OF SLAVES.

FRANKLIN & ARMFIELD'S SLAVE PRISON.

"CASH FOR 200 NEGROES"

JOSEPH W. NEAL & CO.

ALEXANDRIA AND NEW ORLEANS PACKETS.

FRANKLIN & ARMFIELD.

"CASH FOR 400 NEGROES"

FRANKLIN & ARMFIELD.

People of the United States, Congress alone possess the constitutional power to legislate for the District of Columbia: yet one hundred and sixty-three of your representatives are striving to perpetuate in the Capital of your Republic this system of robbery, cruelty and despotism. *House of Representatives, 8th February 1836.*—Certain petitions and resolutions respecting the Abolition of Slavery in the District of Columbia were referred to a Select Committee with instructions to report. "THAT IS THE OPINION OF THIS HOUSE CONGRESS OUGHT NOT IN ANY WAY TO INTERFERE WITH SLAVERY IN THE DISTRICT OF COLUMBIA." Yeas 163—Nays 47.—The following are the Yeas.

Published by the American Anti-Slavery Society, 144 Nassau-street, New-York, 1836.

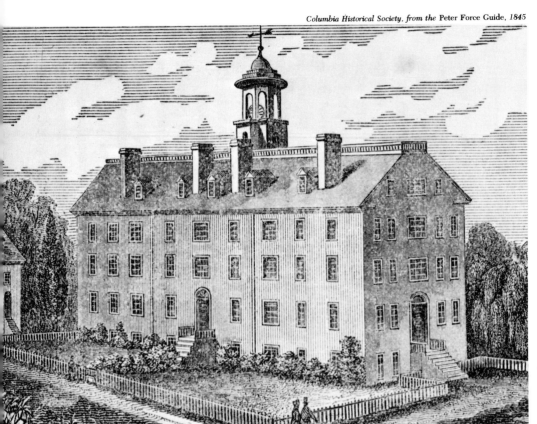

Columbia Historical Society, from the Peter Force Guide, *1845*

Columbian College, which later became George Washington University, was the home of the city's first medical school (opened in 1825) and law school. Opened in 1826, the law school was afterward discontinued but was reopened in 1865.

The college was founded by a group of Baptist ministers and laymen, inspired largely by the zeal and energy of the Reverend Luther Rice. Having raised funds for the purchase of a site, the founders petitioned Congress for a charter. A denominational charter was refused, but eventually a nondenominational one was granted. It was signed by President Monroe on February 9, 1821, and the college opened eleven months later. For entrance to the Classical Department an applicant was required

> "to sustain a reputable examination in English Grammar, Geography, Arithmetic, Latin Grammar, Greek Grammar, Virgil, Sallust, Caesar's commentaries, Cicero's select orations, Latin and Greek Testament, etc. . . . and produce satisfactory evidence of a good moral character."

For years the campus was on the heights above the city, near 14th Street and Columbia Road.

Moorland-Spingarn Research Center, Prints and Photographs Collection, Howard University

"Honorable and gentlemanly deportment to be maintained in all respects . . . playing dice, cards, billiards, backgammon, contentious falsehood, intemperance, injustice, profaneness, immodesty, uncleanliness, any kind of immorality would be punished."

—Rules of Columbian College, c. 1825

The only secondary school for blacks in the city was set up in 1834 by John Francis Cook (left). Cook had been a slave until eight years before, when his freedom was purchased by his aunt, Alethia Tanner. At his school, Cook instructed young men wishing to enter the ministry. In 1841 he founded the Fifteenth Street Presbyterian Church (still an important downtown church) and was its pastor until his death in 1856. One of his sons became Washington's first Superintendent of Colored Schools; another was elected alderman in 1868.

During the 1840s, according to a paper read before the Columbia Historical Society in 1901 by Mrs. Jennie Tree Rives, educating blacks in the District was made punishable by a fine. Passage of the law, Mrs. Rives had been told, came about as a result of an incident at the Fourth Presbyterian Church, on Ninth Street NW:

> "The white Sunday-school, of one hundred and fifty pupils, had morning session, and the colored held afternoon session; there were over three hundred colored pupils in the Sunday-school. A man from the North asked permission to address the colored school. After a few preliminary remarks he launched into a furious tirade against the South, and finally wound up by telling the negroes that they had three remedies in their hands, 'the bowl, the knife, and the torch,' poison, murder and incendiarism. This speech created such intense feeling that a law was passed forbidding the education of negroes."

This 1860 lithograph shows "The Government Hospital for the Insane of the Army and Navy and the District of Columbia," better known as St. Elizabeth's, which was the name given the land grant in 1663. (Blue Plains, 1662, and Giesborough, 1663, are close by.) Washington historian Constance McLaughlin Green called it "the fruit of Dorothea Dix's long crusade for humane treatment of the mentally ill . . . as epoch-making in its way as the founding of the Smithsonian Institution." Another Washington historian described the hospital as apart but not isolated: "when one looks upon the moving panorama of the boats upon the river, and there is society in the evening lights of the City beyond, it is the calm presence of the world outside without its distracting roar." Dorothea Dix is seen in the portrait below.

"On high ground on the south side of the Anacostia River, near the point where it mingles its waters with the Potomac, is the Government Hospital for the Insane, which was erected in 1855, at a cost of nearly $1,000,000. It has a commanding site, overlooking the city of Washington, and from its grounds the finest view of the Capitol can be obtained."

—J.W. Moore, 1884

The Washington Infirmary, in Judiciary Square, was established in 1806, "the more effectively to provide for the poor, disabled and infirm persons." It occupied the remodeled city jail, which is believed to have been designed by English architect George Hadfield in 1803. For many years it bore the stigma of a "poor house," and efforts were made to build a real hospital for the people of Washington and Georgetown—one that would also serve as a teaching center. The Infirmary did become a teaching hospital in 1844, when it was assigned by Congress to the Medical Faculty of Columbian College "for medical instruction, and for scientific purposes." But it remained the city's only hospital until the Civil War. During the cholera epidemic of 1832 Margaret Bayard Smith noted that her nephew

"Bayard says it makes his heart ache as he goes along the avenue, to see the poor creatures (street laborers, mostly Irish) . . . working in the midst of disease in continual apprehension of its attack, and without any hope beyond that of being, when attacked, thrown in a cart and carried to a Hospital, which they fear as they fear the grave itself. So averse are the poor generally . . . to going there, that they conceal the first symptoms, so that when the last stage comes on, it is commonly fatal. Even then, they are carried by force, for voluntarily they will not go."

Journal of the Cholera Year

The services of the Washington Infirmary and of the city's doctors were sorely strained during the cholera epidemic of 1832. The severity of the epidemic is evident from the "Mortality Books" kept by William King, the Georgetown cabinet-maker (see page 142).

The following account is taken from the unpublished journal of Alfred Mason Badger, a neighbor of King who came to Georgetown from Portsmouth, New Hampshire, in 1830 to work for Libbey's lumberyard and who later owned a foundry:

"July 6: . . . we hear that the Collery is in New York . . . we may now expect to have the visiter in this our city verry shortly.

"Monday 9: we hear that the collery is in Baltimore dont know how true it is hope not shall know tomorrow. There was a child died this morning at ten o'clock on Water Street right opposite the Lumber Yard after an illness of ten hours, the doctors say it is the simptoms of the collery in every way if it is in Geotown it will sweep the place i expect, for it is very filthy.

"Friday 27: Frank [Badger's infant son] is verry sick think he gets worse every day. . . . I thought he would not live till morning. I wished for my mother a dozen times.

"Thursday August 9: Frank is no better today . . . there has ben two doctors here twiste today and say that he will not live . . .

"Wednesday morning nine oclock . . . my dear Frank has died at five minutes before eight oclock.

"Wednesday 22: The collery is raging in Washington Verry bad four new cases, two deaths chiefly those that are taken with the collery are Irish men that are at work on the avenue in Washington Macadamizing the avenue between the Capitol and the President's house.

"September Wed 5. . . . There is many cases of the collery today, Some estimate to be one hundred and sixty in Washington and Geo town.

"Saturday October 6: we have had but three cases of collery this week. . . . Mr. King has been telling my wife and myself the number of Coffins he made in one month in the month of September he says he made ninety-two Coffins in his shop, the verry next door to us, he says he made nine in one day and they are amakeing one in the shop now."

Marcia Burns Van Ness and her daughter, a victim of the cholera epidemic of 1832, lie in this mausoleum (right). As Montgomery Meigs noted on his sketch, the tomb was located at H Street, between 9th and 10th streets NW, in one of the small burial grounds then scattered throughout the city. The tomb, designed by George Hadfield, is now in Oak Hill Cemetery in Georgetown.

The Congressional Cemetery (below) is situated on a high bluff above the Anacostia River, at 18th Street and Pennsylvania Avenue SE. It was established in 1812 by Christ Church Capitol Hill. In this watercolor, Benjamin Latrobe shows the cenotaphs he designed for deceased members of Congress. The monuments, said Senator Hoar of Massachusetts, "add a new terror to death." There are memorials to Tobias Lear, George Hadfield, William Thornton and Elbridge Gerry. Frances Trollope, who observed a Congressman's funeral during her 1827 visit to Washington, wrote that

"I was surprised by the ceremony and dignity of his funeral. It seems that whenever a senator or member of Congress dies during the session, he is buried at the expense of the government (this ceremony not coming under the head of internal improvement). . . .
"The procession was of considerable extent, but not on foot, and the majority of the carriages were hired for the occasion. The body was interred in an open 'graveyard' near the city. I did not see the monument erected on this occasion, but I presume it was in the same style as several others I had remarked in the same burying-ground, inscribed to the memory of members who had died at Washington. These were square blocks of masonry, without any pretension to splendour."

"This is how it is in Washington—streets not paved, swept or lighted."

—the Chevalier de Bacourt
on a visit to Washington, 1840

Plans for Pennsylvania Avenue, like this one of 1853 (below), have brought high hopes but few results in two centuries. The federal government did little to improve the condition of the city's streets and alleyways, and the city itself was unable to raise the necessary funds, despite revenues from property taxes, slave taxes, dog taxes and licensing fees for stores, theaters, carriages, peddlers and billiard tables. Consequently, Pennsylvania Avenue and most of the other streets in Washington were rough roads to travel. One indication of how bad the early roads were is found in a Decatur House inventory, which shows that in a four-month period Susan Decatur had to buy eleven pairs of "Prunell Shoes"—high, cloth-topped boots. A French visitor, the Chevalier de Bacourt, recorded his impressions of the city in 1840:

"I went to see Mr. and Mrs Charles Hill, who live at the extreme end of the city [near 14th and Massachusetts Avenue]; my carriage sank up to the axle-tree in the snow and mud; it was necessary to leave the carriage, which had to be dragged out and scraped to remove the mud and slush which stuck to it like glue. I don't know how anyone can get to the Hill's on Monday next, when they give a ball; they count on the moon shining that night to save their necks. . . . The nights are so noisy that one can scarcely sleep. There is a continual uproar, the reason for which is that the inhabitants all own cows and pigs, but no stables, and these animals wander about all day and all night through the city, and go to their owners' houses only in the morning and evening to be fed; the women milk their cows on the sidewalk and sprinkle the passers-by. The nocturnal wanderings of these beasts create an infernal racket, in which they are joined by dogs and cats."

The Old Print Shop, New York

In 1848 the White House and Capitol were lighted by gas. A lantern six feet in diameter on an eighty-foot mast glowed atop the Capitol dome. In 1842 Pennsylvania Avenue, between the White House and the Capitol, had been lighted with oil but for seven years remained the only lighted street in the city. This view of the White House from Lafayette Square was done by August Köllner.

In 1851 there were forty-seven appointed policemen (there was one, "the Superintendant of Police," in 1803). The Metropolitan Police were organized in 1861. The city fire department was begun in the 1870s. Before that there were volunteer groups who were frequently bitter rivals.

"I was delighted with the whole aspect of Washington; light, cheerful, and airy, it reminded me of our fashionable watering-places. It has been laughed at by foreigners, and even by natives, because the original plan of the city was upon an enormous scale, and but a very small part of it has been as yet executed. But I confess I see nothing in the least degree ridiculous about it; the original design, which was as beautiful as it was extensive, has been in no way departed from, and all that has been done has been done well. From the base of the hill on which the capitol stands extends a street of most magnificent width, planted on each side with trees, and ornamented by many splendid shops. This street, which is called Pennsylvania avenue, is above a mile in length, and at the end of it is the handsome mansion of the president; conveniently near to his residence are the various public offices, all handsome, simple, and commodious; ample areas are left round each, where grass and shrubs refresh the eye. In another of the principal streets is the general post-office, and not far from it is a very noble townhall. Towards the quarter of the president's house are several handsome dwellings, which are chiefly occupied by the foreign ministers. The houses in the other parts of the city are scattered, but without ever losing sight of the regularity of the original plan; and to a person who has been travelling much through the country, and marked the immense quantity of new manufactories, new canals, new rail-roads, new towns, and new cities, which are springing, as it were, from the earth in every part of it, the appearance of the metropolis rising gradually into life and splendour, is a spectacle of high historic interest."

—Frances Trollope, 1831

"Let our aqueduct be worthy of the nation; and, emulous as we are of the ancient Roman republic, let us show that the rulers chosen by the people are not less careful of the safety, health and beauty of their capital than the emperors who . . . caused their names to be remembered with respect and affection by those who still drink the water supplied by their magnificent aqueducts."

—Montgomery Meigs, 1852

DeLancey Gill sketched this picturesque well in Washington. The artist was the illustrator for the Smithsonian's Bureau of American Ethnology. Through the kindness of his decendants, several of his previously unpublished drawings appear elsewhere in this book. It was DeLancey Gill who discovered the Rock Creek Indian quarry (see page 12) while sketching beech trees, a favorite subject.

Prior to the mid-nineteenth century, when a municipal water system was developed, wells and springs were Washington's primary sources of water. Pierre L'Enfant's plan for the city noted that "there are within the limits of the City about 25 good springs of excellent water abundantly supplied in the driest season of the year." Having a well or spring on one's property was a great asset. A handwritten receipt owned by the Laird-Dunlop family assigns rights to a spring at 30th and N streets NW:

"This 21 July 1809 of John Laird, Esq. the sum of twenty dollars in full for the fair uses of a spring near Washington Street near a lot sold Henry Upperman in T. Beall's first addition. The free use of said spring is to John Laird, Esq. and his heirs forever."

Wooden pipes were used to convey the water from the springs to whichever nearby houses could afford the expense. The Van Ness House (see page 121) was reputedly the first in the city to have running water, beginning in 1820. The first completely indoor plumbing in a private house appeared in the 1850s. The White House had it somewhat earlier.

In 1852, engineer Montgomery Cunningham Meigs, a West Point graduate, was appointed to devise a water supply for the city and was given the rank of captain by Jefferson Davis, the Secretary of War. His design for the aqueduct to carry water from Great Falls to Washington took over ten years to complete; it was built on a grand scale, which Meigs felt did honor to the city and the man for whom the city was named.

The workings of the aqueduct were explained in an article published in *Harper's Weekly*, September 29, 1860:

"The Washington Aqueduct Bridge over Rock Creek, at the western end of Pennsylvania Avenue, now near completed . . . is a cast-iron arch of twenty feet rise and two hundred feet clear span between the abutments. . . . Upon these girders rest cross beams of timber, supporting the roadway of the bridge, which embraces two city railroad and carriage tracks, and two paths for foot-passengers.

"This bridge is particularly remarkable for the double duty which the arch performs. While it supports a roadway, forming a beautiful and much-needed communication . . . between the cities of Washington and Georgetown . . . the water of the Washington Aqueduct is conveyed into the city of Washington through the pipes of which the arch is composed. To guard against all danger of freezing the pipes are lined with staves of resinous pine timber, three inches in thickness, leaving a clear water-way in each rib of three and a half feet in diameter.

"The abutments contain vaults, in which are the connecting pipes and stop-cocks for regulating the flow and discharge of water; and in the western abutment, on the Georgetown side, one of the vaults serves as an engineroom, and contains a water-pressure engine—the first, it is believed, erected in this country.

"This engine, drawing its supply from the cast-iron street mains of the Washington Aqueduct, pumps ten thousand gallons of water per hour into a reservoir on the heights of Georgetown, a mile distant, and two hundred and four feet above the machine. This reservoir supplies that portion of Georgetown which is above the level of the great store and distributing reservoirs. . . ."

The bridge that carried the aqueduct pipes over Cabin John Run, a tributary of the Potomac, is still in use today. Seen at the center of the engraving below, the bridge was built of granite and seneca stone and was the longest masonry arch in existence at the time it was constructed. The reservoir at Georgetown (top left in the engraving) was removed in the 1930s, and the Georgetown library was built on the site. But the wall shown in the sketch (below and to the left of the reservoir) can still be seen along Wisconsin Avenue, and water is still conducted through the original pipes lying under the "conduit" road, MacArthur Boulevard. The above sketch by Meigs shows the interior of one of the pipes when the aqueduct was under construction.

One of Robert Mills' sketches for the Washington Monument

A sketch from the notebook of Robert Mills showing a crane with which four men could lift tons—an enormously important consideration with the grading, draining, canal building, transporting and lifting of stone going on in the city.

"The public sentiment just now runs almost exclusively and popularly into the Grecian school. We build little besides temples for our churches, our banks, our taverns, our court houses, and our dwellings. A friend of mine has just built a brewery on the model of the Temple of the Winds."

—Aristabulus Bragg, in James Fenimore Cooper's
Home as Found, 1828

During the 1840s and 1850s the Washington landscape began to be filled out by the erection of several major government buildings, including the Patent Office, the Post Office and the Treasury. The Washington Monument was begun about the same time. All these were designed principally by Robert Mills.

Mills was among the first native American architects. His classical tendencies were encouraged during his formative years in Washington, where he was draftsman under Hoban and assistant to Latrobe. The latter job came to him at the recommendation of Jefferson, with whom he lived for two years. Jefferson gave Mills encouragement and shared his knowledge and the use of his superior architectural library.

In 1836, after establishing himself as an architect of national prominence, Mills returned to Washington and was appointed by President Jackson to be "Federal Architect of Public Buildings." He remained in this post for fifteen years. Each of his three public buildings was under construction for nearly thirty years, under the supervision of a succession of architects.

Latrobe's influence is readily apparent in Mills's work. Writing of his mentor, Mills noted that Latrobe's style "was purely Greek," adding:

"It was fortunate that this style was so early introduced into our country, both on the ground of economy and of correct taste, as it exactly suited the character of our political institutions and pecuniary means. . . .

"The example and influence of Mr. Jefferson at first operated in favour of the introduction of the Roman style into the country, and it required all the talents and good taste of such a man as Mr. Latrobe to correct it by introducing a better. The natural good taste and the unprejudiced eye of our citizens required only a few examples of the Greek style to convince them of its superiority over the Roman for public structures, and its simplicity recommended its introduction into their private dwellings."

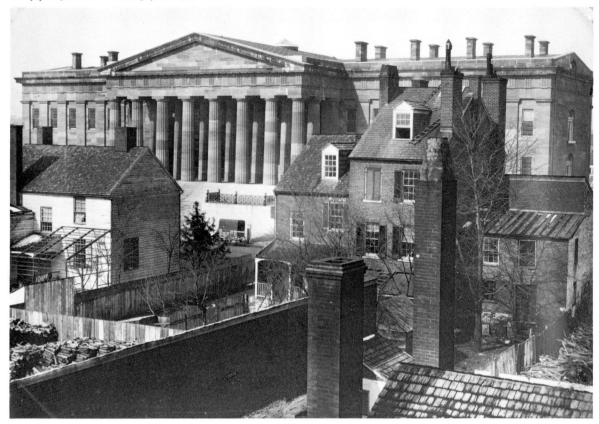

The Patent Office, begun in 1836 and completed in 1867, is shown above in one of the first known daguerreotypes, made by John Plumbe, Jr., in 1846. The porticos of the building are said to be exact reproductions of the Parthenon. Dickens found that

> "The Patent Office . . . furnishes an extraordinary example of American enterprise and ingenuity; for the immense number of models it contains are the accumulated inventions of only five years; the whole of the previous collection having been destroyed by fire. The elegant structure in which they are arranged is one of design rather than execution, for there is but one side erected out of four."

> "The Post office is a very compact and very beautiful building," wrote Charles Dickens during his visit to Washington in 1842. Built between 1839 and 1869, the Post Office (below) stands between 7th and 8th streets and between E and F on the site of Blodgett's Hotel (see page 86).

The Treasury Department (above) was the first major departure from the L'Enfant plan, interrupting as it did the grand vista of Pennsylvania Avenue from the White House to the Capitol. Legend has it that the building site was chosen by Andrew Jackson. Wishing to end the dispute over where the building should go, Jackson walked from the White House to the site and, pointing with his cane, said: "Build it here!" Beside the Treasury in this engraving is the small brick building that housed the State Department. The *Wm. Q. Force Guide* of 1845 wrote: "Hard is the lot of the Department of State. [It] still occupies one of the four plain brick buildings erected years ago." Force described the Treasury Department as

"a noble structure—pity it were not built of something more durable than sand-stone. . . . When completed, by the addition of the north and south wings, its length will be four hundred and fifty seven feet. In front is an imposing colonnade, stretching the entire length of the building, after the architecture of the temple of Minerva Polias, at Athens."

"Venturing outside into the air reeking with the thick odor of the catalpa trees, he found himself on an earth-road, or village street, with wheel-tracks meandering from the colonnade of the Treasury hard by, to the white marble columns and fronts of the Post Office and Patent Office which faced each other in the distance, like white Greek temples in the abandoned gravel-pits of a deserted Syrian city."

—Henry Adams, 1850

Begun in 1836, the Treasury Department took thirty-three years to be completed. The scene above, photographed near the building site, shows the thirteen teams of horses and oxen that were needed to move one of the building's seventy-four granite columns, which had been brought by ship from Maine. The bottom photo, taken in 1861, shows one of the columns being raised into position.

Washington's original City Hall, at 4th and D streets, was designed by English architect George Hadfield. After a lottery scheme failed to raise enough money to finish the building, Congress contributed ten thousand dollars, on the condition that the federal government be allowed to use one wing. The building was completed in 1853, without the central dome of Hadfield's design. It stands in the center of Judiciary Square.

The city of Washington has gone through a number of experiments in self-government. In 1802 the city was run by a mayor appointed by the President and by an elected council. After 1812 elected council members appointed the city's mayor. Eight years later the city began electing its mayor, as well as its councilmen and a Board of Aldermen. Washington and Georgetown then had separate city governments, but in 1871 all D.C. jurisdictions were united under a single territorial government, with an appointed governor, a bicameral legislature (half appointed, half elected) and a nonvoting delegate to Congress. During the fiscal crisis of 1874, three commissioners were temporarily appointed to run the District. Subsequent legislation made the appointed Board of Commissioners a permanent institution. It remained as such until the Reorganization Act of 1967, when the city began being run by an appointed commissioner (who was given the courtesy title of mayor), his assistant and a nine-member City Council. In 1975 the District of Columbia Self-Government Reorganization Act provided for the election of a mayor and of a City Council consisting of a chairman, four members at large and eight ward representatives.

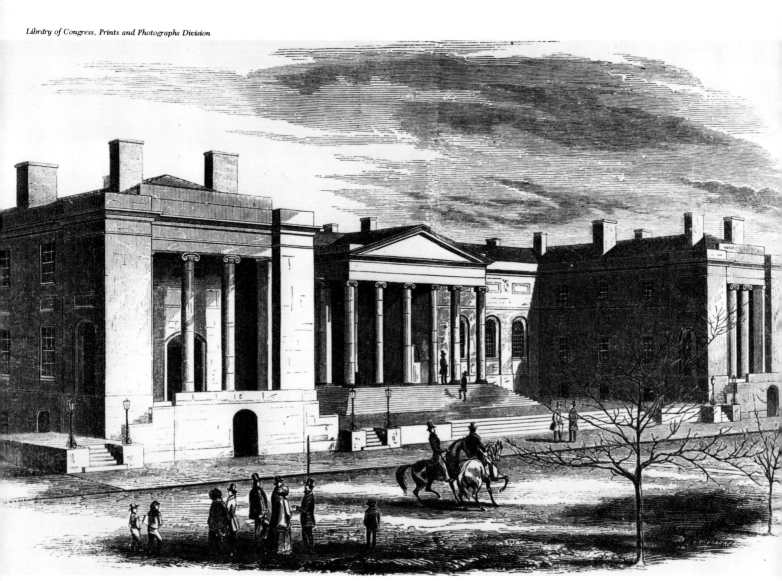

William Thornton's Capitol building, seen here in an 1848 view from the roof of the White House, had been finished scarcely twenty years, but already it was too small to house the growing country's growing number of representatives. Congress therefore authorized another competition, this time for the Capitol's enlargement. The winning design, by architect Thomas U. Walter, called for the extension of the two wings and the addition of an iron dome. The dome was inspired by that of St. Isaac's Cathedral in Leningrad (below), which was the world's first iron dome. (The plan of St. Isaac's had been brought to America by Walter's assistant, a German immigrant.) His enlarged Capitol was completed in 1863.

OVERLEAF: An artist's projection of 1852 shows the Capitol as it was to look after the addition of the Senate and House wings (center and right, respectively) but before the completion of the new iron dome. The view looks down Pennsylvania Avenue toward the Treasury Department and the White House. The colonnaded building at right, behind the House wing, is Washington's City Hall, with the Patent Office behind it. On the Mall, to the left of Pennsylvania Avenue, is the Smithsonian Institution, which was finished in 1855; and the Washington Monument, which would finally be completed in 1885 (but without the temple base of Mills' original design). The Washington Canal borders the Mall on the north, where Constitution Avenue was later laid down.

Dickens, in a dyspeptic mood, had this to say about the shortcomings of the City of Washington:

> "It is sometimes called the City of Magnificent Distances, but it might with greater propriety be termed the City of Magnificent Intentions; for it is only on taking a bird's-eye view of it from the top of the Capitol that one can at all comprehend the vast designs of its projector, an aspiring Frenchman. Spacious avenues, that begin in nothing, and lead nowhere; streets, mile-long, that only want houses, roads, and inhabitants; public buildings that need but a public to be complete; and ornaments of great thoroughfares, which only lack great thoroughfares to ornament—are its leading features. One might fancy the season over, and most of the houses gone out of town forever, with their masters."

185

186

"The means of acquiring knowledge is . . . the greatest benefit that can be conferred upon mankind."

—John Quincy Adams, championing the cause of building the Smithsonian Institution and an observatory, 1836

"An establishment for the increase and diffusion of knowledge among men" was what James Smithson wanted built in his name. The natural son of aristocratic English parents, Smithson was apparently much in sympathy with America's egalitarian ideals. Although he never visited the United States, he specified in his 1826 will that should his nephew and heir die without issue (which he did in 1835), the entire Smithson fortune was to be given to the United States. Accordingly, in 1838, 105 bags of gold sovereigns—worth some half a million dollars—arrived by packet boat in New York.

Congress spent the next eight years debating the intent of the bequest. Should it be used to build a library? An orphanage? To support agrarian reform? Finally, in 1846, under the Act of Establishment, Regents were appointed and a building authorized. The Institution was to include a chemical laboratory, library, gallery of

The main entrance of the Smithsonian Institution.

The 1885 engraving (right) shows the signal office of the U.S. Weather Bureau, which was founded by Congress as a result of the pioneering work in telegraphic weather reporting done by Joseph Henry. Seizing on Samuel F. B. Morse's new concept of telegraphic communication, Henry had persuaded the telegraph companies to transmit the daily reports of 150 volunteer weather observers throughout the country. In 1847, Henry proposed

> "to organize a system of observation which will extend as far as possible over the North American continent. . . . The extended lines of the telegraph will furnish a ready means of warning the more northern and eastern observers [weather in the eastern United States usually moves from the west or southwest] to be on the watch from the first appearance of an advancing storm."

In 1857 the Smithsonian began furnishing Henry's telegraphic weather reports to the Washington *Evening Star*, thus making the paper the first to publish daily weather news. Meanwhile, coastal authorities were warned of approaching storms by signals from the Smithsonian's tower.

Columbia Historical Society; from Ten Years in Washington *by Mary Clemmer Ames*

The National Observatory

art, lecture rooms, a museum and a collection of scientific materials. By 1855 the "Castle" was substantially complete.

Civic pride swelled at the sight of James Renwick, Jr.'s, red brick Gothic edifice, with its nine towers and campaniles and its plethora of niches, traceries and vaulted arches. Robert Dale Owen, chairman of the Smithsonian Building Committee, declared that the building deserved "to be named as a National Style of Architecture for America." But Joseph Henry, the first Secretary of the Smithsonian, complained of the building's "peculiar style . . . and its points of peculiar exposure to injuries of weather."

Henry, who was distinguished for his research in the interchangeability of magnetism and electricity, the electromagnet, electric meter and the electromagnetic telegraph, shaped the course of the Smithsonian for thirty-one years. He was instrumental in making basic scientific research an "essential function" of the Institution. There was no money to pay scientists and scholars a salary, but they were offered laboratory space and a bed in the tower (if they brought their own linen). Henry and his family lived on the second floor of the Castle, where apartments were also available for his colleagues.

Although Henry's own orientation was toward research and publication, he did offer a series of lectures for the general public: "The object has been to give instruction rather than amusement—to improve the public taste rather

"The intention is to make a contribution to Astronomy worthy of the nation and the age," wrote Matthew Fontaine Maury, who was the first superintendent of the United States Naval Observatory in Washington (above). The original 1844 building stands where the Marines camped in 1800, in Foggy Botton (see page 110).

At the Observatory, Maury, who began his naval career in 1825 as a midshipman, became internationally known for his work in hydrography, astronomy and meteorology. He proposed the first International Maritime Meteorological Conference, which met in Brussels in 1853, with Maury giving the opening address. He described the conference as a "sublime spectacle. . . . All nations agreeing to unite and co-operate. . . . Though they may be enemies in all else, here they are to be friends. Every ship that navigates the high seas, with these charts and blank abstract logs on board, may henceforth be regarded as a floating observatory, a temple of science." By1854 he reported that "nations owning more than nine-tenths of all the shipping in the world have come into this plan." His researches revolutionized the science of navigation and earned him the name "Pathfinder of the Seas." For more than a hundred years every navigational chart bore this note: "Founded upon the researches made in the early part of the 19th century by Matthew Fontaine Maury, while serving as a lieutenant in the U.S. Navy."·

From scientific studies of the logs of sailing ships over a period of years, Maury made charts to indicate the winds and currents, the weather in different seasons, the locations of dangerous reefs and of the world's whale-fishing grounds. He suggested one-way traffic lanes across the Atlantic to reduce collisions. His deep-sea soundings made possible the laying of the Atlantic Cable in 1866. And it was he who first charted the Gulf Stream—an immeasurable aid to shipping.

than to elicit popular applause." The lectures were so successful that a larger lecture hall had to be built; and the public also thronged to the Institution's museum exhibits, which Henry opened reluctantly, giving them a very minor role. In time they became the largest and best known of the Smithsonian's many programs.

189

The Corcoran Legacy . . .

William Wilson Corcoran, founder of the Corcoran Gallery of Art, was known as "Washington's First Philanthropist." Having inherited a fortune from his Irish-born father (who had been twice elected mayor of Georgetown), Corcoran increased his wealth as a member of the banking firm of Corcoran and Riggs (later Riggs Bank). After his retirement in 1854, he spent the rest of his life as a philanthropist and as a patron of American art. In addition to building a notable collection of American painting and sculpture, he supported many Washington charities and several Virginia colleges and gave Columbian College a new medical school.

The Corcoran's first building (below), which the philanthropist gave "for the encouragement of the Fine Arts," was designed by James Renwick and stands at the northeast corner of 17th Street and Pennsylvania Avenue. Begun in 1859, "it was about ready for occupancy in the early Sixties when the government, wanting clerical space, asked no questions and took it," according to the *Recollections* of Albion Keith Parris: "Mr. Corcoran, a sympathizer with the South, had little to say, and went to Europe." After the Civil War, when the building was returned by the government, Corcoran gave the deed to a board of trustees, writing (in 1869):

> "As soon as the interior of the building shall have been completed, according to the original plans (which will be placed at your disposal), for which the rents in arrears will more than suffice, I shall ask you to receive as a nucleus my own gallery of art, which has been collected at no inconsiderable pains, and I have assurances from friends in other cities whose tastes and liberality have taken this direction that they will contribute fine works of art from their respective collections."

The trustees were able to collect $125,000 in back rent—less than half what Corcoran thought he was owed by the government.

The Corcoran Gallery was finally opened in 1871, with a grand ball attended by more than 2,000 guests. The ball also celebrated George Washington's birthday and helped raise money for completion of the Washington Monument.

And a Washington Memorial

"We regard Mr. Greenough's Washington as one of the greatest works of sculpture of modern times. . . . Mr. Greenough has adopted a drapery which meets all the requirements of delicacy which is sanctioned by the authority of the greatest masters of art in ancient and modern times, and to which the public is now reconciled and familiarized in busts, which are almost invariably made either wholly nude, or with an artistical drapery unlike any thing actually worn."

—*Morrison's Stranger's Guide,* 1844

Black schoolchildren visit Horatio Greenough's sculpture of Washington, which is now displayed at the Smithsonian's Museum of History and Technology.

L'Enfant's plans for the city called for an equestrian statue to memorialize the nation's first President. The day after Washington was buried, John Marshall of Virginia rose in the House of Representatives to call for "measures suitable to the occasion and expressive of the profound sorrow with which Congress is penetrated." Measures were not taken. Congress rejected numerous bills to erect a memorial. In the affecting and thrifty argument of one Congressman who voted against an appropriation: "When foreigners inquire of us 'Where is his monument?' our answer is, 'In our hearts, our deep, all-pervading, overwhelming gratitude to the great benefactor of our country.'"

Centenary celebrations of Washington's birth sparked new interest in a memorial, and an appropriation was passed in 1832. Describing the outcome, Frank G. Carpenter, writing some forty years later in the Cleveland *Leader,* reported that

> "it took eight years for Horatio Greenough to make [the statue]. He did the work in Florence, Italy, where he chiseled out the Father of our Country in a sitting posture instead of standing, as the Act of Congress demanded.

"When the statue was completed, in 1840, the next question was how to get it from Italy to America. Congress haggled over the matter for weeks, finally sending a man-of-war to bring the statue across the Atlantic Ocean. But the marble George weighed twelve tons, and it took twenty-two yoke of oxen to haul him over the Italian roads. . . . When it arrived at the Washington Navy Yard, Congressmen were horrified to see that our great hero had been carved, sitting in a chair, nude to the waist. The Virginia statesman General Henry A. Wise remarked at the time, 'The man does not live, and never did live, who saw Washington without his shirt.' . . . At the Capitol doors, it was found that the statue was too large. . . . The masonry had to be cut away and the door enlarged. When it was finally installed the Rotunda floor began to sink, so a pedestal was built under it to support it. It was soon decided that the Rotunda was not a suitable place for the statue, and at last, after a number of removals, it was taken to . . . the bitter cold, bleak air of the Capitol plateau. . . . One jokester, commenting on the outstretched sword in the figure's hand, says he is sure Washington is crying, 'Take my sword if you will, but bring me some clothes!' "

191

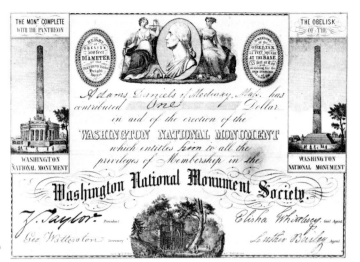

A certificate of membership in the Washington National Monument Society (at left) was issued to contributors to the monument building fund. The Society's goal was to collet one dollar from every citizen. Robert Mills's original design is seen in the upper left-hand corner of the certificate.

Perhaps foreseeing the disappointments of the Greenough Statue, a group of prominent Washingtonians formed the Washington National Monument Society in 1833. George Watterston, Librarian of Congress, was the strongest force behind the effort, but the Society also included former mayors Thomas Carberry, Joseph Gales, Jr., Peter Force and W. W. Seaton. Electing seventy-eight-year-old Chief Justice Marshall to be the Society's president and Judge William Cranch (Abigail Adams' nephew) to be its vice-president, the members raised enough money and sponsored a competition for the monument's design. Robert Mills, who had designed many prominent Washington buildings (see pages 180–183) as well as Baltimore's monument to the first President, offered the winning entry, a 600-foot obelisk that was to rise from a colonnaded temple 100 feet high. The cornerstone was laid in 1848. As reported in the diary of Michael Shiner, a Washington slave who had obtained his freedom and was an employee of the Navy Yard:

"all the Mechanic and laberors of Washington Navy yard volinteer ther selves to carry the corner stone of general Washington Monument and They carried from fourteenth street Bridge and Brigaddire Gen Archabel Henderson of the U S Merines and they walked of with it By the tune of hial Columbia and yankee doodle on the 7 of June 1848 on Wensday ther wher it Remains and they had to get the truck out the Navy yard and they it off the stone wagan and put it on the truck and walk off with it Hamsomily

"The Coner Stone of general Washington Monument wher laid in Washington by the Hon Colonel James R. polk ex president of the United States on the forth of July 1848 tuesday and they wher a great prosesion that day diferent volinteer company and the United States draggones from Carlile Barracks Pensyilvanes 3 or 4 company of them under ther command of lietenant Colonel Charles May United States armmy and one Battery of flying artilry several volunteer company from alexandria and from difererent parts of the country and ex governers of states and teriroty and sentors and Repasentive wher present and the mayo of the City Washington and the alldermen Camman Concilmen and the Citizyens of Washington and Georgetown and Alexandria and it wher a splendrd day and evvy thing went on peacebul and quite that day and they a grert dissplay of fier Works that night and the fier works wher supiretend by and gentleman By the of Mr. George Marshal as guner in the United States Navy the hold of the Milatary force that wher out that day wher commanded By magor general John a Quitman"

By 1851 it was being reported that the monument "is now up to eighty feet above the surface, thirty-eight feet of which have been put up in the year, at a cost of $900 a foot." Memorial stones were contributed by various states and societies. One of these, a marble block from Rome's Temple of Concord, which was sent by Pope Pius IX, turned out to be the rock on which the monument's fortunes foundered. In March 1854 the stone was stolen by members of the American Party, the chauvinistic, anti-immigration, anti-Catholic group that was also called the Know-Nothings. The following February, on the eve of Washington's birthday, the Know-Nothings "stole" the whole monument by seizing the Monument Society's records and fraudulently electing their own members to the highest offices. Their antics put a halt to Congressional funding and public subscriptions. The Know-Nothings managed to raise the shaft from 152 to 156 feet. But the masonry they used was so poor that in 1880, after the Centennial spurred interest to finish the building, Army engineers had to remove the Know-Nothings' four-foot section and start building anew from the 152-foot level.

The view at top, by Seth Eastman, shows the monument under construction in 1851. In the background rise the Gothic towers of the Smithsonian and the domes of the Capitol. At right is a more familiar view of the monument as it was being built.

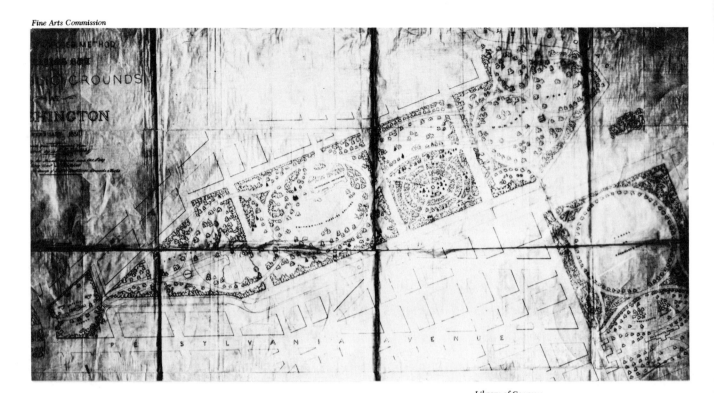

The City's Pleasure Grounds

The Mall, the core around which Pierre L'Enfant had laid out his plan for the city, was intended by the French designer to be the model of all federal parks. L'Enfant envisioned two parks, each a third of a mile wide, which were to stretch along two converging axes. One was to be built along a line extending westward from the Capitol to the Potomac River and the other leading from the White House south to the river. A Washington memorial was to be situated at their intersection. "This," according to historian H. P. Caemmerer, "was an innovation and a departure from the usual development of a city about a commercial street."

Forgotten for fifty years, while the city grew around it, the area designated for the Mall began to take shape in the early 1850s, when President Millard Fillmore appointed architect Andrew Jackson Downing to develop the swampy acreage on which bordered the newly built Smithsonian Institution. Downing's Mall—all tangled bowers and curling pathways—was to embody "the beauty of curved lines and natural groups of trees."

194

Andrew Jackson Downing's plan for the Mall (opposite) is dated February 1851. In the drawing the Capitol is at left, the White House at lower right. The fanciful engraving (below) presents a vision of Washington as it never was. Robert Mills's colonnade adorns the base of the Washington Monument, and ships under full sail ply an idealized Washington canal. In the allegorical view of the Mall and Capitol (right), printed in 1847, the canal and towpath are seen at left, the Smithsonian at right. The view illustrates the "Elements of National Thrift and Empire: Public Lands, Railroads, Canals, Rivers, and Harbors; Agriculture, Manufacture, and Mechanical Arts; Science and Art, the Parents of Emulation and Enterprise."

A Washington street scene, 1851

A Washington Diary

The private diary kept by Elizabeth Lindsay Lomax in the 1850s and 1860s conveys a sense of what life was like when Washington was both a sleepy Southern town (as in the 1851 Seth Eastman sketch above) and, increasingly, a capital divided by the threat of secession. Mrs. Lomax was the widow of an Army officer, living with her daughters, worrying about her son Lindsay Lomax, who was also an Army officer, supplementing her income by her work as a copyist. Her diary, published in 1943 by E. P. Dutton and Company, Inc., as *Leaves from an Old Washington Diary, 1854–1863* (edited by Lindsay Lomax Wood), is excerpted below.

MONDAY, JUNE 19, 1854. Very warm today, overcast, with clouds hanging low. . . .

Lindsay dined at Willards this evening with Custis Lee and several of his classmates, later they gathered here for a dancing party.

WEDNESDAY, DECEMBER 20, 1854. This afternoon . . . attended a large reception at Colonel Cooper's where we met many old friends in the city for the holidays. Among others, Colonel R. E. Lee, Superintendent of West Point. I had forgotten that he was such a handsome man, though Lindsay wrote me from West Point that Colonel Lee was the handsomest man he had ever known, just like a "marble model"—Handsome yes, but not like marble. Colonel Lee is "very human, kind, calm and definite."

TUESDAY, MAY 1, 1855. Beautiful day—and a festive one. An old English custom which still prevails in this country.

The fire engines turned out in force, their fine horses

decked with garlands of flowers. The children had Maypoles and daisy chains and the whole world seemed to be in holiday attire.

The girls have gone fishing with Chandler and the Gordon boys, and will have their picnic lunch in the woods near Rock Creek.

NEW YEAR'S DAY, 1856. The visiting commenced today at an early hour and continued until late. Everyone seemed happy and gay. Our house must have been the last "port o call"—So many lingered on for supper and dancing.

SUNDAY, OCTOBER 26, 1856. Miss Emily Mason was here this afternoon, she said the reason I lost my writing was because the Government was obliged to reduce expenses and diminish the number of clerks, but Mr. Claxton was here also and said he was present when the President said to Mr. McClellan that he must give me more writing to do.

I hope and pray it may be true.

FRIDAY, NOVEMBER 21, 1856. Mrs. Davidge, Mrs. Pendergast and Mrs. Peter came in for tea and talked at length about the beauty and charm of Georgetown—endeavored to persuade me to build in Georgetown. I admit all of the advantages, but it is too far from my work.

WEDNESDAY, DECEMBER 10, 1856. A message from the War Department brought me a note from Mr. Campbell, the chief clerk, asking if I could copy the paper sent by twelve o'clock tomorrow. I commenced work at once and finished the paper by one o'clock the same night.

FRIDAY, DECEMBER 25, 1857. Snowing hard, cold and Christmasy. . . .

We are dining at the Octagon House this evening, which is sure to be an enjoyable occasion—As Virginia Tayloe has the rare gift of collecting together guests with congenial minds and spirits.

TUESDAY, MARCH 16, 1858. . . . Mrs. Cabell invited me to go to the Smithsonian this evening to hear Mr. Everett's lecture on Charity. I was greatly interested. Two thousand people were present and after Dr. Everett's lecture the Marine Band played wonderfully good music.

SUNDAY, APRIL 17, 1858. I had a letter from Mr. Thornton this morning asking if I would write an article giving my views on education for women. I shall do so with pleasure. It gives me an opportunity to say what I have long believed—that men and women should have the same advantages of education. Any mind not cultivated and permitted to vegetate will deteriorate—and that is the fate of the average feminine mind—but some not far distant day women will come into their own.

SATURDAY, JUNE 4, 1859. The gas was turned on this evening at seven o'clock and burned beautifully.

TUESDAY, JUNE 14, 1859. Lieutenant [Jeb] Stuart of Lindsay's regiment came to see me today—he is on leave, having been wounded slightly in a battle with the Comanche Indians—I never met a more interesting and charming young man. He is very musical and sang many songs with Virginia and Vic.

Tomorrow is the day for the German musical festival at Arlington Springs—I pray the weather will be propitious—they usually have wonderful music.

FRIDAY, DECEMBER 2, 1859. This is the unhappy day that [John] Brown, the conspirator, is to be hanged —God have mercy on his soul.

ASH WEDNESDAY, FEBRUARY 22, 1860. Bright overhead, but ground still covered with snow.

Great celebrations today—the unveiling of the statue of General Washington at Washington Circle —A large crowd expected—Bands and regiments of soldiers.

THURSDAY, MARCH 1, 1860. . . . I am enjoying the quiet of Lent—Quiet is essential to mental repose and mental repose is essential to harmony in living.

FRIDAY, APRIL, 6, 1860. The water pipes are now laid on—We shall have a real bathroom—a great luxury.

SATURDAY, MAY 19, 1860. A pleasant morning.

I was out on our small front lawn this morning cutting lilacs for the drawing room, when the Japanese princes passed by. They were on their way to see the statue of General Washington at the Circle, were escorted by Lieutenant Alexander.

TUESDAY, JUNE 5, 1860. The roses we bought from Saul are already in bloom and are fragrant and lovely—they do Virginia credit for she is the one who works over them so lovingly.

Barrett is re-elected Mayor over Magruder and Wallack.

FRIDAY, AUGUST 17, 1860. Anne brought a sewing machine yesterday, the agent is coming today to give the girls instruction. They say it requires a good deal of practice. I shall try my hand at it when no one is watching.

THURSDAY, OCTOBER 4, 1860. Mr. Steele and Marshall Crawford called for Anne and Vic to go to the White House to the reception for the Prince of Wales from twelve until one o'clock. The crowd was very great but they met the Prince, said he was not tall or handsome, but had great charm of manner.

WEDNESDAY, OCTOBER 24, 1860. The tone of the newspapers within the last few days has been very strange and gives one cause for anxiety as to the present state of the country. . . .

The unveiling of Clark Mills's statue of Washington by President Buchanan, February 22, 1860

The idea of secession or disunion is terrific and *appalling. God defend us from such a calamity.*

WEDNESDAY, OCTOBER 31, 1860. This morning I went to see Mr. Fisher about transferring my stock even at a great loss. The times are so dubious that I prefer having the money—I drove to the Bank of the Metropolis and arranged it . . .

Major and Mrs. Buell, Mrs. Greenough, Kate Andrews, Mr. and Mrs. Pendleton, Bob and Marshall Crawford, and Chandler spent the evening with us. We had some music but were not very merry. I believe that everyone is subconsciously conscious of a dark cloud upon the horizon—the appalling war cloud growing darker each day.

FRIDAY, NOVEMBER 9, 1860. Great excitement—Mr. Lincoln elected President of the United States.

The papers speak of the dissolution of the Union as an accomplished fact—*God spare us from such a disaster.*

WEDNESDAY, DECEMBER 5, 1860. The first snow of the season this morning.

The country is still in a *distracted* state. Many persons have gone to the Capitol to hear the debate in Congress. Much excitement expected. One retires at night with the feeling anything may happen tomorrow.

SATURDAY, DECEMBER 8, 1860. Bright day.

Exciting times are anticipated in the House on Monday. The general opinion seems to be that there is little hope of preserving the Union. . . . Snowden and Kate Andrews spent the afternoon with me. They think, as so many do, that a war between the North and the South is to be the result of the present maladjustments. Snowden does not seem depressed by the prospect—to me it seem a frightful and tragic calamity.

TUESDAY, DECEMBER 18, 1860. *Snowing.*

I am, after much thought and deliberation, *definitely for the Union with some amendments to the Constitution. . . .*

THURSDAY, DECEMBER 20, 1860. South Carolina has seceded—God defend us from civil war.

TUESDAY, DECEMBER 25, 1860. Christmas Day—Very cold.

This is the most eventful Christmas that I have ever spent. It is true that I have Lindsay and my dear girls with me to cheer my lonely heart, but in the background is the terrible feeling of uncertainty—and fear. Fear of separation, fear of danger to those we love, fear for our beloved country. God grant us peace.

Churchill Gordon sent us a beautiful wild turkey from Virginia and we had a large family gathering for dinner, a great many presents for the young people, and after dinner they danced until one o'clock.

THURSDAY, DECEMBER 27, 1860. Bright cold day.

Major Anderson has spiked the guns! He has moved his troops from Fort Sumter to Fort Moultrie which is considered a much stronger fort.

TUESDAY, JANUARY 1, 1861. This is usually a gala day in Washington—but this day is oh, so different. No social calling, everyone looks harassed and anxious—the state of our beloved country is the cause.

MONDAY, JANUARY 28, 1861. Bright day. The political horizon very, very gloomy.

Great preparations being made on Dr. Lawson's lot for Government troops—building quarters and stables. Last night was dreadfully rowdy, one could not sleep.

A battery of light artillery arrived about eleven o'clock and are quartered in the Lawson house on this street [G Street NW].

SATURDAY, FEBRUARY 23, 1861. The President is to arrive here today. The reception will be a very quiet one.

Have just heard that President Lincoln arrived in the six o'clock train—Mrs. Lincoln and son came in the afternoon.

THURSDAY, FEBRUARY 28, 1861. Bob Lincoln [son of President Lincoln] and Lieutenant Griffin and Lieutenant Alexander came home with Lindsay this afternoon and dined with us.

MONDAY, MARCH 4, 1861. This dreaded day [Lincoln's inauguration day] has at last arrived. Thank Heaven all is peaceful and quiet.

The girls left about nine o'clock to go down to Perry's to see the procession.

They said there was a large crowd, a great many strangers, but that everything was perfectly orderly and quiet. My dear son commanded the escort for President Lincoln.

We did not get our *Star* until very late this evening, due to the fact that it contained President Lincoln's inaugural address. We read it aloud. Many and varied opinions were the opinions expressed by our friends. I thought there was not doubt of its sanity and its excellence.

SATURDAY, APRIL 13, 1861. Fort Sumter was attacked yesterday—greatest excitement.

The news from the South makes me wretched—God help us!

TUESDAY, APRIL 16, 1861. This has been a frightfully exciting day. Riots here and in Baltimore, many persons shot, also a heartrending day for Lindsay and for me.

Colonel John Bankhead Magruder, Ogle Tayloe and Custis Lee spent the morning in a serious consideration.

This evening Lindsay told me that he had sent in his resignation; Colonel Magruder has also sent in his resignation from the army and will go to Virginia where Lindsay will join him. It will be a sad, sad parting from my darling son. I greatly deplore the necessity for his resignation, but after he gave me the following letter to read I felt that I had no right to try to persuade him to do otherwise. He wrote to his classmate whom he loved so dearly: "I cannot stand it any longer and feel it my duty to resign. My State is out of the Union and when she calls for my services I feel that I must go. I regret it very much, realizing that the whole thing is suicidal.

"As long as I could believe in a war on the Union and the flag I was willing to stay, but it is a war between sections—the North and the South and I must go with my own people. I beg of you not to let my decision alter the friendship between us."

TUESDAY, MAY 7, 1861. . . . This afternoon Virginia Tayloe came to take me for a drive. We drove out to the Soldiers' Home and on our return stopped at the Stone's lovely place where the Seventh Regiment is encamped. They have a charming military band and are a wonderful looking body of men. We stayed to see them drill but oh to think they are drilling to kill—and to kill my own people.

THURSDAY, MAY 9, 1861. A letter from my dear son, he writes that he has been promoted to a captain in the Virginia Army and attached to Gen. J. E. Johnston's staff. This we hope is good news.

AUGUST 27, 1862. Yesterday I had a visit from my old servant, Ailsa. She looks well and has seen a great deal of the world since she became free. She has selected Boston as her future home. This family of negroes has been in my family for generations. Her grandfather was my father's body servant, attended him throughout the Revolution.

Ailsa was given to me by my mother early in life as my personal maid. I raised her with great care, teaching her not only her duties, but her lessons and the religion and prayers of the Episcopal Church. She repaid me fully with her devotion and care of my children. It grieved me to part with Ailsa, but she was persuaded that it was the right thing for her to do.

Ailsa looked at me very wistfully when she said good-bye. I am sure there were tears in my eyes, but I had no money to offer her to remain with me. I feel that I shall never see her again.

SATURDAY, AUGUST 30, 1862. Soldiers very drunk and rowdy last night. We were obliged to lock our windows at an early hour. Oh, day of days! News was brought to the city about one o'clock that a terrible fight was in progress across the river—the firing could be heard distinctly.

Hundreds of ambulances getting grain from the storehouses and taking up clerks to convey them to the scene of action to assist eight thousand wounded men.

Every physician in the city hurried across the river and every one seems frantic.

MONDAY, SEPTEMBER 1, 1862. The Government has notified Tom Green that they will confiscate his beautiful home, the Van Ness Place, as a hospital for the wounded.

Also Mr. Corcoran's fine residence as well as the handsome home of Mr. Hill, and they call this a free country.

The wounded pouring in by the hundreds.

THURSDAY, SEPTEMBER 4, 1862. The United States are in my debt to the extent of five hundred and forty dollars this day. Although I have no winter fuel, and my necessities are very great, with no money to support or supply these needs, and by taking the oath of allegiance I could draw the amount due me—never will I sacrifice principle to interest and disgrace my children and ancestry.

MONDAY, DECEMBER 15, 1862. Lindsay's great friend and classmate, General Bayard, was killed [at] Fredericksburg. He was an only son. Poor fellow—Lindsay will be heart-broken. . . .

The papers and reports say that Fredericksburg and dear old Port Royal are both in ashes—Oh, when will this dreadful war ever cease.

MONDAY, FEBRUARY 2, 1863. A dismal day . . . Yesterday Anne and Julia were arrested as Southern sympathizers, sent to Old Point to be imprisoned in the casements there—Virginia was sent to the Old Capitol in Washington.

Here the diary ends—but the story does not. The girls were released from prison. Scholarly, musical Anne married Tom Johnson and was mistress of the Van Ness mansion after the war. Lindsay Lunsford Lomax survived the war and moved his mother and sisters to Belle Vie, a farm near Warrenton, Virginia, where Mrs. Lomax later died. Vic, the Belle, never married; she and Julia successfully launched The Young Ladies Seminary in Warrenton. Lindsay later served on the Gettysburg Battlefield Commission. He lived until 1913.

Lincoln's first inaugural parade.

199

*"This City is one great Camp,
we see and hear
nothing but the well ordered
tramp of the Soldier."*

—Major Daniel McCook of Ohio, May 4, 1861

Marching up Pennsylvania Avenue, a Union regiment passes in review before President Lincoln and General Winfield Scott early in 1861 (below). In the engraving above, New York's 71st Regiment arrives at the Washington railroad depot. Writing to a friend in May 1861, newspaperman Francis Preston Blair declared that by sending troops New Yorkers were "giving earnest that the north would not suffer the capitol to be sacrificed by the mob of Baltimore and the conspirators of D.C."

4 War and Reconstruction (1860–1875)

The divisiveness of the Civil War bore down on Washington as on no other city. Here, where most people were natives of Maryland and Virginia, Southern sentiments prevailed. Many Washingtonians had kin in the Confederate Army, including Mrs. Lincoln, whose brothers fought under the C.S.A. banner. There were those who, like W. W. Corcoran, the banker and art collector, left the country rather than repress their anti-Union views. Others, like Elizabeth Lomax (whose diary is quoted on the preceding pages), remained in Washington but refused to take the oath of allegiance to the Union—a requisite for receiving payment for freed slaves. (The District slaves were freed nine months before the Emancipation Proclamation. It was the only place in the country where slaveowners were legally compensated, but they had to swear the oath to get the money.)

As the war began, the first action taken by Union forces was to capture Alexandria, Arlington and the Virginia hills commanding the capital city. Major Daniel McCook, who described himself as "one of the first to volunteer to defend the President's Mansion in the darkest hours of this 'irrepresible conflict,'" stated a general Northern belief when he wrote that "our troubles will not be of long duration." Writing to a friend in Connecticut in May 1861, McCook said that

> "this question of secession or rebellion must now be settled for all time to come. The unity of Northern sentiment shall soon bring it about."

But the Confederate threat was still very real. Indeed, the Union capital was so near Confederate lines that a balloonist could ascend from the Mall to reconnoiter enemy gun emplacements across the Potomac; and the first big battle of the war, Bull Run (Manassas), in July 1861, drew streams of Washington carriages to watch the ac-

tion. The battle ended in an astonishing defeat for Union forces, prompting Union generals to hasten the construction of a series of forts and batteries to defend the city.

Washington became the primary point of embarkation for troops and supplies moving south. Moreover, since it was the Union-held city nearest the fighting, it became a major receiving station for the wounded, the rooms of its great public and private buildings being converted to convalescent wards and operating rooms. Hundreds of Northerners, including Walt Whitman and Louisa May Alcott, came to town to nurse the wounded. The major change in the city's demographic profile came as more and more blacks fled the South; Washington's black population more than doubled.

The presence of the military wrought enormous physical changes in the city. Trees were felled so they could not be used for cover or impede Union fire. Roads were torn up by the passage of heavy military equipment. New roads were built to link the city's defense positions. Although the only military action in the District was a skirmish at Fort Stevens, a few miles north of the capital, in July 1864, Washington's buildings and institutions, as well as its landscape, were a shambles by the war's end. Several years later, cries of "shame" greeted the suggestion that the nation celebrate its Centennial in the shabby capital. But when improvements came, they came almost overnight. Thanks to Alexander Shepherd, a governor of the District, Washington was reborn. Shepherd's ambitious program of installing gas lights and sewers and of paving the streets and planting trees incurred a huge debt. This prompted Congress to revoke the city's territorial status, dispense with a governor and take to itself the task of running the capital. But Shepherd's improvements made the city a beautiful and comfortable place to live.

"The Seat of War"

Plans to defend the capital from attack, either by Confederate ships on the Potomac or by troops, were quickly implemented. The bluffs on the Virginia side were secured, and the three Potomac bridges were put under close guard, as were the two Anacostia bridges leading to the Maryland side. In Georgetown, the Aqueduct Bridge was covered with planks and used as a roadway. At night, planks on this and other bridges were removed as a further precaution against a Confederate assault.

By the middle of July 1861, General Irvin McDowell, commanding 30,000 Union troops; was ordered to advance against a Confederate force stationed at Manassas Junction, Virginia, some twenty miles southwest of Washington. As reported in the *Washington Star*, on July 16 the scene around Arlington Heights and the Columbia Turnpike was all

"activity and bustle, and officers were continually coming and going, every one seeming anxious to be on the march and in the van. The numerous companies of regulars in the vicinity of Arlington House, comprising artillery, cavalry, and infantry, soon had their tents struck, and formed a column. . . . The scene from the hills . . . was grand. Looking toward Washington, regiment after regiment was seen coming along the road and across the Long Bridge, their arms gleaming in the sun. . . . Cheer after cheer was heard as regiment greeted regiment, and this with the martial music and sharp clear orders of commanding officers made a combination of sounds very pleasant to the ear of a Union man."

In the early hours of May 24, 1861, little more than a month after the first shots of the Civil War were fired at Fort Sumter, the Twelfth New York Regiment crossed the Potomac over Long Bridge (below), becoming the first Union regiment to enter Virginia. As reported by an officer:

"It was a beautiful moonlight night and the moonbeams glittered brightly on the flashing muskets as the Regiment silently advanced across the bridge. The Engineer Corps, commanded by Captain B. S. Church, led the column, driving in the picket line stationed near the bridge as they advanced. The Regiment proceeded toward Alexandria for a considerable distance, and then partially retraced its steps and marched to Roach's Mills, a point some six miles from Washington, where it occupied the advance post of honor."

Arlington House, the home of Colonel and Mrs. Robert E. Lee, became Union headquarters. Lee and his wife had left the house for the last time after Lee resigned his commission to take up arms for Virginia.

"The Seat of War"—a view of the Washington area published in the early 1860s.

On July 21, the first battle of Bull Run (Manassas) was fought. Rose O'Neal Greenhow, who lived on Lafayette Square and was later accused of being a spy for the Confederate Army, wrote afterwards that the battle

"ended in the total defeat of the entire 'Grand Army.' In the world's history such a sight was never witnessed: statesmen, Senators, Congressmen, generals and officers of every grade, soldiers, teamsters—all rushing in frantic flight, as if pursued by countless demons. For miles, the country was thick with ambulances, accoutrements of war, etc. . . . The news of the disastrous rout of the Yankee army was cried through the streets. . . . For days the wildest disorder reigned in the Capital. The streets of Washington were filled with stragglers, telling the doleful tale."

Contrary to expectations, Southern troops failed to follow up their advantage. Union forces took the opportunity to further strengthen the capital's defenses. For days after Bull Run, however, Washington remained in a state of confusion—as Walt Whitman recorded:

"Fourteenth street etc., crowded, jammed with citizens, darkies, clerks, everybody, lookers-on, women in the windows, curious expressions from faces, as those swarms of dirt-cover'd return'd soldiers there (will they never end?) move by. . . . During the forenoon Washington gets all over motley with these defeated soldiers— queer-looking objects, strange eyes and faces drenched (the steady rain drizzles on all day) and fearfully worn, hungry, haggard, blister'd in the feet. Good people . . . hurry up something for their grub. They put wash kettles on the fire, for soup, for coffee. They set tables on the sidewalks—wagon-loads of bread are purchas'd, swiftly cut in stout chunks. Here are two aged ladies, beautiful, the first in the city for culture and charm, they stand with store of eating and drink at an improvis'd table of rough plank, and give food, and have the store replenish'd from their house every half-hour all that day: and there in the rain they stand, active, silent, white-hair'd and give food, though the tears stream down their cheeks . . . it seems strange to see . . . the soldiers sleeping—in the midst of all, sleeping sound. They drop down anywhere, on the steps of houses, up close by the basements or fences, on the sidewalk, on some vacant lot, and deeply sleep."

"I propose to strengthen the garrisons of Fort Corcoran, Fort Bennett, the redoubt on Arlington road, and the blockhouses," Colonel William Tecumseh Sherman reported to General McDowell the day after the Union defeat at Bull Run. Fort Jackson (left) was built to protect the Virginia end of the Long Bridge, the approach to which lies beyond the battlements in the background at right.

On the Washington side of the Potomac, Union Army camps proliferated. The panoramic view below was taken in 1861 from the top of the Capitol, looking down East Capitol Street toward the Eastern Branch (the Anacostia River). The regiments in view are those of Vermont, New York and New Jersey.

The network of forts and batteries that encircled the city is shown on the map opposite. Under the supervision of Generals Barnard, Meigs, Barry, Cullum and Totten, Washington rapidly became the most heavily fortified city in the world. By the end of the war it was ringed with sixty-eight forts and twenty-two batteries. Eighteen forts were concentrated between Fort Lincoln on the Anacostia and Fort Sumner on the city's western border. In the same area, wrote General Barnard, four batteries of heavy artillery and twenty-three light artillery batteries formed "a connected system of fortifications in which every point at intervals of 800–1000 yards was occupied by an enclosed field fort." Seen from a hotel window in the center of town, the city would literally have been encircled with a ring of camp fires. It was this scene that inspired Julia Ward Howe to write, in "The Battle Hymn of the Republic,"

> "I have seen Him in the watch fires of a hundred circling camps;
> They have builded Him an altar in the evening dews and damps . . ."

A friend afterward recalled how Mrs. Howe came to write the hymn:

> "1861 was a very dark time in the history of our Country. No decisive victories had been won and the divided nation held its breath in fear of what the dim and uncertain future would bring forth. One day James Freeman Clarke was driving with Dr. and Mrs. Howe through the streets of Washington, and the carriage stopped to allow a regiment of troops to pass. The soldiers were singing 'John Brown's Body Lies A-Mouldering in the Grave'—Dr. Clarke turned to Mrs. Howe and said: 'I wish you could write a poem for that tune.' Mrs. Howe replied that she wished she could; she returned to Willard's Hotel that night and went to bed and to sleep. The next morning just before dawn, she suddenly awakened as though some one had laid a hand upon her shoulder, and the great Battle Hymn of the Republic came sweeping through her mind. . . ."

> "All's quiet along the Potomac tonight
> Where the soldiers lie peacefully dreaming:
> Their tents in the rays of the clear autumn moon,
> In the light of the watch fires are gleaming:
> A tremulous sigh, as the gentle night wind,
> Through the forest leaves softly is creeping:
> While stars up above, with their glittering eyes,
> Keep guard—for the Army's sleeping."

—Ethel Beers, 1879

Columbia Historical Society

DEFENSES OF WASHINGTON

Extract of Military Map
of N. E. Virginia

SCALE OF MILES

0   ¼ ½ ¾ 1   2 Miles

National Park Service

Soldiers and their tents spread to the distant hills in "The Army of the Potomac" (below), painted by James Hope between 1860 and 1865. In the engraving at left, a Pennsylvania artillery unit shells Confederate cavalry across the Potomac on October 4, 1861. Ordered to shell a barn in which Confederate supplies were believed to be stored, the artillery men had placed a Parrot gun on the heights above Great Falls and had begun their shelling. Several shells fell into the barn, which, according to the picture's original caption, "had the effect of unhousing a number of Confederate Cavalry, who rode with all speed for the neighboring woods."

The pencil sketch opposite, by G. A. Harker, shows a Union camp overlooking the Capitol. Writing home about Washington's summer climate, a Michigan soldier commented wryly that "the sun is so damned near Washington that it is the next place to Hell. The Fourth of July is around here somewhere but we can't get a hold of it. The Black Bottle is empty on the shelf and our throats seems as dry as the contributions to the Soldiers Aid Society. Nothing to do but lay and sweat out old times." Mary Clemmer Ames, a resident of Washington during the war, described the city this way:

> "Capitol Hill, dreary, desolate and dirty, stretched away into an uninhabited desert, high above the mud of the West End. Arid hill, and sodden plain showed alike the horrid trail of war. Forts bristled above every hill-top. Soldiers were entrenched at every gate-way. Shed hospitals covered acres on acres in every suburb. Churches, art-halls and private mansions were filled with the wounded and dying of the American armies. The endless roll of the army wagon seemed never still. The rattle of the anguish-laden ambulance, the piercing cries of the sufferers . . . made morning, noon and night too dreadul to be borne."

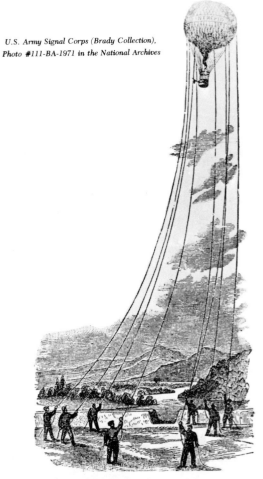

When Thaddeus S. C. Lowe of New Hampshire suggested that balloons be used for military purposes, the Army at first resisted. But Lowe found an ally in Joseph Henry, who, as the first Secretary of the Smithsonian, had seen the usefulness of balloons in weather science. Henry put in a word to President Lincoln, and Lowe's equipment was soon set up near the Smithsonian's "Red Brick Castle." Launching his silk ballon *Intrepid*, Lowe crossed the Potomac to observe Confederate troops.

Lowe, who later founded the Lowe Observatory in California, not only organized the Army's Aeronautical Corps; he also became a founder of naval aviation, for he sometimes made his aerial observations from a balloon tethered to a steamer in mid-Potomac. On a mission in 1861, Lowe had his balloon towed through the streets of Washington and Georgetown and across Chain Bridge (above):

"Our progress was slow, the night being very dark, and we were constantly apprehensive of running the balloon against trees or other obstacles. . . . We arrived at the Chain Bridge about three o'clock the next (Sunday) morning, and found it filled with artillery and cavalry going to Virginia. In order to take the balloon over, my men were obliged to mount the trestle-work and walk along the stringers, only eighteen inches wide and nearly a hundred feet above the bed of the river. Thus, with the balloon above their heads, myself in the car directing the management of the ropes, the men getting on and off the trestle-work, with a column of artillery moving below, and a hundred feet still lower the deep strong current rushing over the rocks, while the sky was dark above, the scene was novel, exciting, and not a little dangerous."

In this aerial view of Washington in 1862, important points in the city's defense perimeter are clearly visible: the Potomac bridges, which carried troops and supplies to the Virginia shore, and the forts and batteries that dotted the hilltops. Points of interest include:

1. Matthias Point
2. Aquia Creek
3. Shipping Point
4. Fredericksburg
5. Mount Vernon
6. Alexandria
7. Orange & Alexandria R.R.
8. Loudon & Hampshire R.R.
9. Manassas Junction
10. Bull Run
11. Centreville
12. Fairfax Court House
13. Vienna
14. Falls Church
15. Arlington House
16. Chain Bridge
17. Aqueduct Bridge
18. Long Bridge
19. Georgetown
20. Washington
21. White House
22. Smithsonian Institution
23. Patent Office
24. General Post Office
25. Capitol
26. Navy Yard
27. Arsenal
28. Maryland shore
29. Fort Washington
30. Indian Head
31. Maryland Point
32. Port Tobacco
33. Forts Scott, Albany, Runyon, Richardson, Craig, Woodbury, Corcoran, Bennett, etc.

Base of Operation

Washington was a vital embarkation and supply point for the Army of the Potomac in carrying the war to the South. The logistics overwhelmed the city. Troop arrivals and departures swamped the wharves and railroad stations. Guns moving through the streets tore up what pavement there was. The quartermaster corps put cattle on the Mall and a bakery in the Capitol. Since no other Union-held city was so near the field of combat, the capital became a major medical center.

Meanwhile, the capital took on new meaning for the rest of the country, becoming the symbol of the Union as well as its political and administra-

The Sixth Street Wharf, on the southwest waterfront, as it appeared during the Civil War. The oversize flag flies over the Law House (see page 73).

tive center. As Mary Clemmer Ames wrote in her 1874 memoir, *Ten Years in Washington:*

> "How many an American boy, marching to its defense, beholding for the first time the great dome of the Capitol rising before his eyes, comprehended in one deep gaze, as he never had in his whole life before, *all* that the Capitol meant to him and to every free man. . . . 'Washington city' . . . was no longer a name to the mother waiting and praying in the distant hamlet; her boy was camped on the floor of the rotunda. No longer a far off myth to the lonely wife; her husband held guard on the heights defending the capital. No longer a place good for nothing but political schemes to the village sage; his boy, wrapped in a blanket, slept on the stone steps of the great treasury.
>
> "Never, till that hour, did the Federal city become to the heart of the American people what it had so long been in the eyes of the world—truly the capital of the nation."

When the war started almost every public building, church and large private house was commandeered by the Army—including the newly completed Corcoran Gallery. Tudor Place was turned into a boardinghouse for Union officers by its owner, Britannia Wellington Peter Kennon (below), one of Martha Washington's great-grandchildren. Born at Tudor Place in 1815 (her name celebrates Wellington's victory at Waterloo), she was widowed when her husband, Captain Beverly Kennon, was killed in the *Princeton* explosion in 1844 (see page 169). She took in Union officers as boarders as a way of keeping the house from being requisitioned for government use. When a long-time family friend asked what her mother would think of such a turn of events, Mrs. Kennon replied that her mother would think that she was doing her best under the circumstances. Mrs. Kennon continued living at Tudor Place until her death in 1911. The engraving below shows the Georgetown barracks of the 69th New York Regiment. J. Holdsworth Gordon, a Georgetown resident, wrote:

> "We boys fraternised with the soldiers, to a certain extent, many of whom were fine fellows and loved to talk with 'the little Rebs' as some of us were dubbed. . . . Indeed, these poor fellows, many of them almost boys, just from home and home surroundings, were glad enough to find any one with whom they might pass a word of friendship or fellowship. As we would see the sick and wounded brought in, our hearts could but go out to them in their suffering, and make us very anxious for the loved one away from us, who might at any moment be in their condition and not under such favorable surroundings, as the United States soldiers had everything that money could buy to alleviate their sufferings and supply their wants while the Confederates had almost nothing."

"Among other sights are immense droves of cattle with their drivers, passing through the streets of the city. Some of the men have a way of leading the cattle by a peculiar call, a wild, pensive hoot, quite musical, prolong'd, indescribably, sounding something between the cooing of a pigeon and the hoot of an owl. I like to stand and look at the sight of one of these immense droves—a little way off—(as the dust is great). There are always men on horseback, cracking their whips and shouting—the cattle low—some obstinate ox or steer attempts to escape—then a lively scene—the mounted men, always excellent riders and on good horses, dash after the recusant, and wheel and turn—a dozen mounted drovers, their great slouch'd, broad-brim'd hats, very picturesque—another dozen on foot—everybody cover'd with dust—long goads in their hands—an immense drove of perhaps 1000 cattle—the shouting, hooting, movement etc."

—Walt Whitman

An Arthur Lumley sketch from the *New York Illustrated News* titled "A Stormy Day at the Aqueduct Bridge, Georgetown, D.C." shows how the "water trough" bridge was adapted to military use. At right, a canal barge. Across the Potomac are the fields and hills that today are Rosslyn, Virginia.

United States artillery units drill near the Washington Monument. The engraving is from a sketch by Thomas Nast.

"*You would not know this God-forsaken city, our beautiful capital, with all its artistic wealth, desecrated, disgraced with Lincoln's low soldiery. The respectable part [of the soldiers] view it also in the same spirit, for one of the Seventh Regiment told me that never in his life had he seen such ruin going on as is now enacted in the halls of our once honoured Capitol!*"

—Mrs. Philip Phillips of Washington,
in a letter dated Spring, 1861

The Capitol Rotunda served as barracks for Massachusetts' Eighth Regiment (left). The engraving below shows the workings of the Army bakery that was set up in the basement of the Capitol. Barrels of flour, shuttled down the stairs, were stored beneath the vaulting of the Rotunda floor. The flour was baked into bread in these basement ovens, and the bread was then shipped to the front by wagon.

A Rhode Island regiment had its sleeping quarters in the Patent Office (right). During the war the Patent Office also served as an Army hospital, litters and cots being placed in the aisles between the glass display cases. In the photograph below, an ox team hauls a fifteen-inch Rodman gun, weighing twenty-five tons, through the streets of Washington. The city's streets, most of which were unpaved at the time, were so cut up by the wagons, cavalry and artillery that, remembered Holdsworth Gordon, "the mud was in many places clear up to the bodies of the horses, and it was difficult to get along. This was especially the case on Fourteenth Street." There were other hazards in the streets as well, as Albion K. Parris recalled:

> "One day, about three or four hundred government mules were being driven out from Twentieth Street when an intrepid woman carrying a little basket undertook to cross the street before the drove had hardly passed. The onlookers were horrified to see a big brute of a mule kick up his hind legs and throw the woman up in the air. The poor soul landed flat down in the dirt road. . . . She was unconscious and there was the animal's hoof print on her forehead."

"Vividly I recall the conversion of the city . . . into one vast hospital," wrote Washingtonian Henry E. Davis. "Not only were many of the public reservations and other vacant lots occupied by temporary hospitals, but also many of the churches and . . . a large part of the Patent Office building." The Armory Square Hospital (above) was at Seventh Street, next to the Smithsonian. Volunteers came from all over the country to help nurse the wounded. One physician was Dr. Mary Walker (left), who, as one Alexandrian wrote,

"was a strong advocate of dress reform, and always appeared in a complete masculine outfit. Ordinarily, this consisted of long trousers, with frock coat and tall, silk hat. She was very punctilious in raising her hat to a casual acquaintance, and in removing it when custom required. . . . As a young woman, she had studied medicine and received a physician's degree. At the time of the Civil War she served as a volunteer nurse in the Union Army, and was later detailed to a surgeon's duty, with the rank of First Lieutenant. In this capacity she wore the full uniform of the Army officer, with gold stripes, and a hat with gold cord. . . . Alas, her career was interrupted when she was captured by the enemy, and consigned, for some months, to Libby Prison, in Richmond. She was eventually exchanged for a man of equal rank in the Confederate Army. . . .

"The career of Dr. Walker was not without its drawbacks. She was arrested several times for masquerading in men's clothing; this even after Congress had bestowed upon her the right to wear trousers. Her costume was certainly misleading, and at times she created considerable consternation by appearing suddenly in ladies' dressing rooms about town."

218

In the photo above, an Armory Square ward is hung with Christmas decorations. As the photograph suggests, amputation was the usual treatment for arm and leg wounds. Recovery was slow and chancy, and the hospitals were always crowded.

In letters to her husband, a Union officer, Harriet Ward Foote Hawley of Connecticut wrote the following vivid account of her days as a nurse in the Armory Square Hospital, where she worked from six in the morning until ten at night:

"I am glad and thankful that I am here, just as I am that you are there, yet the days drift by in one long agony. I am learning not to let myself *feel* as much as I did at first, yet I can never get used to it. . . . O, my men are dying so fast! The truth is this Hospital is so near the boat that it is always filled up with the very worst cases, and this time they all say they have never had men whose systems seemed in such a low bad state. There comes a man to tell me 'Capt. Bell is bleeding,' a secondary hemorrhage, and I thought his amputated leg was doing so nicely. . . .

July 24. "You see what the Sanitary Commission does and I see what the Soldier's Aid does. One of the nurses who had been here more than a year said to me to-day, that she couldn't have made her men comfortable if it had not been for the Hartford Aid. The Government provides all the *essentials,* food, and medicine, and surgeons and nurses, but I don't think Uncle Sam provides pocket handkerchiefs or easy chairs when the sick boys first begin to sit up, or carpet slippers, or

lemonade when they are feverish, or jelly to tempt their appetites a little when they're sick of Hospital tea . . . or books and games . . . to help along the weary hours of a slow convalescence.

Dec. 25, 1864. "We trimmed the ward by way of keeping Christmas. A wreath of evergreens hangs on each of the twelve pillars, festoons across the center of the hall, a large garrison flag looped across the far end, while at this end are crosses and stars. Mrs. Foster sent me eight beautiful flowering plants which stand in the windows, and a bouquet of fresh flowers from Miss Dixon on the piano. I have rarely enjoyed anything more than sitting and chatting with my men and tying greens yesterday. The Commissary and I clubbed together and gave all the full diet patients a plum pudding, and we lady nurses did the same by all the others. . . .

Feb. 19, 1865. "There comes that odious Walt Whitman to talk evil and unbelief to my boys. I think I would rather see the evil one himself—at least if he had horns and hoofs—in my ward. I shall get him out as soon as possible.

February 23rd. "Glorious victories! I stood and listened to the salutes yesterday. There are so many fortifications in and around Washington that the roar and thunder was grand."

219

A devoted father, who tried to make the White House a happy home for his sons despite the tribulations of war, Abraham Lincoln is seen in the portrait at left with his son Tad. At the toy store above, on New York Avenue NW, the President bought toys for his young children. (Robert, the only one of Lincoln's four sons to live to manhood, was away at college during the war.) In the engraving below, Lincoln reviews a brigade of New Jersey troops with Tad by his side. Walt Whitman wrote of seeing the President

"almost every day, as I happen to live where he passes to and from his lodgings out of town. He never sleeps at the White House during the hot season, but has quarters at a health location some three miles north . . . the Soldiers' Home.

"I saw him this morning about 8:30 coming in to business, riding on Vermont Avenue, near L Street. He always has a company of twenty-five or thirty cavalry, with sabres drawn and held upright over their shoulders. They say the guard was against his personal wish, but he let his counselors have their way. . . . Sometimes one of his sons, a boy of ten or twelve, accompaines him, riding at his right on a pony."

"Though the Union was more to him [Lincoln] than our black freedom or our future, under his wise and beneficent rule we saw ourselves gradually lifted from the depth of slavery to the heights of liberty and manhood; . . . under his rule we saw two hundred thousand of our dark and dusky people responding to the call of Abraham Lincoln, and with muskets on their shoulders, and eagles on their buttons, timing their high footsteps to liberty and union under the national flag; . . . under his rule we saw the internal slave-trade, which so long disgraced the nation, abolished, and slavery abolished in the District of Columbia; under his rule we saw for the first time the law enforced against the foreign slave trade, and the first slave-trader hanged like any other pirate or murderer; under his rule, assisted by the greatest captain of our age, and his inspiration, we saw the Confederate States, based upon the idea that our race must be slaves, and slave forever, battered to pieces and scattered to the four winds; under his rule and in the fullness of time, we saw Abraham Lincoln . . . penning the immortal paper, making slavery forever impossible in the United States."

—Frederick Douglass, speaking at the dedication of the Lincoln statue in Lincoln Park, April 14, 1876

Martin Luther King Library, Washingtoniana Collection

Seamstress to both Mrs. Jefferson Davis and Mrs. Lincoln, Elizabeth Keckley (above) had been born a slave but had purchased her freedom and her son's (for $1,200). As founder of the Contraband Relief Organization, she raised funds for blacks in New York, Boston, Philadelphia and Washington. Later she taught at Wilberforce University. In 1868 Mrs. Keckley published her reminiscences of family life in the Lincoln White House. Called *Behind the Scenes*, the book included the following description of the "sad, anxious days" of 1863, when the "the Confederates were flushed with victory":

"Those who saw [Lincoln] in privacy only, could tell how much he suffered. One day he came into the room where I was fitting a dress on Mrs. Lincoln. His step was slow and heavy, and his face sad. Like a tired child he threw himself upon a sofa, and shaded his eyes with his hands. He was a complete picture of dejection. Mrs. Lincoln, observing his troubled look, asked,
"'Where have you been father?'
"'To the War Department' was the brief, almost sullen answer.
"' Any news?'
"' Yes, plenty of news, but no good news. It is dark, dark everywhere.'
"He reached forth one of his long arms, and took a small Bible from the stand near the head of the sofa, opened the pages of the holy book. . . . I discovered that Mr. Lincoln was reading the divine comforter, Job."

Anderson Cottage, the center building in the picture below, was the summer White House of Presidents Lincoln, Hayes and Arthur. Here, in 1862, Lincoln prepared the final draft of the Emancipation Proclamation. The neo-Gothic cottage, Corn Rigs, was built in 1842 as the country house of banker George Washington Riggs. It stands on the grounds of the U. S. Soldiers' Home.

Kiplinger, Washington Collection

Contrabands coming into camp: a pencil sketch by A. R. Waud, 1862.

"On the first day of January, in the year of our Lord one thousand eight hundred and sixty-three, all persons held as slaves within any State, or designated part of a State, the people Whereof shall then be in rebellion against the United States, shall be then, thenceforward, and forever free."

—Emancipation Proclamation

During the Civil War, many blacks sought refuge in Washington. "They came," said a former slave, "with great hope in their hearts, and with all their worldly goods on their backs. Fresh from the bonds of slavery, fresh from the benighted regions of the plantations, they came to the Capital looking for Liberty."

Slaves who had thus fled or been abandoned by their masters during the war came to be known as "contrabands." The nickname originated in a ruling by General Benjamin F. Butler, commander of Fort Monroe, Virginia, who declared in May 1861 that slaves escaping to his lines were "contraband of war" and would not be returned to their masters.

Slavery was outlawed in the District of Columbia on April 16, 1862. The reaction of a Washington slave to the news that she was free is recorded in a letter to Christian Fleetwood, a black sergeant major:

"This indeed has been a happy day to me. Sights have I witnessed that I never anticipated one of which I will relate. The Chambermaid at Smiths (my former place) (who is a sweet lovely creature in disposition . . .) is a Slave. So this morning I went there to inform her of the passage of the Bill. When I entered the Cook . . . and another Slave woman who has a slave son were talking relative to the Bill, expressing doubts of its passage. When I entered they perceived that something was ahead and . . . asked me 'What's the news?' 'The District's free,' says I pulling out the *National Republican* and reading its editorial. When I had finished the chambermaid had left the room sobbing for joy. The slave woman clapped her hands and shouted . . . left the house, saying, 'Let me go and tell my husband that Jesus has done all things well.' While the cook who is free retired to another room to offer thanks for the blessing sent. Should I not feel glad to see so much rejoicing around me? Were I a drinker I would get on a jolly spree today but as a Christian, I can but kneel in prayer and bless God. . . ."

Nine months after the slaves were freed in the District, Lincoln signed the Emancipation Proclamation. Although the Proclamation actually freed no slaves (it applied only to areas still in rebellion, where the federal government had no authority), it confirmed the government's opposition to slavery, offering hope of total abolition.

Company E of the 4th U. S. Colored Infantry was photographed at Washington's Fort Lincoln on November 17, 1865. Although many blacks throughout the country volunteered to serve in the Union Army, they were at first refused because the militia act of 1792 specified that only "Free white males" were to be accepted. After 1862, however, blacks were permitted to join. Eventually there were 166 black regiments, most of them infantry but also including cavalry and engineer units. A group of Washington blacks, recruited by John F. Cook, Jr. (see page 172), Rev. Henry McNeil Turner (pastor of the Israel A.M.E. Church) and Anthony Bowen, joined the first U. S. Colored Troops, with Turner serving as their chaplain. Earlier in the war, meanwhile, Michael Shiner, a Washington black who worked at the Navy Yard, had noted in his diary that

"on The first Day of June 1861 on Satturday Justice Clark was Sent Down to the Washington navy yard For to administer the oath of allegiance to The mechinics and The Labouring Class of working men with out Distincsion of Colour for them to Stand By the Stars and Stripes and defend for the union and Captain Dalgreen Present and I Believe at that time I michael Shiner was the first Colored man That Taken The oath in washington DC and that oath still Remains in my heart and when I taken that oath I taken it in the presence of my God without predudice or enmity to any man And I intend to Sustain that oath with the assistance of the Allmighty God until I die for when a man Takes an oath For a just cause it is more than taking a Drink of water Sitting Down to his breakfast"

All: Library of Congress, Prints and Photographs Division

The Freedman's Village at Arlington, built by the government in 1863 to provide housing for contrabands, was sketched for *Harper's Weekly* by A. R. Waud. Both public and private organizations—notably the Freedman's Relief Association, founded in March 1862—mobilized to provide clothing, housing and jobs for the contrabands. The F.R.A. also made an effort to teach the newcomers to read and write and to "bring them under moral influences." The government's "contraband department," organized in June 1862, with headquarters in an army barracks on the outskirts of Washington, registered the contrabands and gave them passes that guaranteed them military protection.

The number of contrabands in the Washington area grew rapidly: from 400 in April 1862 to 4,200 in October, to 17,000 the following spring and to an estimated 40,000 by 1865. The Freedman's Village erected at Arlington was an early instance of the government providing housing and other forms of public assistance.

In July 1864 the war came to Washington's doorstep, when Confederate General Jubal A. Early crossed the upper Potomac and then marched southeast toward the capital. He reached the District of Columbia on July 11 but was held off by Union troops at Fort Stevens, in a battle witnessed by President Lincoln (above). Two days later, the Confederate invaders were driven back into Virginia.

Lincoln, meanwhile, had been nominated by the Republican, or National Union, Party for a second term as President. One of the most active political arenas in Washington was the lobby of Willard's Hotel, seen here in a sketch by Thomas Nast. As reported by Nathaniel Hawthorne for the readers of *Atlantic Monthly*, Willard's

"may be much more justly called the centre of Washington and the Union than either the Capitol, the White House, or the State Department. Everybody may be seen there. It is the meeting-place of the true representatives of this country—not such as are chosen blindly and amiss by electors who take a folded ballot from the hand of a local politican, and thrust it into the ballot-box unread, but men who gravitate or are attracted hither by real business, or a native impulse to breathe the intensest atmosphere of the nation's life, or a genuine anxiety to see how this life-and-death struggle is going to deal with us. Nor these only, but all manner of loafers. Never, in any other spot, was there such a miscellany of people. You exchange nods with governors of sovereign states; you elbow illustrious men, and tread on the toes of generals; you hear statesmen and orators speaking in their familiar tones. You are mixed up with office-seekers, wire-pullers, inventors, artists, poets, prosers, (including editors, army-correspondents, attaches of foreign journals, and long-winded talkers), clerks, diplomats, mail contractors, railway directors, until your own identity is lost among them."

224

The House of Representatives erupts in celebration after the passage, on January 31, 1865, of the Thirteenth Amendment to the Constitution, which abolished slavery in the United States. (The Amendment became law on December 18, after it was ratified by twenty-seven states.) The photograph at right was taken during Lincoln's second inauguration, which was held on March 4, 1865, on the steps of the still unfinished Capitol. "The most significant thing to me in the celebration," wrote Harriet Ward Foote Hawley in her diary, "was the batallion of *colored* brass band and the delegation (a large one) from the colored Odd Fellows." Early in April, Richmond fell to the Union Army. On April 9 Lee surrendered to Grant at Appomattox.

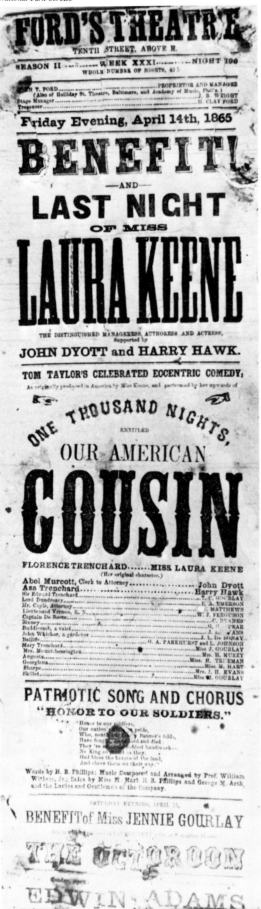

On April 14, 1865, five days after the news reached Washington that Lee had surrendered at Appomattox, President Lincoln attended the final performance at Ford's Theatre of *Our American Cousin*. While sitting in his box at the theater, Lincoln was shot by John Wilkes Booth, who jumped to the stage and fled. The President, mortally wounded, was carried to a house across the street from the theater (opposite page), where he died on the morning of April 15. The *Evening Star*'s account of the assassination appeared shortly before the President's death. A Georgetown resident, J. Holdsworth Gordon, afterward remembered the effect of the assassination on the city—and on his family—on that Good Friday:

"I had that evening gone to the National Theatre, being Friday night. While the play was going on some one made a cry; we could not tell if it was 'fire', 'murder', or what. The immense audience, as if impressed with the fact that something terrible had occurred, rose to their feet, and there was a rush for the doors. I was but a boy, not particularly strong, and was carried along with the crowd, fairly lifted off my feet. When we reached the open street, after a great deal of struggling and shouting, we witnessed a scene of indescribable excitement. Soldiers, guards and police were dashing here and there and in all directions, gazing into the faces of the men in the crowd, and a word was almost as much as one's life was worth. We soon found that Mr. Lincoln had been assassinated at Ford's Opera House, a few blocks away. It was a terrible night in Washington. I joined the crowd and ran first up to Ford's and then back to the theatre, and then to the White House. The streets were soon filled with negroes, many of them inflamed with liquor, shouting, sobbing and yelling for 'death to the rebels'. After a time I beat a hasty retreat to home. When I reached there, I woke father and told him what had occurred. . . . My father was filled with horror at the story, and as we expected Will to be home in a short time, was greatly agitated, being much concerned for the future safety of the Confederates, in view of the frenzied condition of mind that must naturally result in the North.

"The next morning we were notified by a delegation of negroes that unless we immediately festooned our house with crepe, the house would be attacked and our family imprisoned. It was known that Will was in the Southern army and that our feelings were with that cause. It was impossible to purchase crepe or evidences of mourning, the demand being so much greater than the supply, and we had to resort to tearing up some of mother's old dark clothing, in order to use the same as mourning emblems. Every house was draped, and all were required to show at least outward sorrow. Later on we learned to appreciate the fact that in the death of Mr. Lincoln, the truly great man, the South and her people had lost a good friend; one whose kindly heart would have spared them many of the sufferings and tyrannies they were subsequently obliged to undergo as a result of his death."

At the war's end, men of the Union Army march down Pennsylvania Avenue during the Grand Review of May 23–24, 1865. In the engraving above, General Sherman leads his troops past the reviewing stand. President Andrew Johnson is at the center of the stand, with General Grant on the left and Secretary of War Stanton on his right. As one newspaper account noted, "The army marched through Washington and then, as an army, disappeared forever; absorbed into the body-politic, a million men of war turned men of peace in a single day." Harriet Riddle Davis wrote:

> "The liveliest recollection I have of this grand review is of seeing General Custer thrown from his horse in the presence of two armies and of several hundred thousand spectators. This horse with its gallant rider came prancing along the avenue, the horse's neck being literally hung with wreaths of flowers, as were all the officers' horses in that vast procession. An over-enthusiastic young woman threw still another wreath towards Custer which struck his horse, a big black charger, full in the face, causing it to rear and landing the unsuspecting General upon the dusty roadway. I also remember the delight we children took in all the queer things that followed in the wake of the different divisions. There were eagles perched aloft on flag poles, some of them with scarce a feather left on them. There were dogs, cats, pigs, cows, owls and monkeys, all marching as proudly as the troops themselves."

"The Georgetown Election—the Negro at the Ballot Box" by Thomas Nast was published in *Harper's Weekly* in 1867.

"From the Depths of Slavery"

What Frederick Douglass called "the immediate, complete, and universal enfranchisement of the colored people of the whole country" was the cause that drew black leaders to Washington toward the end of the Civil War and that stirred the black community of the District of Columbia. Since 1864 black leaders had been petitioning Congress for the vote. A meeting at the Fifteenth Street Presbyterian Church in 1866 drew black delegates from as far away as Wisconsin, Alabama and six New England states to discuss and press the issue. In Congress, the chief proponents of black enfranchisement were Radical Republicans, who wanted the South punished for its rebellion and reconstructed in a new image. Considering Washington to be part of the defeated South, they made the capital a testing ground for their Reconstruction program.

Early in 1867, nineteen months before the Fourteenth Amendment granted blacks full United States citizenship, Congress passed a bill to enfranchise blacks in the District of Columbia. Washington and Georgetown voters protested. In January 1866 Washington's mayor had reported to the President that in an election "to ascertain the opinion of the people . . . on the question of negro suffrage," the vote was 6,591 against, 35 in favor. In Georgetown the results were 712 against, 1 in favor. President Johnson vetoed the enfranchisement bill, but it was immediately overridden by Congress. In 1867 thousands of blacks voted in District elections. In 1868 blacks were elected to local office for the first time. By 1869 there were seven black councilmen. By 1870 the City Council prohibited discrimination in hotels, bars, restaurants and places of amusement. For a short time, at least, segregation was officially ended.

Meanwhile, Washington still faced pressing problems stemming from the plight of the thousands of former slaves who had crowded into the city. During the war years the city's population had doubled, and so had the cost of living. The need for housing, employment and health facilities strained the resources of the long-established black and white communities alike. Yet the development of education was given first priority. The School Board Report of 1864 said:

> ". . . in this city, burdened with extraordinary expenses, distracted by the convulsions of a civil war, thronged with passing troops, in close proximity to great armies, at times within the sound of hostile cannon, and almost in a state of siege, the public schools, in the midst of all these adverse circumstances, have not only steadily continued to dispense their benefits to the community, but . . . mark the three years just ended as the beginning of a new and proud era in their history."

Buildings were turned into makeshift schools, volunteer teachers came forward, and classes for adults and children were organized on a large scale by private groups, particularly the black churches. The District of Columbia, required by Congress in 1862 to establish public schools for blacks as well as whites, started a school building program (supported by local taxes) even before the war was over. Classes began in the first black public school building—part of a row of small frame houses on Capitol Hill—in May 1865. The next decade brought an ambitious building program for black and white schools throughout the city. At the first dedication, Mayor Wallach pledged that the school would be used so "that our own as well as the children of the thousands who were flocking to the metropolis of the Union might reap the advantage."

Frederick Douglass, the abolitionist lecturer and newspaper editor who was known as "The Sage of Anacostia," came to Washington in 1871 as an editor of the *New National Era.* He served as secretary of the Santo Domingo Commission in 1871, marshal of the District of Columbia from 1877 to 1881, Recorder of Deeds of the District of Columbia from 1881 to 1886 and minister to Haiti from 1889 to 1891. He was photographed with his family in front of his Washington home, at 316–318 A Street NE, which became the Museum of African Art in 1964. His large suburban house, Cedar Hill, on the hilltop at 14th and W streets SE in Anacostia, was preserved and maintained for years by the Frederick Douglass Memorial and Historical Association, together with the National Association of Colored Women's Clubs. It has now been restored and opened to the public by the Park Service.

Howard University, "the capstone of Negro education" (as it came to be called), was conceived as an "institution for the training of preachers (colored) with a view to service among freedmen." Located on a high plateau above Florida Avenue at Seventh Street NW, the university was established in 1867 by a special act of Congress which provided funds through the Freedmen's Bureau headed by General Oliver O. Howard, the university's main founder. (The First Congregational Church at 10th and G streets, with its strong New England Abolitionist heritage, gave the impetus.) Soon after its founding the university had 400 students. Its six departments included theology, medicine, law, college, normal and preparatory. Freedmen's Hospital, started in 1862, became affiliated with the University Medical School. (The new 500-bed Howard University Hospital opened in 1975.) While the university included white trustees, faculty and students from the first, the education of black leadership has always been foremost among its goals. Howard graduates and faculty have played a major role in local and national life, and the university has also attracted many students from Africa and the Caribbean.

In the 1865 engraving above, based on a sketch by A. R. Waud, clerks leave the Treasury Department at the end of their work day. In the days before the Civil War, recalled Sara E. Vedder, "No female could get employment in government offices. . . . Men were employed exclusively." The situation changed during the war, when men were needed at the front.

Postwar Scenes

The grounds of the White House on a Saturday in June 1868. "Olivia," the pen name of a Washington correspondent, wrote this description of a Presidential reception in 1870:

> "A Presidential levee is public. . . . A perfect river of human life pours through the Executive Mansion. Human beings are packed together just as solid as sardines in a box, whilst the President and Mrs. Grant are obliged to take each separate atom by the hand. . . . After two hours of this kind of work, its ravage begins to show its effect upon the person of the Chief Magistrate. His eyes begin to have a far-off look, great drops of perspiration stand on his forehead, and his thin, quivering nostrils rise and sink. . . .
> "Mrs. Grant stands a little way from the President—'fair, fat and forty.' She appears in grace and manner just as any other sensible woman would who has been lifted from the ranks of the people to such an exalted position."

Harper's Weekly, on March 4, 1868, printed this picture of the Reporters' Gallery of the House of Representatives ("with more than fifty recognized reporters") and wrote:

"Very few persons have any distinct idea of a reporter. . . . The nature of his labor makes him unobtrusive, though prying; quiet, though busy; a listener rather than a talker; the observer rather than the observed; his identity is swallowed up in that of his journal; he is known less by his name than his title; and, finally, he is a night-hawk, sleeping when others wake, and working and *preying* when others sleep.

"And yet what would society do without these unobtrusive, meddling spies upon itself? It would come to an end, or nearly so; for what would an American newspaper be without its reports of Congressional proceedings, its White House scandal, its army bulletin, its police accidents, its harrowing disasters? And what would any American community be without its newspaper?"

Privately owned

Below, photographer Mathew Brady (1823–1896), as seen in an 1857 portrait by Charles Loring Elliott. Seen at right is a view of Brady's gallery. Already a successful chronicler of the Washington political and social scene in the years before the war, Brady acquired his greatest fame as a photographer during the Civil War. "I felt I had to go," he recalled later. "A spirit in my feet said 'go' and I went." He maintained his Washington studio until well into the Nineties. The building is on Pennsylvania Avenue near 7th Street.

The Metropolitan Museum of Art, New York

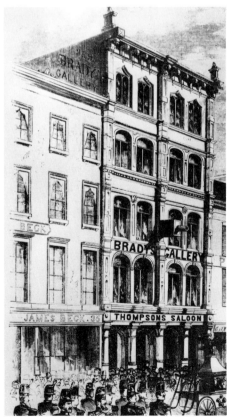

Library of Congress, Prints and Photographs Division

In 1868 Vermont Avenue near N Street and Logan Circle still had the appearance of a country lane when it was sketched by General Montgomery Meigs. As late as 1870 a notice was published by the Mayor's office giving warning "to the owners of hogs, geese and goats that . . . the laws against allowing these animals to run at large within the Corporation will be strictly enforced." Improvements were already being made, however, such as the new horse-drawn streetcars that traveled a line from the Navy Yard to the Capitol and on to Georgetown. Others ran on 11th and 7th streets from the wharves and along F Street. A railroad line, built during the war for the transport of troops and supplies, now carried travelers across a Potomac bridge to Southern destinations. Less of an improvement from an aesthetic point of view was the rail line—also a wartime necessity—that carried trains across the Mall.

The City Rebuilds

After the war the City of Washington faced an immense task of rebuilding. It took years before many of the public and private buildings were again in use. The Smithsonian and the Washington Infirmary had suffered devastating fires. The Corcoran Gallery, which General Meigs used as his headquarters, was kept by the government until about 1870. W. W. Corcoran's country house, Harewood, just south of the Soldiers' Home, had just been finished when the government took it over. It was so damaged by the war's end that Corcoran refused to accept it back and it became a permanent part of the Soldiers' Home. Kalorama (see pages 102–103), which was used as a smallpox hospital during the war, was burned almost to the ground on the night of a farewell ball for the troops. The damage done to Giesboro during its occupation by Union officers, including the "destruction of fences, buildings, and the cutting of timber," was assessed at $37,000, according to a member of the family who owned the property. As late as 1900 the claim was still unpaid. In the Lafayette Square area the Blair,

Cutts-Madison and Decatur houses had all been commandeered; this last was not returned to its owners for eleven years.

A few improvements were made, among them streetcars and better train service. The Department of Agriculture was built in the Sixties, as were Freedmen's Hospital, Columbia Hospital for Women and Lying-in-Asylum, and Providence Hospital. A new YMCA, Masonic Hall and a few churches were also built.

But much of the town was still in a state of ruin. In 1867 the Chief of Police reported: "Here crime, filth and poverty seem to vie with each other in a career of degradation and death. . . . Whole families are crowded into mere apologies for shanties, which are without light and ventilation." Describing a private relief center that was founded by Josephine Griffing, a former abolitionist and crusader, Frances Dana Gage wrote: "A cloud of darkness, poverty, rags, hunger, cold and suffering confronted me." Proposals to move the capital to some other city met with considerable support. And derision greeted those who tried to promote a major Centennial celebration in the capital. Calling Washington "the ugliest city in the whole country," Senator Stewart of Nevada declared, "The idea of inviting the world to see this town, with its want of railroads and its muddy streets, seems to me altogether out of the question."

In 1870 the first concerted effort was made to improve the city, thanks to the energy (some said the greed) of Alexander R. Shepherd. First an alderman, then vice-president of the Board of Public Works and finally (in 1873) governor of the District of Columbia, Shepherd "conceived the idea of making the Federal City worthy of being in fact, as well as in name, the Capital of the nation." So said a committee report that sought to erect a memorial in his honor. The report continued:

> "In three years the Board of Public Works, under the initiative and guidance of Shepherd and in the face of vigorous and weighty opposition, performed a work of such marvelous magnitude in the way of public improvements as to re-create the city, cause all agitation for the removal of the Capital to cease and make possible the new Washington of today. In these brief three years, under the controlling genius of this man, public works were accomplished of such magnitude as under ordinary circumstances would have required at least half a century."

Alexander Robey Shepherd (1835–1902), Governor of the District of Columbia, was both praised and damned for the improvements he brought to Washington. One newspaper cheered his "indomitable courage" in making the capital "the most attractive and beautiful" city in the country. Another railed: "Under his energetic administration Washington was rendered practically bankrupt. Even now himself and his confederates are striving to make the government assume the responsibility for the gigantic debt which is represented by the Boss's rotting pavements and crumbling sewers and overgrown private fortune."

Gas lamps, sewers, graded and paved roads, street sweepers and new trees appeared under Shepherd's steam-roller administration, transforming the war-ravaged city into a showplace.

For years the debate would continue: was Shepherd a crook or a visionary? ("If anybody knows all about sewers, it must be BOSS SHEPHERD," gibed one critic.) Cronyism was his *modus operandi*. He thought big, lived high and took good care of his friends. While it was never proved that he pocketed an illegal dime, he was nevertheless hounded to Mexico by charges of corruption. Meanwhile, Washington went on bicycling on his glorious new pavements, strolling under his shade trees and paying the piper. The enormous cost of Shepherd's improvements bankrupted the city. The debt, which had to be assumed by Congress, helped put the District under Congressional management for the next century.

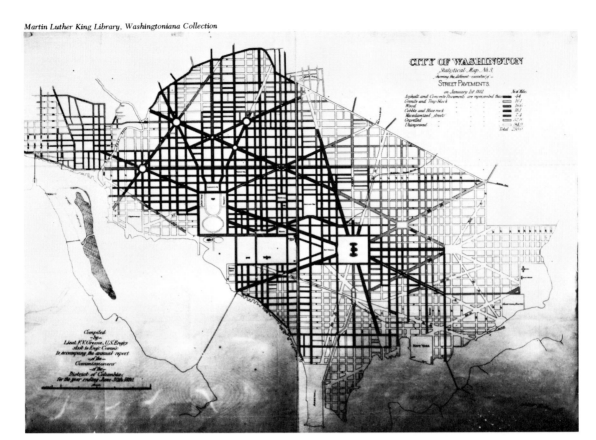

The improvements wrought by Alexander Shepherd on the city of Washington during the 1870s are shown by the 1881 Corps of Engineers map of paved streets (above) and by the keys to other city services mapped at the same time (left). As the *Graphic* reported in November 1875:

"The improvements in the District of Columbia within a few years have been marked. Its broad and elegant avenues and parks and drives in all directions, its splendid public buildings and rapidly increasing number of fine dwellings, its climate, libraries, society, and direct connection with all parts of the country, combine to make it one of the most attractive cities on the continent. People who remember it as it was in the old days before the war can hardly believe that it has been transformed into the new and elegant city of to-day. But its prosperity has kept pace with its growth and improvement, and its population is increasing. There is a constant demand for houses at increased rentage, while rents in other cities have fallen. New buildings are rising everywhere, and the prospect of growth is better than ever before. There is no question that the City of Washington is at the beginning of a long period of growth and prosperity, which in a few years will make it one of the most important, as it will be one of the most beautiful, cities in the Union."

Street grading marooned some houses, such as this one on 23rd Street near P, NW, sketched by DeLancey W. Gill in 1883. Throughout Georgetown and Washington today the effect of altered street levels from the Shepherd years is still evident.

Owned by a descendant of the artist

236

The mansion Shepherd built for himself was at Connecticut Avenue and K Street, facing the northwest corner of Farragut Square (right). The house, which later in the nineteenth century served as both the Russian and Chinese embassies (and finally in the 1930s and 1940s as a nightclub, The Troika), was described by one newspaper reporter as having been two years a-building. It was, said the reporter, built of Ohio, a type of stone that had a "cool, high-bred, pale blue tint, like a very respectable bride's travelling dress."

The Shepherds' combination wedding-anniversary and house-warming party (below), held in February 1876, was attended by, among others, President Grant (here being received by Mrs. Shepherd), "the entire Cabinet except the Secretary of the Interior, as well as most of the ladies and gentlemen of the diplomatic corps." Grant's attendance at the affair, at a time when Shepherd was under suspicion of corruption, raised the ire of the *New York Sun*, which noted that

> "The President not only gave this fellow the countenance of his official presence, but he took his whole family with him, and sat down on a level with the thieving contractors, fraudulent measurers, notorious jobbers, and colluding clerks, who made up a large part of the 'distinguished company.'"

This bird's-eye view of Washington was printed by Currier & Ives in 1880. In March a reporter for *The Century Magazine* wrote:

"Within the past ten years Washington has ceased to be a village. Whether it has yet become a city depends on 'the point of view'. It has no elevated railroads, no palace hotels, no mammoth elevators, no great commercial establishments; it has no opera and but indifferent theaters, and for a park it borrows the grounds of the old soldiers of the army. . . . On the other hand it has large public buildings and monuments and numerous statues; it has a mild climate, clean, well paved streets, and no 'local politics.' Its chief inhabitants are those persons who guide the action and control the interests of fifty millions of people. . . . Washington is thus a place quite out of the ordinary run; whether city or no, it is certainly unlike other cities."

5 A Tour of the Capital (1880–1900)

"One of these days this will be a very great city if nothing happens to it."

—Henry Adams, 1877

By the 1880s Washington had been transformed from a provincial town into a cosmopolitan capital. "The Capital of the Great Republic," wrote Mark Twain in *The Gilded Age*, "gathered its people from the four winds of heaven, and so the manners, the faces and the fashions there, presented a variety that was infinite." In the capital, wrote Joseph West Moore in his 1884 look at *Picturesque Washington*, were "ponderous domes and majestic spires, countless turrets and rooftops, emerald-tinted parks, massive monuments, and all the evidence of a great and prosperous city."

In the years since the Civil War government had grown and so had the number of federal job holders. More and more houses, shops and services were springing up every day. In the West End, which had increasingly become Washington's fashionable residential section, newly rich industrialists used their vast wealth to build what Moore called "palatial edifices embodying the highest architectural genius of the age." Meanwhile, suburbs began spreading beyond the boundaries of the L'Enfant city and out into the neighboring farmlands and country estates.

As a seat of government the city became not only more functional but also more livable. Dredging may have cleared up the malarial swamps in the area, but "Potomac Fever" became worse: people once elected or stationed or appointed to a Washington post seldom left. The journalist Frank Carpenter wrote that his editor in Toledo "told me the other day that this city reminds him of one vast boardinghouse. Most of its people do not really live in it; they merely stay for a time." But Carp might be surprised to find that his own great-grandchildren still live in Washington.

Even foreign diplomats have occasionally stayed on. The presence of the Diplomatic Corps brings the city a special flavor. One outstanding character was Queen Victoria's first minister to Washington, Henry Stephen Fox. He was selected as "climate proof," having served in Brazil. He stayed up all night playing cards and

Martin Luther King Library, Washingtoniana Collection

gambling, tended his roses in the late afternoon and presented them to random passers-by. When the Russian minister, Baron Alexander de Bodisco, married a Georgetown schoolgirl, Fox arrived at the wedding in a rented hearse. "How peculiar we all look in the daytime," he observed. As Frank Carpenter wrote:

> "The great charm of society in Washington is that it is not entirely founded on wealth. Its principal interest comes from the fact that the most important and successful men in all branches of activity come here. Instead of there being one lion to roar at a party, there may be ten or twenty or thirty. So many men and women of brains and brilliance give Washington gatherings a sparkle that is found nowhere else, except perhaps in the capitals of Europe. There is a frankness and a lack of snobbishness as regards wealth and fashion."

On another occasion, in a slightly different tone, he noted: "Washington seldom bothers itself about the skeletons in the inhabitants' closets. Lucifer himself will be welcomed if he will dress well, keep his hoofs hidden in patent leathers, and his tail out of sight."

Daredevils on high wheels and shutterbugs on the White House lawn became part of the Washington scene in the Eighties. President Taft was to complain: "I have come to the conclusion that the major part of the work of a President is to increase the gate receipt of expositions and fairs and bring tourists into the town."

Getting Around Town

In the engraving opposite, a blithe spirit tours Pennsylvania Avenue. Downtown Washington is seen on the map below. The Washington Canal skirts the Mall on the site of present-day Constitution Avenue. Logan Circle is at the upper left, where Vermont Avenue crosses Rhode Island. Dupont Circle is far left, at the intersection of Massachusetts, Connecticut and New Hampshire avenues.

The map below is a detail of a celebrated map of 1859, drawn by German-born Albert Boschke. Boschke worked for the Coast Survey until he was fired for devoting too much time to his map-making ventures: Washington City, published in 1857, and the District of Columbia, published in 1859. He himself hired a corps of surveyors to depict accurately every extant building and road. Afterward, Boschke sold his interest in the maps to the firm that engraved them. As the only such detailed topographical maps of the area, they were wanted by the government when the Civil War broke out. Refusing to pay the engraver's price, Secretary of War Edwin Stanton sent troops to the engraver's LeDroit Park house to seize the maps. The Committee of War Claims eventually paid the engraving firm less than half its asking price.

CENTER CITY PLAN MAP FOR 1880s TOUR

1. Blaine Mansion, 1881
2. British Legation
3. Corcoran Gallery (now Renwick)
4. Corcoran Gallery (present site)
5. Corcoran House
6. Decatur House
7. Department of Agriculture
8. Duddington
9. Dupont Circle
10. Logan Circle
11. Luther Place Memorial Church, 1870
12. The Maples (Friendship House), 1795
13. The Mall (A. J. Downing design)
14. John Marshall house
15. National Museum (Arts and Industries)
16. The Octagon
17. Olmsted's Grotto
18. Pension Building, 1883
19. Portland Apartments
20. Post Office
21. St. John's Church
22. Scott Circle
23. State, War and Navy Building
24. Stewart's Castle
25. Thomas Circle
26. Tiber Creek
27. Washington Canal
28. Daniel Webster statue
29. Wormley's Hotel
30. Willard Hotel

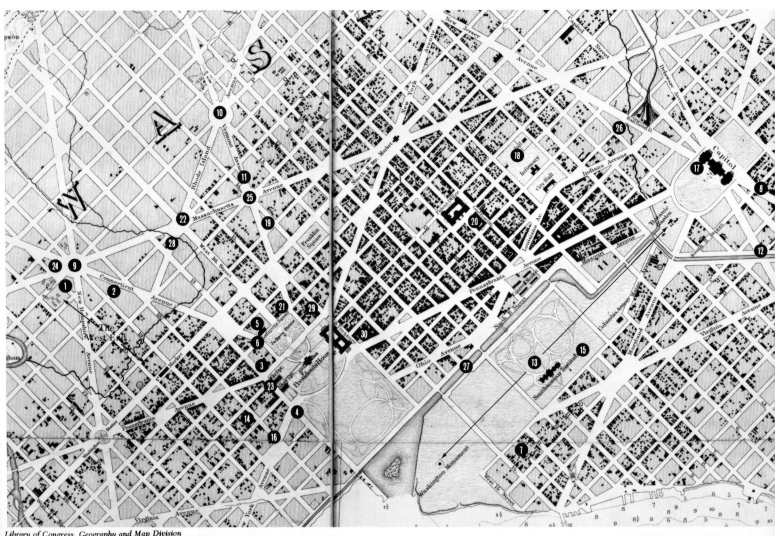

Baggage – Express Men

The Monument

A Typical Sandwich Man

On Pennsylvania Avenue

The Market
and Glimpse of

The League of American Wheelmen parades down Pennsylvania Avenue during a Washington meet. Bicycles, invented in England in 1868, had been introduced to the United States at the 1876 Centennial Exposition. In their infinite variety of styles they became immensely popular in Washington. "Sir Julian Pauncefote, the British Ambassador, is a famous cyclist and a notable figure in the procession of wheelmen when he rides," reported one Washingtonian. Historian Samuel Clagett Busey noted in 1897: "The wheel is a favorite with the Chinese legation. Several of the attaches are expert. All ride ladies' wheels on account of their flowing robes."

The "Eckington and Soldiers Home Railway," the first electric railway established in the District of Columbia, provided transportation to the suburbs. The house on the hill is Joseph Gales's country place, Eckington.

Modern versions of these old excursion boats still dock along the southwest waterfront. Boats similar to these, with staterooms, made overnight trips to Norfolk several times a week until 1957. Before the highway and airline boom that followed World War II, one of the main ways of reaching Washington was by ship, just as it had been in 1800. Ordinary travelers and ceremonial visitors, such as the King and Queen of England in 1939, landed at the wharfs on Maine Avenue or at the Navy Yard.

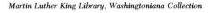

Herdic cabs, named for their inventor, Peter Herdic, were the taxis of the Eighties and were still being used in the early 1900s. In 1884 Joseph West Moore suggested a good way to begin sightseeing in Washington:

"take a carriage with an intelligent driver, or one of the many hansom cabs, and leisurely ride through the centre of the city—the northwest quarter. A ride like this will enable a stranger to obtain a general view of the prominent localities in a short time, and serve to fix them in the memory. The route should be taken through the central portions of Pennsylvania Avenue, and Seventh, Ninth, and F streets, and afterward through the fashionable West End."

"The principal hotels are the Ebbitt House, Riggs' House, Willard's Hotel, Wormley's Hotel, Metropolitan Hotel, and National Hotel. There are numerous smaller hotels for the general public, as well as a number of what are called family hotels, many of which are very elegant in their appointments."

—Joseph West Moore, 1884

The Ebbitt House, which stood until 1925 at the southeast corner of 14th and F streets NW, was the first hotel to stay open all summer, instead of closing when Congress adjourned. According to Morrison's *Stranger's Guide*, a room here cost four dollars in 1875.

The Wormley Hotel, on the southwest corner of 15th and H streets NW, was owned and managed by a prominent local black family. In the words of its founder, James Wormley, "We are not a Negro firm; we are first of all a business organization . . . which just happens to be owned by Negroes." Said an 1884 account, the Wormley Hotel

"ranks at the head of Washington's best establishments of that kind. Elegant in all its appointments and most efficiently managed, it has gradually won the reputation it enjoys at present. For years it has been patronized by our most eminent men, and is the general rendezvous for the foreign aristocracy visiting our country. All the late presidents, Mr. Hayes excepted, enjoyed the hospitality of its well-known proprietor. The hotel was established in 1871 by Mr. Wormley; it was fitted up elegantly in all its appointments and considerably enlarged in 1881. A large number of sleeping apartments and dining rooms for private dinner parties have been located in this addition. . . . The house is arranged for the accomodation of 150 guests, and is provided with all the newest improvements as to elevators, telephone, and heating apparatus; electric bells are introduced throughout the premises; and to be short, its general management is such that nowhere, neither in the United States nor abroad, can a better appointed hotel be found."

Pennsylvania Avenue at Ninth Street, looking west.

Columbia Historical Society;
New Standard Guide, 1886

Fifteenth Street, looking north
from Pennsylvania Avenue.

"The Fashionable West End"

"By riding the entire length of Connecticut Avenue from Lafayette Park to Dupont Circle, and then returning through Massachusetts Avenue, much of the 'palatial section' will be traversed."

—Joseph West Moore, 1884

"When the British Government in 1875 erected its splendid Legation," wrote Stilson Hutchins and Joseph West Moore, "a great impetus was given to building in the West End, and in rapid succession, fine mansions were erected over its territory and the price of land advanced constantly." The legation, seen at left in the engraving below, stood on the corner of Connecticut Avenue and N Street. At left: an embassy lawn party. Moore, writing in 1886, described it as being "one of the notable mansions of Washington. It has broad halls, a great ball room illuminated by three chandeliers, a spacious dining room, and elegant parlors." The present British Embassy on Massachusetts Avenue replaced this building in 1931.

The legations of Russia (top) and of Spain. "What have I done to deserve such a place of exile!" lamented Minister Barcourt of France of his appointment to Washington. Another French minister, named Prevost, felt even more strongly and committed suicide. He wrote in his diary that he "suffered from the heat of mid-summer and couldn't stand the iced drinks." Washington, in turn, had its problems with the diplomats. As the *Evening Star* reported in 1890:

> "Some diplomats are addicted to much faster driving than the law permits. One attache drives a beautiful stallion the avenues at break-neck speed: another secretary of legation has a playful way of riding his horse up to the doors of shops across the sidewalks. . . . Sir Julian Pauncefote cannot be made to clear the snow off his sidewalk, although Attorney General Brewster was arrested for not clearing his."

During her years in Washington the temptress Countess Marguerite Cassini enjoyed *Never a Dull Moment* (as she titled her memoir). The daughter of the Russian ambassador, she served as his hostess at the embassy. "Could there be a better place or a happier time to have been a young girl than Washington at the turn of the century?" she wrote, remembering "the Coaching Parades, the spanking horses behind which we rode in sleighs in the winter, the private yachts on which we cruised in the summer, the private railroad cars that whisked us from Washington to New York or Newport or Boston for a weekend or a special ball." In the photograph at left, the Countess is dressed for a tableaux at Mrs. Albert Barney's (see page 340):

> "Wearing a costume made from a pair of lace curtains, some Chinese brocade, the jade earrings the Buriat chieftain's daughter had given me for a pot of cold cream, and a Japanese sword . . . I appeared as a dramatic and sultry Judith. Despite my qualms I got curtain call after curtain call, to my great joy . . . I felt I did not do too bad for Russia that night."

"Fashion has firmly set its seal upon this district, and all those improvements which come with opulence have been lavished upon it," Joseph West Moore wrote of Dupont Circle. The statue of Admiral Samuel Francis duPont (above) was erected in 1884, on the spot previously known as Pacific Circle. The duPont family removed the statue to Wilmington later and commissioned Daniel Chester French to design the fountain there today. In the background, on the right, is "Stewart's Castle"; on the left, Blaine House.

The center of each Square will admit of Statues, Columns, Obelisks, or any other ornament such as the different States may choose to erect: to perpetuate not only the memory of such individuals whose counsels or Military achievements were conspicuous in giving liberty and independence to this Country; but also those whose usefulness hath rendered them worthy of general imitation, to invite the youth of succeeding generations to tread in the paths of those sages, or heroes whom their country has thought proper to celebrate."

—L'Enfant's plan for Washington

The Blaine mansion (left), which still stands at 2000 Massachusetts Avenue NW, was built in 1881 for James G. Blaine, who served variously as Speaker of the House, Senator from Maine, U.S. Secretary of State and three times candidate for President.

Mansions and hovels stood almost side by side near Dupont Circle. In the sketch at left, by DeLancey Gill, a shack stands near "Stewart's Castle," built in 1875 by silver king William Morris Stewart, who was then Senator from Nevada. As newspaperman Frank ("Carp") Carpenter wrote in 1883:

"The shanty says to the palace, 'This is a free country. We are equals. My master may be bigger than yours during the next administration; then perhaps I shall be built up, and you'll be sold for that mortgage which you know very well is now on your roof.'"

Carp reported that Stewart's lavish receptions made him feel like Marco Polo at the court of Kublai Khan.

The photograph above, taken on a wintry day in 1900, shows the unveiling of the statue of Daniel Webster just west of Scott Circle.

Thomas Circle (right), at Vermont and Massachusetts avenues NW, honors Civil War hero George H. Thomas. Behind the statue rises the Luther Place Memorial Church, built in 1870 as a thanksgiving for the end of the war. Samuel H. Kauffmann, editor of the *Star*, recalled in a 1902 paper for the Columbia Historical Society:

"Doubtless the most elaborate and imposing ceremonies that ever marked an occasion of the kind in Washington, or perhaps anywhere in this country, were those attending the inauguration of the statue of Major General George H. Thomas . . . on the 19th of November, 1879. . . .The procession was two hours in passing a given point, and the brilliant military display embraced such celebrities as are rarely brought together."

251

The Capitol and Public Buildings

"The Halls of Congress should be closely studied, and if an opportunity is afforded to attend a night session of Congress, it should be improved. By no means fail to ascend the dome of the Capitol, even if it does require rather severe exercise. A guide can be profitably employed in the building, as it is one to easily 'get lost' in."

—Joseph West Moore, 1886

Opposite is the Rotunda.

Visiting the Capitol in about 1900, students of the District of Columbia's Third Division School were photographed by Frances Benjamin Johnston.

The Capitol's west terrace is seen below as it looked about 1875.

Mr. Bassett
Doorkeeper
of the Senate

Senate pages sit at the feet of Isaac Bassett, the Senate Doorkeeper, in this sketch by Henry Farny. Frank Carpenter described Bassett as "the prince of pages" and wrote that "Fifty five years ago when he was a black-haired boy of twelve, Daniel Webster, then a Senator, took him on his knee, and asked him if he would not like to be a page. He has been in the employ of the Senate ever since, and during his whole service he has not been absent from duty twenty days."

From 1819 to 1860 this room, designed by Latrobe, was the Senate's meeting place. When the Senate moved to its new wing, the Supreme Court moved into the "Old Senate Chamber" and met there until 1935, when it moved from the Capitol to its present building. Mary Clemmer Ames, a reporter who covered Washington in the 1860s and 1870s, called this "one of the few rooms in the Capitol wherein harmony and beauty meet and mingle":

"Here Clay, and Webster, and Calhoun—those giants of the past . . . once held high conclave. Defiance and defeat, battle and triumph, argument and oratory, wisdom and folly once held here their court. It is now the chamber of peace. Tangled questions concerning life, liberty and the pursuit of personal happiness are still argued within these walls, but never in tones which would drown the sound of a dropping pin. . . .

"In the Court room itself we seem to have reached an atmosphere where it is always afternoon. The door swings to and fro noiselessly, at the pull of the usher's string. The spectators move over a velvet carpet, which send back no echo, to their velvet cushioned seats ranged against the outer-walls. A single lawyer arguing some constitutional question, drones on within the railed inclosure of the Court; or a single judge in measured tones mumbles over the pages of his learned decision in some case long drawn out. Unless you are deeply interested in it, you will not stay long. The atmosphere is too soporific, you soon weary of absolute silence and decorum, and depart."

From The National Capital Past and Present, by Stilson Hutchins and Joseph West Moore; 1885

A rigger's shop (above) and a blacksmith's shop (right) were among the subterranean surprises that flourished deep beneath Capitol Hill. Others included an 800-ton coal vault, the Centennial Safe (an 1876 time capsule of iron that was opened in 1976) and a large reservoir, which lay under the East Plaza but was abandoned when the Capitol was hooked up to the city water system.

255

Library of Congress, Prints and Photographs Division

By the early 1870s the Library of Congress was fast outgrowing its quarters within the Capitol (left). The library had been started in 1800, with 3,000 books chosen in London. The original collection had been destroyed by fire in 1814, but Thomas Jefferson provided the nucleus for a new library when he sold his own 6,000-volume library to the government for $23,950. In 1873 General Lew Wallace, author of *Ben Hur*, wrote in a family letter that "the library grows visibly":

"Books, books—a mountain of books! How very delightful to sit among them, and lift your eyes from page or picture to the alcoves and balconies stories in height, and follow the shelves extending into dim perspective! How the gold lettering on the ground of scarlet and green illuminates the shadow and seem to people the silences. How intuitively visitors, entering the charmed space, uncover their heads, and move across the tiling on tiptoe and speak in whispers! 250,000 volumes! What labor they represent, and what laborers, the thinkers of all lettered times, and of all nations! They overflow the walls. A new building is projected. Sixty plans are already submitted by as many architects. The site chosen is the northwest corner of the garden adjoining the Capitol. Think of a building four stories, a quadrangle 400 feet on each side, in the centre a circular reading room 100 feet in diameter, from which in all directions the deep alcoves radiate—a building to hold 3,000,000 volumes. Such is the design!"

The present-day library, begun in 1886 and completed in 1897, is in the Italian Renaissance style. The plans were by J. J. Smithmeyer and Paul Pelz, modified by Edward F. Casey.

Martin Luther King Library, Washingtoniana Collection

257

"One of the most interesting places for evening amusements during the summer is the parks. The city fathers have thoughtfully provided benches not only along the thoroughfares, but in secluded nooks where lovers may at all hours of the night indulge their whims. . . . Some very interesting things may be witnessed by the quiet prowler."

—From an 1890s guide to the city

Frederick Law Olmsted, seen here as painted by John Singer Sargent, was the landscape architect who designed the grounds and terraces of the Capitol in 1872. Wrote Joseph West Moore of Olmsted's work:

"The grounds of the Capitol comprise an open court on the eastern, and a grand terrace on the western side—in all, forty-six acres of park, laid out in an attractive manner, and planted with a great variety of luxuriant trees and a wide range of shrubbery, which afford pleasing contrasts of form and color. . . . For many years it was merely an open common, with roads and paths crossing it in all directions. At the base of the hill, on the west, flowed the Tiber Creek, a little stream with rugged sycamore trees overhanging its banks. In the early spring it was not fordable, and the small bridge was often washed away by freshets. Congressmen in riding to the Capitol were frequently compelled to secure their horses on the farther side, and to pick their way across the swollen stream on fallen trees. Ten years ago the Tiber Creek was utilized for the sewer system of the city, and now forms a natural sewer much larger than the famous sewers of Paris. . . . Its course is covered by streets, under which the tide ebbs and flows."

The spring within this grotto was used by Indians when they camped at the foot of Capitol Hill and by early travelers following the trail that led from the Eastern Branch to Georgetown. The grotto was part of Olmsted's plan for the Capitol grounds.

The Botanic Garden, wrote Joseph West Moore in 1886, "adjoins the Capitol grounds on the west":

"It was originally an alder swamp, with the Tiber Creek flowing through . . . The first attempt to establish a garden here was made about fifty years ago. It was begun with a small collection of trees and plants carelessly brought together, and of no special value; and it was not until 1850 when the first building was erected, that it began to claim attention. At that time Congress commenced to make annual appropriations for it, and it was enriched by having placed in it the extensive and valuable botanical collections brought to Washington . . . from southern climes. . . . During the past twenty years the rarest and most beautiful plants have been gathered from all parts of the world, and the national garden is at present the equal in many respects of the famous gardens of Europe. North of the main conservatory is the celebrated Bartholdi fountain [right], which was exhibited at the Philadelphia Centennial. . . .

From The National Capital Past and Present,
by Stilson Hutchins and Joseph West Moore; 1885

"Visitors throng the garden in winter as well as summer, and it is regarded as one of the attractions of Washington. It is often jocosely called the "Bouquet garden" for Congressmen. During the annual session of Congress as many as two thousand bouquets are sent from it to the wives and fair friends of the statesmen, and when the season is finished, each Congressman is entitled to take to his home one large box of choice plants, which privilege is seldom neglected, particularly as the government pays the cost of transporting the 'botanical specimens' anywhere throughout the United States."

The Pension Building, shown at left on an Inaugural Ball Dance Card and in the photograph below, was completed in 1885, at G Street between Fourth and Fifth. It was designed by General Montgomery C. Meigs, who had built the Washington Aqueduct and many of the forts that surrounded Washington during the Civil War and who had established the National Cemetery at Arlington. The design, based on the Farnese Palace in Rome, was criticized as being "an example to our national legislators of what not to do." General Sherman declared: "The worst of it is, it is fireproof." But a crowd of 9,000 danced here at President Cleveland's first Inaugural Ball, and the building was the site of all subsequent Inaugural Balls through that of William Howard Taft. Once scheduled for demolition, the Pension Office is now designated a National Landmark.

Library of Congress, Prints and Photographs Division

National Collection of Fine Arts, Library, Smithsonian Institution

At the Museum of Models in the Patent Office, Carp found that "side by side with the greatest inventions of the age, are some of the craziest products of the human brain. . . . One is surprised at the wisdom and foolishness of man's intellect . . . from the foolish point of view it would seem that when an idea of a patent creeps into an inventor's head, common sense flies out of the window." The Patent Office, begun in 1836, burned in 1877, in a fire of such intensity that firefighting equipment was brought from as far away as Alexandria and Baltimore. Much of the damaged interior was restored, but the top floor had to be rebuilt; it was done in the style of the 1880s by the architect Adolph Cluss. The Patent Office until 1932, the building was for thirty years after that occupied by the Civil Service Commission. It was scheduled for demolition in the 1950s, but the chairman of the Fine Arts Commission, David Finley, persuaded President Eisenhower to intervene. Newly restored, in 1968 it became the headquarters of the National Collection of Fine Arts and the National Portrait Gallery.

261

The Romanesque tower of the new Post Office rises above Pennsylvania Avenue in this 1903 view from the Treasury. The Post Office, described by one Senator as "a cross between a cathedral and a cotton mill," was erected in the Nineties, capping the effort to clean up the bawdy section known as "Hooker's Division"—the area extending south of Pennsylvania Avenue between Tenth and Fifteenth streets. As explained in *Night Side*, an 1894 guide to Washington:

"This region is called Hooker's Division because of General Hooker's commmand being quartered here during the war. . . .

"If you are so lost to all self respect as to go there to witness drunkenness, ribald song, vulgarity, immodesty, and all the other vices, do not, as you value truth and honor, take any innocent youths with you. It has been the ruin of thousands of the bright and talented young men of this city. Watches, honor and happiness have been left there innumerable times. Only a fool complains of his losses. Wise men stay away."

262

Public Buildings Service, photograph number 121-BD-54H, in the National Archives

The elevator machinery (right) was used to complete the building of the Washington Monument, on which the capstone was set December 6, 1884 (as seen in the engraving below). As *Harper's Weekly* reported:

> "The visitor will be seized upon by the genius of steam, and raised in a few moments in a comfortable elevator almost to the copper [actually aluminum] apex at its top.
>
> "No one can examine this remarkable column without feeling that a new advance has been made in architecture. . . . Why should we not have houses as tall? Why abandon the upper regions of the air and cling so closely to the tainted earth?"

SETTING THE CAP STONE.

IN THE ELEVATOR.

Library of Congress, Prints and Photographs Division

263

It took twelve years to repair the Smithsonian after fire gutted the Castle in January 1865. Most of the art collection had been lost, including many of the famous Indian portraits by Charles Bird King (see page 165); some were later redone from the artist's sketches. The paintings that survived the fire went to the Corcoran Gallery. The library was also moved to other quarters, but the museum collections were reinstated in the Castle after it was rebuilt from designs by Adolph Cluss.

The Smithsonian's porte-cochere (below) provides the backdrop for an 1888 demonstration of the Copeland steam tricycle. The woman is Washington photographer Frances Benjamin Johnston, who photographed the school tour on page 250 and other scenes in this book.

The National Museum (now the Smithsonian's Arts and Industries Building) is shown on a dance card (opposite) from James A. Garfield's Inaugural Ball, which was held at the new museum in 1881. The building, which was authorized by Congress in 1879 and designed by Adolph Cluss, was intended to house whatever specimens of scientific value were collected by government agencies. The Smithsonian was given custody of the collections. Soon after the museum was completed, much of its two and a half acres of floor space were taken up by forty-five freight-car loads of exhibits shipped from Philadelphia's Centennial Exposition.

This vast acquisition was the work of Spencer Fullerton Baird, Under Secretary of the Smithsonian from 1850 to 1878 and Secretary until 1887. Baird was responsible for amassing much of the Institution's scientific collection (he contributed his own collection of 4,000 bird skins). Under his leadership the Smithsonian became a leading center of biological and geological research. Specimens poured in from all over the country, with acquisitions coming from a vast network of collectors and government expeditions. As Baird's daughter wrote, "No bride ever devoted more thought and attention to her trousseau than did my father to fitting out each of these explorers." The resulting natural-history collection was the best in the country. The building was restored to Victorian splendor for the Bicentennial.

Smithsonian Institution

KENDALL BANK NOTE CO. 100 CHURCH ST. N.Y.

President Garfield's inaugural parade moves up Pennsylvania Avenue in this view (opposite) from the dome of the Capitol. A few months later the scene had changed dramatically, as Jane Gemmill reported in her *Notes on Washington: Six Years in the National Capital:*

"July 4, 1881. What a remarkable country this is, and how rapidly events follow each other, keeping one in a perpetual state of excitement! . . . Yesterday the city was radiant with inaugural festivities, today it is dark, gloomy, uncertain! The President has been stricken down by the hand of an assassin, and no one can foretell the result.

"I stood on Saturday morning last on the same spot where I was standing the 4th day of March, as the newly made President rose in his carriage, bowed to the cheering multitude, and was swirled in through the south gate leading to the Executive Mansion. . . .

"I stopped for a few moments at the White House gate, about sunset, to learn the latest tidings from the sick chamber. Groups were standing all along the square waiting for the same purpose. High and low were there, and each seemed equally interested.

"September. If the contrast between the journey of the President on March 4th and July 2nd was very great, I think the early morning ride of yesterday greater still. Lifted from his couch by tender and loving hands, laid upon a mattress in an express wagon, and driven between daybreak and sunrise . . . the patient slowly, slowly dying and longing, longing for the sight of the sea. The President has longed so much to go to the seashore that his physicians decided to gratify him, and the preparations for the journey were begun some days ago. . . .

"In order to avoid driving over rough cobble-stones to the car, the railroad company kindly ordered a branch track laid up to the very edge of the concrete pavement on Pennsylvania Avenue.

"September 23. Pennsylvania Avenue is clothed today in the habiliments of mourning. With muffled drums, measured steps, and bowed heads, the people have paid the last sad honor to James A. Garfield."

The first large postwar government building, the Department of Agriculture, designed by Adolph Cluss, was finished in 1868. Surrounded by gardens and conservatories, it stood along the Mall between the Smithsonian Castle and the Washington Monument. The origin and growth of the department was sketched by Mary Clemmer Ames in her 1882 memoir:

"Thirty years ago, the merely nominal sum of $1,000 was, at the instance of the Commissioner of Patents, Hon. H. L. Ellsworth, devoted by Congress for the purposes of Agriculture. For two years before, this patriotic gentleman had been distributing seeds and plants gratuitously, and for nine years, during his entire term of office, he continued his good work. His successors in the Patent-Office kept up the practice; but it was not until 1862 that the Department of Agriculture was formally organized."

The State, War and Navy Building (now the Executive Office Building) was begun in 1871, on the spot where the first State, War and Navy office was erected in 1800. Thomas U. Walter drew the plans of the new building to match the Treasury, but the exterior was completely redesigned by A. B. Mullett, a member of the Board of Public Works under Governor Shepherd and Supervising Architect of the Treasury. The building, completed in 1887, "is said to be the largest granite structure in the world," Carp wrote. "It is so built that it will almost outlast the ages." He added: "As I stand here on this marble pavement and think of the lives that will be eaten up in this building, and of the enterprise shriveled into inertia, it makes me shudder."

267

"My husband said to the coachman, 'Drive to Senator Keans, come back at ten, and take us to the White House. Come back at twelve and take us to the British Embassy.' Then wearily, half to himself, 'Come back at two and take us to the Insane Asylum.'"

—Julia B. Foraker, 1932

Frances Benjamin Johnston photographed this scene outside the north portico of the White House during a reception in 1889.

A public reception at the White House was described this way by Ben Perley Poore, a correspondent for *Harper's Weekly:*

"the Army, the Navy, the Diplomatic Corps, and the Judiciary were out in full force. There were nice people, questionable people, and people who were not nice at all in the crowd. Every state, every age, every social class, both sexes, and all human colors were represented. There were wealthy bankers, and a poor, blind, black beggar led by a boy; men in broadcloth and men in homespun; men with beards and men without beards; members of the press and of the lobby; contractors and claim agents; office-holders and office-seekers; there were ladies from Paris in elegant attire, and ladies from the interior in calico; ladies whose cheeks were tinged with rouge, and others whose faces were weather-bronzed by out-door work; ladies as lovely as Eve, and others as naughty as Mary Magdalene; ladies in diamonds, and others in dollar jewelry; chambermaids elbowed countesses, and all enjoyed themselves."

The White House conservatory was visited in 1885 by a young visitor from New Zealand named Russell Carr, who recorded the event in her diary:

"Papa, Edward, Emily, and self went with Senator Wilson. We were a little early and were shown all through the house. The private sitting-rooms are not very large, but so homelike. . . .

"Papa found the head gardener and he took us all through the potting houses, and, I am sure, I have seen more of the White House than many old residents of Washington.

"I say 'I spent the day last Saturday at the White House'; anyway, I seemed to have been there and felt quite at home, as we left after everyone else had gone, for we had forgotten the time while with the gardener, and were the last to leave. He gave us each a memento in the form of a flower."

This was the White House stable until 1871, when it was demolished to make room for the State, War and Navy Building. Mrs. John A. Logan, who was the wife of the Civil War general and was herself a civic and social leader for thirty years, noted in her 1901 memoir:

"The President is a potentate who can not with safety make the rules of his own household—not even of the stable which he pays for. He must drive behind horses whose tails are not docked, and his coachman must not be put in livery. When you see a stylish liveried turnout on the streets of Washington some day, therefore, you may know it is not the President's."

269

Off the Beaten Track

"For a while I tried to have 'days at home', but soon had to give them up, as they amounted to keeping open house for the passers-by. Sightseeing stages actually used to stop and let off their passengers, who would come in, wander around, have tea, and occasionally depart with a souvenir such as a doily or a small spoon."

—Alice Roosevelt Longworth, writing
of her life as a bride, *Crowded Hours*, 1933

A neighborhood market stall, complete with barefoot urchins.

Martin Luther King Library, Washingtoniana Collection

"SEEING WASHINGTON" No 2

STARTING POINT, 1417 G ST. N.W.
Telephone 3019 Main.

Blooming with bonnets and bowlers, visitors pause for a group photograph aboard a Washington tour bus.

271

Logan Circle, at 13th Street and Rhode Island Avenue NW, was one of L'Enfant's "special places." Ringed with handsome houses built between 1872 and 1880, it was at first a smart residential section. As the West End became increasingly fashionable, Logan Circle was bypassed and neglected. Many Victorian houses standing in the path of progress were razed to make way for offices, shops and apartments. But Logan Circle survived. Restoration began in the late 1960s, spearheaded by Turner Associates and Nicholas Satterlee and Associates. One of their drawings appears below. According to the architects' report, "The roof line is hectic with turrets, spires, pinnacles, pavillions, balustrades, dormers, cupolas, lacy grill work and elaborately profiled chimneys." Today Logan Circle presents the most complete Victorian facade left in the city, a look that once characterized much of residential Washington.

Library of Congress, Prints and Photographs Division

Columbia Historical Society; Turner Associates & Setterlee Associates

The Portland, which stood on Massachusetts Avenue at Thomas Circle, between Vermont Avenue and 14th Street, was the first apartment house in Washington. Designed by Adolph Cluss and completed in 1880, it was an immediate success. As Carp wrote in the *Cleveland Leader* in 1883, "The Portland Flats, where the Russian Minister and many other prominent people live, have been a paying investment." He noted that several other apartment buildings were then being built, and "the prospect is that 10 years from now the city will be full of them."

From The National Capital Past and Present, *by Stilson Hutchins and Joseph West Moore, 1885*

Members of one of Washington's oldest families, descendants of Daniel Carroll (see page 62), gather on the porch of Duddington—probably in the 1870s. The Carrolls' continuing presence on Capitol Hill helped keep an aristocratic enclave within the neighborhood well after fashionable society began taking up residence in the West End and Georgetown. Emily Edson Briggs, whose newspaper columns—written under the pen name of Olivia—provide charming glimpses of the city's social life, wrote in 1874:

> "At certain hours of the twenty-four the dainty occupants [of Duddington] emerge to go upon their rounds of daily charity. Like so many nuns, yet a part of the world, they bear the same relation to modern society at the capital as the old French regime to the Bonaparte reign. Earlier blossoms of the family tree have worn the proudest coronets of England; and these lovely silver-haired sisters are characterized by the same courtly refinement and queenly grace."

Croquet mallets in hand, a family poses on the lawn at "The Maples," which was built in 1795. Now Friendship House, the building still stands at 630 South Carolina Avenue SE. Emily Edson Briggs, who lived here in the post-Civil War era, wrote in March 1868:

> "The season of Lent has folded its soft, brooding wings over the weary devotees of fashionable Washington. Luxuriant wrappers, weak tea, and soft-boiled eggs have succeeded the Eugenie trains, chicken salad, and all those delicious fluids that are supposed to brace the human form divine. The penitential season of Lent is just as fashionable, in its way, as the brilliant season which preceded it."

273

This painting by August Köllner shows the Navy Yard or Eleventh Street Bridge, which made Anacostia the logical place for Washington's first working-class suburb. Settled by white workmen from the Navy Yard (blacks were excluded until the 1880s), Uniontown was incorporated in 1854. Adjoining Uniontown was Barry Farms, one of the early black housing projects of the Freedman's Bureau. Farms and scattered settlements surrounded these two villages until after the first quarter of the twentieth century. An old part of Anacostia has been designated a Historic District by the Landmarks Commission.

The detail from Albert Boschke's map (below) shows the area around Uniontown (later Anacostia). Writing in 1900, in a memoir now owned by the Young family, Joseph Young, a descendant of the first settlers of the area, described old Anacostia this way:

"Sixty years ago passing across the Anacostia Bridge then an old wooden structure on which the pedestrian of today would tremble to walk and which being the property of a company cost you a quarter to drive over, you landed on what is now the thriving village of Anacostia.

"Then the three hundred acres adjacent were divided into prosperus truck gardens. . . . There was an old time tavern called "White House" which was famous under the management of its genial host Wm. Sanderson a resort for the bon vivants of Washington. . . . Among his patrons were such men as Clay and Webster. . . .

"To the right we had the Pencote woods for a quarter of a mile being a portion of the Estate of Gisboro Manor. This estate contained 665 acres extending along the river road for one and a quarter miles on and was the property of G. W. Young. . . .

"The Good Hope Tavern was at the juncture of the Good Hope and Marlboro roads at the top of Good Hope Hill. . . . It was the rendesvous of the Gentlemen of Washington and the country around in their meets for fox hunting and it was beautiful sight of a frosty October morning to see superbly mounted men in crimson and top boots surrounding the old Hostelrie making the echos ring with their fox horns and encouraging the half hundred hounds in their grumblings and bayings. All independent gentlemen of that date joined in such amusements and it was not thought an ungentlemanly diversion to attend a cock, dog or bear fight."

EASTERN SUBURB MAP

1. Anacostia
2. Anacostia Bridge (1˙th Street Bridge)
3. Barry Farms
4. Bleu Playne
5. Fort Dupont
6. Frederick Douglass House, 1855
7. Giesboro
   Upper Giesboro frame house, 1688
   Lower Giesboro, begun 1738
8. Nonesuch, 1793
9. U.S. Lunatic Asylum (Saint Elizabeth's)

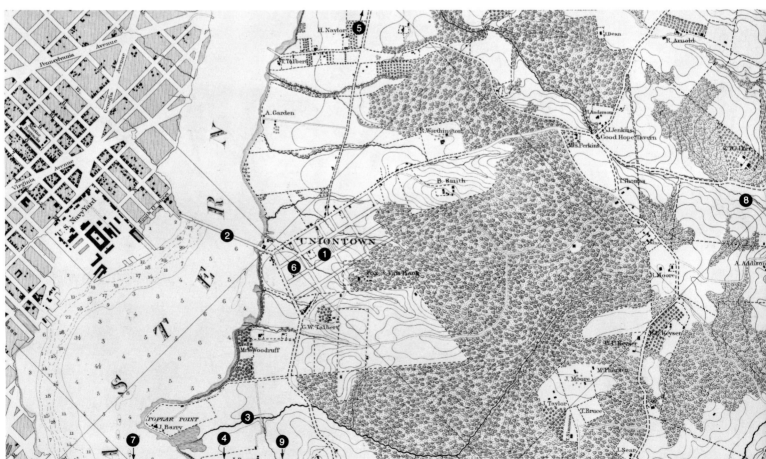

Touring the Suburbs

Giesborough (right) and Nonesuch (below) stood on acreage which, from 1685 to 1921, belonged for the most part to only two families, the Addisons and the Youngs. Notley Young (see page 60) mentioned both places in his will. The painting of Giesborough is by a Young descendant who grew up in the house. Joseph Young recalled that in 1840 the Giesborough estate "was one of the finest around Washington and was a model farm in all respects. It was here that McCormick tested his first reaper." The Nonesuch farm, which contained about 650 acres, became the home of Joseph Young and his wife in 1851. "The old house had not been occupied for three years," Young wrote. "It had been built in 1793 . . . and I suppose to most people would have been dreary and uninviting. To us it was a veritable paradise and we spent very happy years under its roof."

This painting by William MacLeod shows the farmlands on the east side of the Anacostia in 1856. In the distance on the left is the unfinished shaft of the Washington Monument, in the center the Capitol and on the right the Navy Yard. The figure seated on the culvert in the foreground is believed to be the artist himself, who was the first curator of the Corcoran Gallery. Gisboro, St. Elizabeth's, Bleu Playne and some of the road names in the area trace their origins to seventeenth-century land grants.

The White House Collection

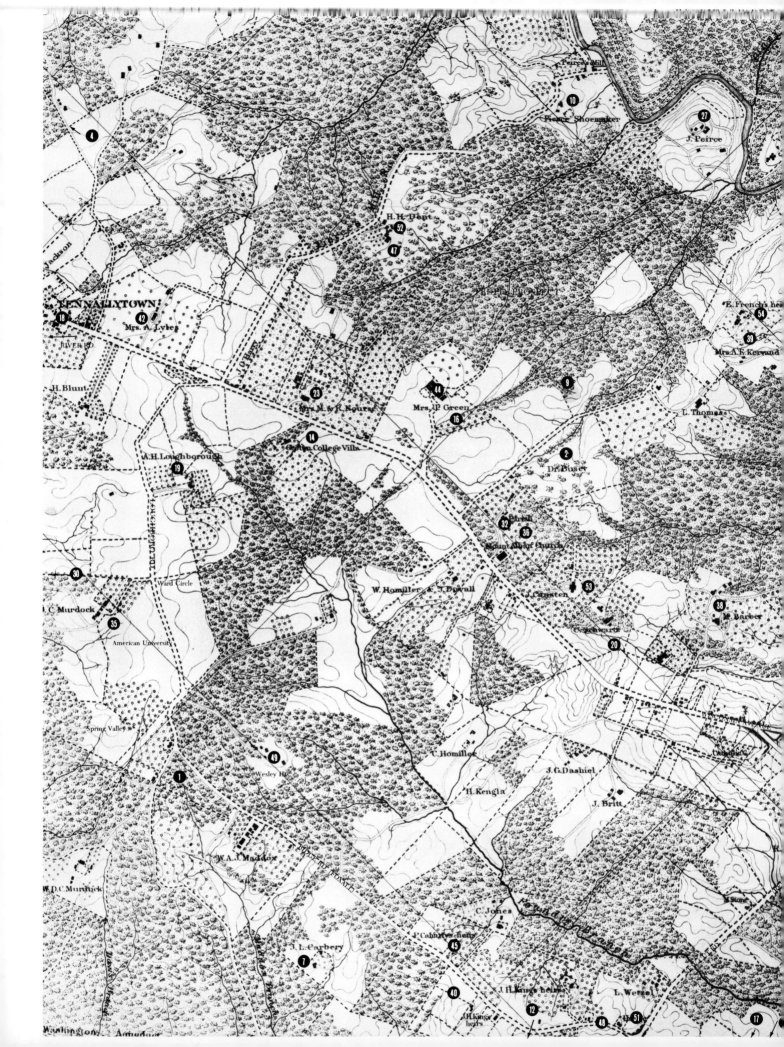

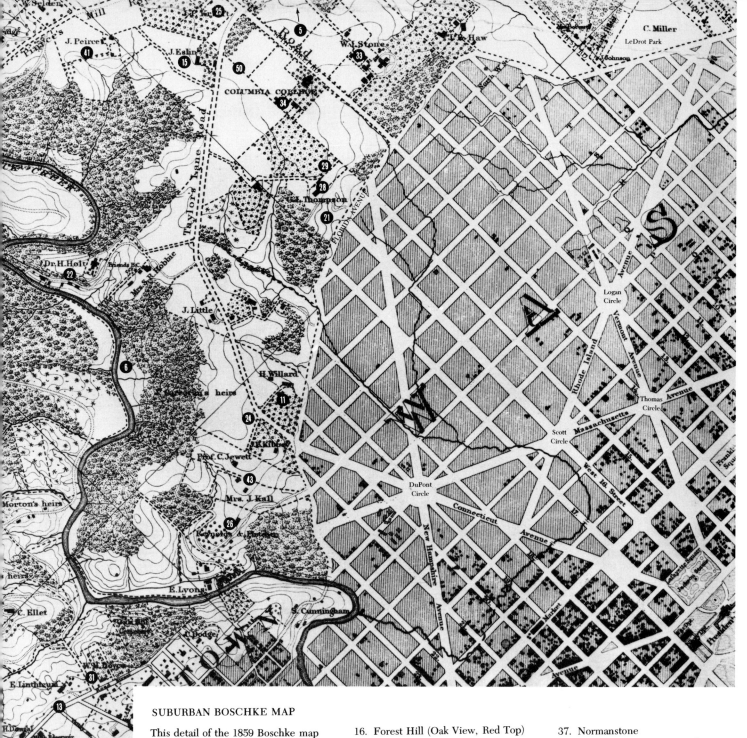

SUBURBAN BOSCHKE MAP

This detail of the 1859 Boschke map shows the city's suburbs from Le-Droit Park west to the Maryland line; names of early country houses and later real-estate developments have been added.

1. Battery Kemble
2. Belvoir (Beauvoir)
3. Berleith, c. 1752
4. Bradley House (Joseph Belt, 1747)
5. Brightwood Driving Park
6. Calvert Street Bridge
7. Carbery Glen (Cincinnati)
8. The Cedars, 1812
9. Cleveland Park
10. Cloverdale (Pierce Shoemaker)
11. Dean's Hill (Oaklawn), c. 1809
12. Drover's Rest (tavern)
13. Dumbarton Oaks (Linthicum)
14. Eden Bower, 1800 (later Friendship)
15. Eslin Tavern

16. Forest Hill (Oak View, Red Top)
17. Foxhall Foundry, 1806
18. Gloria Point
19. Grasslands, 1809
20. Greenwood, 1805
21. Henderson Castle
22. Holt House, 1805 (National Zoo)
23. The Highlands
24. Highlands Apartments
25. Ingleside, 1800
26. Kalorama
27. Linnean Hill (Klingle House), 1821
28. Meridian Hill, 1817 (Park site)
29. Joachim Miller cabin
30. Milton, 1700 with 1849 addition
31. Montrose (Montrose Park)
32. Mount Alban, c. 1800
33. Mount Pleasant, c. 1820 (Calumet)
34. Mount Pleasant Hospital
35. Murdock House
36. National Cathedral

37. Normanstone
38. Northview (Barber House), 1851
39. Oak Hill, 1819 (Redwood)
40. Palisades Dairy Farm (Mount Vernon College)
41. Pierce's Nursery
42. The Rest
43. Rock Hill (Holmead's)
44. Rosedale, 1794
45. Shugrue
46. Spring Hill, 1774
47. Springland, 1845
48. Terrace Heights (Uplands), 1784
49. Tunlaw Farm
50. Unitarian Church
51. Valley View
52. The Vineyard, 1810
53. Weston, 1817 (Ruthven Lodge)
54. Woodley, 1803.

"LeDroit Park . . . fronting along Boundary Street, from Seventh Street eastward to Second Street [is] suburban property; yet only twelve squares from the Post Office, fifteen squares from the Capitol and seventeen squares from the Treasury . . . as soon as Harewood Avenue (3rd Street) is opened northward it will immediately become the popular drive to the Soldiers' Home, and the location of LeDroit Park will become as familiar to the public as that of Franklin Square or the Capitol Grounds."

—From the builder's prospectus, 1877

Harewood Avenue (above) was the main street of LeDroit Park, the suburban development begun in 1873 northwest of Washington. Two LeDroit Park houses are seen at right.

LeDroit Park was named after the son of the proprietor, Anzi L. Barber, a white professor and trustee of Howard University. In January 1877 the builder's prospectus reported that

> "forty-one superior residences and two handsome stables have been erected at a cost of about two hundred thousand dollars. These houses are either built separately or in pairs, and nearly all of brick, are of varied designs . . . no two being alike, either in size, shape, style of finish or color of the exterior. . . . They are supplied with gas, water and sewerage, Latrobe stoves, marble mantles, bells, etc. etc. and will be sold on easy terms, or rented at Low rents to First Class Parties Only."

The development's appeal to prospective buyers was outlined this way:

> "A residence that can be pleasantly occupied by his family during the entire year is best suited for the merchant, professional man or government clerk. One that has sufficient open ground around it, and is so constructed as to admit a free circulation of pure air, so as to be cool and comfortable during the summer months, and yet located convenient enough to his place of business, and surrounded by suitable improvements, to make it desirable for occupancy during the winter. One that's far enough away from the noise & bustle of commercial activity to secure quiet & moderate seclusion, yet near enough to enjoy the luxuries of city conveniences as well as the society of friendly neighbors. All these desirable features are afforded in a residence in Le Droit Park."

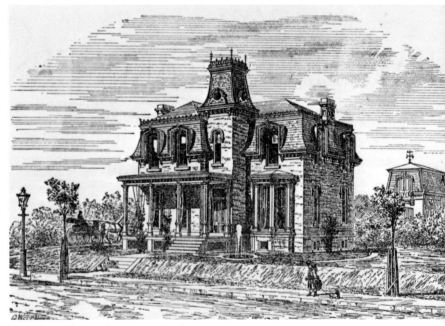

The 1877 advertisement above offers homeowners velvet wallpaper, gilt picture frames and "Special Inducements to Cash Purchasers." LeDroit Park was built for whites only but began attracting black families in the 1890s. Among its advantages was its proximity to Howard University and to Freedman's Hospital. Early black residents included Medal of Honor winner Christian A. Fleetwood (right, top), who was a cashier at the Freedman's Bank and active on behalf of war veterans; his wife, Sara, who was the first black superintendent of nurses at Freedman's Hospital; Robert H. Terrell, who was Washington's first black municipal judge; and *his* wife, Mary Church Terrell, who was a civic leader and a delegate to several international conferences of women's organizations. Active in city affairs throughout her life, Mrs. Terrell is seen in the 1952 photo at right, at age eighty-nine, protesting segregation in Washington stores and restaurants.

Other black residents of LeDroit Park included poet Paul Laurence Dunbar and his wife, writer Alice Moore; Dr. Hattie Riggs, who had earned a medical degree and who taught English at the M Street High School; Fountain Peyton, one of the city's first black lawyers; Dr. Eva B. Dykes, who was one of the first black women to receive a Ph.D.; Dr. Anna J. Cooper, who was awarded a Ph.D. from the Sorbonne in 1925, when she was sixty-two; Dr. Kelly Miller, dean of Howard University; Major James E. Walker, the first black officer to die in World War I; Dr. Ionia Whipper, noted for her work with unwed mothers; and the families of Robert Weaver and Senator Edward Brooke. Mayor and Mrs. Walter Washington live in the house of her father, the Reverend George Bullock. Of the original fifty houses built in LeDroit Park, some forty remain and a few still belong to families who moved in before 1900.

"The beginnings of Mount Pleasant and Meridian Hill must take stock of the old Columbian College, now George Washington University downtown; of popular race courses and rumbling stagecoaches; of swamps whence snakes shimmied across dusty or muddy roads; cows grazing where today are congested blocks. Wooded stretches have merged into farms, farms into separate settlements and suburbs; and suburbs into part and parcel of [the] city."

—Reminiscences of Fred A. Emery, 1930

At left, the 7th Street Road in about 1900. Seventh and 14th streets were two of the major routes to Mount Pleasant, Meridian Hill and northern suburbs. Below, the Brightwood Driving Park near Mount Pleasant. The park, recalled local resident Fred A. Emery, had "a half-mile course on Piney Branch Road. Stagecoaches ran to and from it connecting with downtown hotels."

Mount Pleasant, a name that appears on the earliest maps of the area, is one of the oldest sections of the District. The first farm known to have been located here was Ingleside, with a house built in 1800 for Harry Ingle, a friend of George Washington. At the northeast corner of 13th and Clifton streets NW was Mount Pleasant, the 120-acre country seat of William Stone, who came to town in 1815 to found an engraving business. It was later sold to General John Logan, who renamed it Calumet. The development of the area came after the Civil War, when many New Englanders settled here after serving in the Union Army. The Unitarian Church moved from Pennsylvania Avenue to 16th Street to serve this congregation, which still owns the Paul Revere bell and silver given to the original church by its designer and chief benefactor, Charles Bullfinch.

In the 1870s Mount Pleasant was described as "the most healthy suburb of Washington, proved by its exemption from the chills and autumnal fevers of malarial districts." Some houses of that period still survive, forming a nucleus for a strong restoration movement.

Mount Pleasant Hospital was built during the Civil War. It fronted on 14th Street (the road running along the base of the flagpole). The large building in the right background, back in the trees, is probably Columbian College.

DeLancey Gill's sketches (top, right) of part of Meridian Hill as it looked in 1883, with the Capitol in the distance. The hill was named after the stone placed on it during early surveys of the Federal City to mark a true meridian line. One of the most famous residents of the hill in the Eighties was Joaquin Miller, the "poet of the Sierras," who is seen here on the porch of the cabin he built for himself at the end of 16th Street (below). Carp quoted Miller as saying: "The President's House is at one end of Sixteenth Street and mine is at the other, but while I own a cabin, the President has only his cabin-et." Miller built the cabin with his own hands, layering the floor with bearskin rugs and the walls with newspapers and rejection slips. A favorite in society, he thought himself fitted for the office of Ambassador to Japan, lobbied for it and, when passed over for the appointment, left town for good. In 1912 the California State Association moved the cabin to its present site north of Military Road in Rock Creek Park.

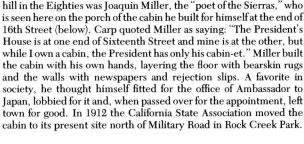

From The National Capital Past and Present, *by Stilson Hutchins and Joseph West Moore, 1885*

In the turn-of-the-century photograph by Frances Benjamin Johnston (right) schoolchildren sketch the gates of Henderson Castle, the Meridian Hill home of Senator and Mrs. John B. Henderson. Mrs. Henderson was the dominant figure in developing upper 16th Street into the palatial neighborhood seen in the 1920s photograph below. In 1888 she and her husband (the Missouri Senator who had drafted the Constitutional amendment abolishing slavery) bought up considerable acreage in what was then a still bucolic Meridian Hill section. Mrs. Henderson and her builders turned out the chateaux and villas that she hoped would make 16th Street the Embassy Row of Washington. For themselves the Hendersons built a Romanesque castle that survived until after World War II. (The castle site became a townhouse development in 1976.) Mrs. Henderson's grandest dream was to have the White House moved out to her end of 16th Street. Her vision culminated in the renaming of the street in 1912 to "The Avenue of the Presidents." But more egalitarian spirits condemned the new name as "pompous, ostentatious, affected," and after one brief year the street lost its grand appellation. By the mid-1920s the 16th Street heights were graced by Meridian Hill Park, designed by Horace Peaslee, and by a variety of splendid houses.

Through the 1880s the heights above Georgetown retained much of the pastoral air that had prompted men of means to build country seats there. Suburban development of these uplands was inevitable, and as the city expanded many country houses disappeared except as names for roads, bus lines, telephone exchanges and real-estate developments.

The view above was probably sketched from what is today Foxhall Road, the core of one of Washington's most prominent residential areas. The road was named for one of America's earliest defense contractors, Henry Foxall, an iron founder who moved his business from Philadelphia to Washington in 1800 at the request of Thomas Jefferson. From his foundry in Georgetown comes the name of Foundry Branch, which enters the Potomac near the Three Sisters Islands. The original foundations and joists of his country seat, Spring Hill Farm, are thought to survive in a

house at 4435 P Street, which was built in 1911. In the present century Foxall's farmland became Foxhall Village.

Uphill from Foxall's farm was land belonging to Benjamin King. Called Valley View, King's house stood near where present-day Hoban Road meets Foxhall. Across the road stands an early-nineteenth-century farmhouse, Terrace Heights, in which Mary Lightfoot Bradford was born in 1874. She lived on the property for more than a century and in 1975 she recalled: "Foxhall Road was a lovely, lonely, light traveled road, just a country road until Daisy Harriman moved out here. Then it became fashionable." Mrs. (Florence Jaffray) Harriman remodeled the house in the early 1920s and renamed it Uplands. (Active politically and socially, Mrs. Harriman was U.S. minister to Norway in the late 1930s.)

Farther uphill is the land where the Malone-Shugrue family ran the Palisades Dairy Farm,

August Köllner's 1861 view from the Georgetown uplands (left) showed the buildings of Georgetown College on the rise at left, at their right Analostan Island and behind them the Long Bridge.

Henry Foxall's foundry (below) is credited with producing the cannon Commodore Perry used at Lake Erie. In 1816 David Baillie Warden described the foundry as being located

> "about a mile beyond Georgetown. About thirty workmen are employed, chiefly emigrants from Europe. Firemen have two dollars; moulders, one dollar and a half; and common workmen, two-thirds of a dollar per day. The iron ore is brought from the banks of the Potomac, near Harper's ferry."

After a providential thunderstorm drenched the threat of British fire in 1814, Henry Foxall built as a thank offering the Foundry Methodist Church at 14th and G streets. The church at bottom was the second building; a third now stands on 16th Street.

Martin Luther King Library, Washingtoniana Collection

Georgetown Public Library, the Peabody Room

now the site of Mount Vernon College. The family had brought its herds here from the 1600 block of 19th Street after cows were forbidden inside Washington's fire limits. Thereafter, the herds grazed in the pastures around the family's summer cottage, which still stands on the east side of Foxhall Road at W Street.

Uphill from the Malone-Shugrue farm was a forty-acre tract called Whitehaven, which was bought by miller Amos Cloud from Benjamin King ("BK" is carved on a barn cornerstone) and sold in 1809 to Colonel Henry Carbery. Artemesia Cloud married Lewis Carbery, and the land remained in the Cloud-Carbery family for 130 years. The house was called Cincinnati or Carbery Glen, and it survives as the east wing of a substantial 1930s house (acquired by Nelson Rockefeller after World War II). Across 49th Street is Battery Kimble. Like other Civil War defense points it is now a park.

"*The [Loughborough] road is bordered by blooming yarrow, that hardy white flower which will accompany you along the dustiest and hottest roads in this section. Chicory is also blooming blue and freshly there, and little splashes of red blaze here and there. There are Deptford pinks and they grow plentifully in the fields around the American University and in the lower lands to the west. You will pass many weedy spaces along the road, where wild roses bloom in masses. Honeysuckle tangles things up now and then, and its blossoms make the air heavily sweet. As your road touches the moist lands along the creek side you come in touch with masses of elder, blooming and fragrant.*"

—"The Rambler," in the *Evening Star*, 1917

Loughborough Road, near the top of Foxhall Road, was named for Nathan Loughborough (left), who came to Washington as Comptroller of the Treasury under President John Adams. Loughborough's property covered 250 acres north and west of present-day Wesley Heights. The 1891 drawing above shows the Loughborough Road site of American University.

Nathan Loughborough built his country seat, Grasslands (right), in 1809. Remodeled late in the century by W. C. Whitney, Grover Cleveland's Secretary of the Navy, the house was famous as the site of lavish parties and figured prominently in the annals of local hunts. The Clevelands were frequent visitors.

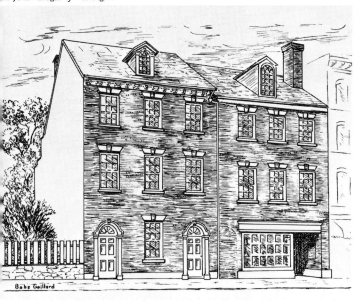

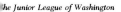

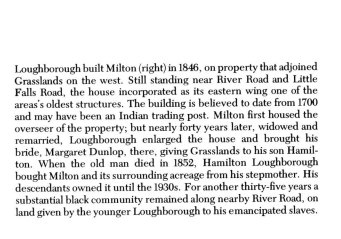

Babs Gaillard

Loughborough's Georgetown houses on M Street (left) were restored in the early 1960s by the Junior League of Washington. Among the first restorations on M Street, they are now the League's headquarters.

Loughborough built Milton (right) in 1846, on property that adjoined Grasslands on the west. Still standing near River Road and Little Falls Road, the house incorporated as its eastern wing one of the areas's oldest structures. The building is believed to date from 1700 and may have been an Indian trading post. Milton first housed the overseer of the property; but nearly forty years later, widowed and remarried, Loughborough enlarged the house and brought his bride, Margaret Dunlop, there, giving Grasslands to his son Hamilton. When the old man died in 1852, Hamilton Loughborough bought Milton and its surrounding acreage from his stepmother. His descendants owned it until the 1930s. For another thirty-five years a substantial black community remained along nearby River Road, on land given by the younger Loughborough to his emancipated slaves.

The Chevy Chase Hunt gathers (circa 1900) at the old Abraham Bradley farmhouse, half a mile beyond Chevy Chase Circle on Connecticut Avenue. The house, built in 1749 by Joseph Belt, was bought by Bradley when he came to Washington in 1800 to serve as John Adams' Postmaster General. It became part of the Chevy Chase Club around the turn of the century. "Somebody had a pack of mangy hounds and got up a hunt" was the wry recollection of Charles Carroll Glover, Jr.

The Chevy Chase Hunt, organized in 1892, had merged with the earlier Dumblane Hunt, which centered around Tenleytown and often ended its meets at Grasslands. Sometimes the field met in Rock Creek Park at Pierce Mill, finishing at Kensington. As *The Rider and Driver* described the New Year's chase of 1894, the fox "headed straight south, giving the riders a stiff in-and-out across the road west of Chevy Chase Circle, and then back again into the Reno Road, whence he was followed south almost to Tennallytown."

But open space was shrinking. In Chevy Chase, "the Villagers began to complain about the baying of the hounds" wrote hunt historian Samuel J. Henry. The pack was removed to M. F. H. Clarence Moore's farm near Kensington. By 1916 Moore, the guiding spirit, had gone down with the *Titanic;* America was at war; and the hunt was disbanded. With it died a tradition that began with the Washington Hunt of the 1830s, whose members dined from time to time with Andrew Jackson in the White House and whose meets began at their kennels a short distance from the Willard Hotel.

Trolley Car No. 9 traveled the "High Street & Tennellytown Road" from Water Street to the District line, passing the great tracts originally known as Pretty Prospect and Friendship. The latter, noted on the Boschke map as Georgetown College Villa, was famous in the 1930s and 1940s as the house called Friendship by Evelyn Walsh McLean (see page 334). Today's Friendship Heights bus still passes the wall of that estate at McLean Gardens on its way to Tenley Circle. Tenleytown (as it is now spelled) was a working-class settlement five miles from the Capitol. It was named for a Charles County blacksmith who plied his trade at Gloria Point, the intersection of Wisconsin Avenue and River Road. It stands on what was originally a 3,000-acre tract granted to Colonel Thomas Addison and James Stoddert in 1711. (Nathan Loughborough's properties, Milton and Grasslands, were also part of this tract.) Listed in city directories as a "post village" in 1899, Tenleytown was by then growing rapidly.

Georgetown Public Library, the Peabody Room

TUNLAW FARM,

NEAR WASHINGTON, D. C.

THOMAS L. HUME, Proprietor.

*Importer and Breeder of Registered Jersey Cattle, Berkshire
and Essex Pigs of the first prize winning families.
Pigs of all ages for sale. Stock guaranteed
as represented or money refunded. No
charge for shipping.*

Between Foxhall Road and the Wisconsin Avenue of today lay Tunlaw Farm, advertised on the card of its owner (left). In the 1870s it was a popular focus for country outings. The farm was a part of the tract acquired in 1862 by Adolphus Pickrell, who was listed in the 1834 City Directory as living in Georgetown "near the Bank" on Prospect Street. Pickrell willed his farm to his "highly esteemed son-in-law," Thomas Levi Hume, who operated a grocery business "Fine Family Groceries, Terms Cash" on Market, between 8th and 9th. The Tunlaw springhouse still stands in a Wesley Heights garden.

Hume is thought to have called the farm Tunlaw—walnut spelled backward—at the suggestion of President Grant; a huge walnut tree was the farm's striking feature. In the photograph below, taken on July 4, 1875, Grant himself sits in the second row in front of the man in the top hat. General William Tecumseh Sherman is three seats to Grant's left.

The punch bowl at left was presented to Hume by a hundred of his friends "as a memorial of the happy hours we have spent under the boughs of the Walnut Tree at Tunlaw." After Hume died in 1881 the Tunlaw land was sold. The name Wesley Heights reflect its nearness to the Methodists' American University.

Uriah Forrest, Revolutionary War general and member of the Continental Congress, built his country seat, Rosedale, on the heights above Georgetown, where it still stands at 34th and Newark streets. The 1793 building incorporates an older structure behind the kitchen; this may be among the city's oldest buildings, perhaps dating from 1740. Descendants of Forrest owned the house until it was sold in 1920.

Spread over a thousand acres, Pretty Prospect formed the early District's most substantial property; here rose several of the country houses that Frances Trollope admired. Pretty Prospect had been part of Ninian Beall's vast holdings. Forrest and his partner, Benjamin Stoddert, acquired it from Beall's grandson, and in 1794 Forrest bought out Stoddert's interest. As his granddaughter Maria Genevieve Green recalled:

> "Mr. Forrest was very rich at that time, the [shipping] firm of Forrest and Stoddert having been very successful, and being of a bright and lavish disposition, he lived in great extravagance. The house lot, as it was called among planters—the family residences, gardens, stables, barns and all out houses—covered five acres.
>
> "My grandfather loved to be among people and have them at his house. . . . All the illustrious men, survivors of an illustrious time, were his friends and around him. They frequently dined with him and our mother tells that on one occasion when General Washington dined here the party railed him unmercifully on his tardiness about selecting the site for the District of Columbia and insisted that he should confide to them the location. He, sitting at the right of his hostess . . . occasionally looking out the window, never answered a word. Perhaps when the site was announced the guests recalled their merry dinner."

Woodley, built about 1800 by Philip Barton Key, was used as a summer White House by Presidents Van Buren, Tyler, Buchanan and Cleveland. In the twentieth century it was owned by Henry Stimson (left), who served in the cabinets of Taft, Hoover and Roosevelt. As late as the end of World War II the land around Woodley was still rural enough for Stimson to ride from his stables into Rock Creek Park. Acquired by the Maret School in 1950, the house still stands at 3000 Cathedral Avenue, a few blocks east of the National Cathedral.

Mt. Alban is seen here in a watercolor by Caroline Nourse Dulaney, granddaughter of the owner of the house, Joseph Nourse. An Englishman born in 1754, Nourse came to Washington with the federal government. He served as Registrar of the Treasury from 1789 to 1829. In 1813 he acquired eighty-two acres that had been part of Uriah Forrest's Pretty Prospect and moved into the frame house that had stood on the property since before 1800. He called it Mt. Alban after the Mount Saint Alban of his Herfordshire birthplace. Deeply religious, he expressed the hope that a house of God would one day stand on his land. Today the Mt. Alban property is the site of the National Cathedral.

The Highlands, on Wisconsin Avenue between Quebec and Sedgewick streets, was originally part of the 130 acres adjoining Rosedale and Mt. Alban. It had been purchased in 1817 by Joseph Nourse. Nourse gave it to his son Charles, who had recently married Rebecca Wister Morris of Philadelphia. For his bride, Charles Nourse built a stone house in the Pennsylvania manner and named it the Highlands after her parents' home near Philadelphia. He enlarged it continually to suit a growing household, which in time included eleven children—among them Caroline Nourse Dulany, who painted this watercolor. The Highlands remained in the Nourse family until 1920, when it was sold to Admiral Cary Grayson, who was President Wilson's physician and later chairman of the American Red Cross. The Admiral's widow sold it in 1956 to Sidwell Friends School, which uses it as an administrative building. Most of the extensive garden is gone, but Wisteria—reminiscent of Charles Nourse's bride—is still there.

St. Albans Church, painted by Rebecca Wister Morris Nourse, derived from Nourse family philanthropy. Joseph Nourse's invalid granddaughter Phoebe Nourse devoted her energies to sewing layettes and other fancywork, which she sold. Secretly she hoarded the profits and, after her death in 1850, left forty gold dollars with a note asking "For a Free Church on Alban Hill." Other donations followed. St. Albans, the first free church in the Diocese of Washington, opened in 1852. It stands today on Wisconsin Avenue, on the Cathedral Close.

*"Very good in its way is the Verzenay
Or the sillery, soft and creamy,
But Catawba wine has a taste more devine
More dulcet, delicious and creamy."*
—Henry Wadsworth Longfellow

East of Charles Nourse's Highlands stood a 200-acre tract known as the Vineyard. Originally part of Pretty Prospect, the tract was owned by Major John Adlum, who is seen here in a portrait by Rembrandt Peale. Adlum was a Pennsylvania surveyor and judge who came to the District in the early 1800s. The Adlum house (the watercolor at right is by Margaret Adlum Barber) was built about 1810 and stood for a hundred years at the place where today Tilden Street meets Reno Road.

Adlum, who was keenly interested in the development of native plants (Adlumia, the smoke vine of the Alleghenies, is named in his honor), produced some twenty-two varieties of grapes in his Rock Creek vineyards. These included the Catawba grape, which Adlum himself developed and which is today one of the major domestic wine grapes. In 1824 a New England Congressman noted that the wines produced at Adlum's vineyard were "of excellent quality" and were "found upon the tables of the Secretaries and other citizens of Washington." The author of two books on winemaking, Adlum wrote in 1826 that whiskey "destroyes both body and mind," but wine "moderately enjoyed leaves a man cheerful, capable of attending to business, happy in himself & benevolent to others; it renders him a kind neighbor, an ardently affectionate husband, a good tempered pleasant companion; and it prepares his heart for the happy & virtuous influence of women."

In this 1920s photograph, the Sterrett clan, descendants of Major Adlum, gather at Springland Farm, which adjoined the Adlum estate in what is now the Cleveland Park section. The patriarch in the clerical collar is the Reverend James MacBride Sterrett. Founder of All Soul's Memorial Episcopal Church and a professor of philosophy at the old Columbian University, Dr. Sterrett was married to Major Adlum's granddaughter and heiress, Adlumia Dent, who is seated beside him in the photograph. Mrs. Sterrett eventually sold many of her acres to residential developers and to the government, which used the land as the site for the Bureau of Standards (now the Washington Technical Institute). But Springland remained in the family until just recently. Members of the Adlum-Dent-Sterrett clan still live in the area, where the family has owned land for almost 170 years.

Forest Hill, also called Oak View or Red Top (because of its red roof), stood on land that had been part of Uriah Forrest's Rosedale, between Newark Street and Mount Alban. In the 1880s the house was owned by President Cleveland and was reigned over by his young wife, Frances Folsom Cleveland (right). "Coming to the White House fresh from college," wrote Frank Carpenter, "she ran the gauntlet of the Washington society critics, but her natural tact and beauty made her at once the most popular woman in the country."

The presence of the Clevelands drew many new residents to the area, which soon was known as Cleveland Park. Real-estate values shot up. As the *Washington Star* reported in 1898:

> "Ex-President Cleveland paid $1,000 per acre for Oak View, comprising thirty acres, and three years later sold it to Mr. Francis G. Newlands for $5,000 per acre, thus clearing over $100,000 after taking out all the money he had spent on improvements. Three years later Mr. Newlands sold two acres of this thirty-acre tract to Col. Robert I. Fleming for $40,000 or $20,000 per acre, and Col. Fleming has recently refused $75,000 for these two acres, which include the old homestead."

Still, for all its popularity, Cleveland Park remained a quiet place. As Robert V. Fleming reported: "It was so quiet that when my father drove from his office at 1018 12th Street, NW, and came across Calvert Street Bridge, then a wooden bridge, as a little fellow I could recognize the sounds of the horses that he drove."

In this 1900 view looking south from Connecticut Avenue near Woodley Road, the Washington Monument can be seen in the distance at right, the Capitol dome at left. At left, in the middle distance, is the Calvert Street Bridge, which, until 1907, was the main upstream crossing over Rock Creek. The tall apartment house to the left of the Washington Monument is the Highlands, which is still standing at Connecticut Avenue and California Street.

The Cleveland Park area, which an early promoter described as being "within 20 minutes of the city by two lines of electric cars," has remained popular. In the 1950s Grace Dunlop Peter and Joyce D. Southwick reported in their book, *Cleveland Park*, that homes in the area "are popular with diplomats because of the proximity to Embassies, the excellent private and public schools, and the spacious homes and grounds. . . . It has also been the home of well-known newspaper correspondents and journalists."

295

A mammoth fireworks display on the South Lawn of the White House celebrates the inauguration of Grover Cleveland on March 4, 1885. The portraits represent Cleveland and his running mate, T. A. Hendricks.

6 Turn-of-the-Century City (c. 1890–1917)

"A new consciousness seems to have come upon us—the consciousness of strength—and with it a new appetite, the yearning to show our strength."

—From an editorial in the *Washington Post*, 1898

Toward the end of the nineteenth century America was being stirred by a new vision of its place in the world. Optimism was in the air, and the spirit was felt in Washington as strongly as anywhere else in the country. Symbolic of the city's mood was a prediction made in 1884 by Joseph West Moore in his *Picturesque Washington*. When the Washington Monument is completed, wrote Moore, "It is believed that the prospect from the top will be sublime beyond conception. On the west the range of vision will probably extend to the Allegheny Mountains, and on the south to the Chesapeake Bay and across it to the oceans."

But the splendid view of the future was far from realized. Prosperity and idealism continued to exist side by side with poverty and social injustice. Progress toward black civil rights suffered a severe setback when, in 1883, the Supreme Court ruled that the Fourth Amendment prohibited discrimination by the states but not by individuals. As journalist Frank Carpenter noted: "Now, innkeepers, managers of public institutions, railroads, and other public carriers need no longer fear penalties for discriminating against the Negroes in the matter of accommodations." Black citizens were to be barred from many Washington stores, restaurants, hotels, theaters and other public facilities until the late 1940s, when such discrimination was judged unconstitutional in a decision against a Washington restaurant.

Yet in other areas progress was being made. The need for an orderly plan for city development came sharply into focus, for instance, over a proposal to put a railroad viaduct across the Mall.

Colonel Theodore A. Bingham, chief of Public Buildings and Grounds, began campaigning to revive interest in Pierre L'Enfant's original plans for the Mall. The American Institute of Architects urged a new look for the city during its annual meeting of 1900, which was held in the capital. And the 1900 centennial celebration of the government's move to Washington further concentrated attention on the city's shortcomings. As Charles Moore pointed out in his 1929 history, *Washington Past and Present*:

> "Questions had arisen as to the location of new public buildings; of preserving spaces for parks in the regions outside of the L'Enfant plan; of connecting existing parks and developing the extensive areas under reclamation from the malarial flats of the Potomac and the Anacostia. . . ."

The call to action was answered by Senator James McMillan, chairman of the Senate Committee on the District of Columbia, at whose urging the committee established a commission to plan for the orderly development of the city's parks and the siting of future government buildings. It included some plans for the offices of business, trade, professional and philanthropic organizations, more and more of which were locating their national headquarters in Washington. It also chose sites for some of the galleries through which philanthropists from all over America would transform the city into a treasure house of art. By its far-ranging efforts, the commission reestablished the principle of planned development that had been laid down by L'Enfant and paved the way for the making of the modern city.

Charles Pepper, Everyday Life in Washington with Pen and Camera, *1900*

On Government Business

"The President's Message Center" in 1900.

Columbia Historical Society Collection

At left, a constituent—perhaps an office-seeker—calls on a Senator. Until President Cleveland began enforcing the 1883 Civil Service Act, government jobs depended on the spoils system. Carp wrote, "The Washington hotels are crowded, and office seekers are as thick as shells on the beach. . . . At Willard's Hotel the gang appears especially seedy and desperate. . . . The city will be overrun with these office seekers until Cleveland has firmly established that Civil Service Reform is to prevail, not only in spirit but in fact." "The civil service idea is the most ridiculous thing ever attempted in the domain of politics," said a Congressional friend of Carp's. In the cartoon below, Cleveland, dressed as Hamlet, hails the ghost of "reform" while being restrained by two "spoilsmen." The caption quotes Hamlet:

> "Still am I called. Unhand me, gentlemen.
> By heaven, I'll make a ghost of him that stops me.
> I say away! Go on; I'll follow thee."

And that is exactly what Cleveland did.

Library of Congress, Prints and Photographs Division

At right, the Justice Department offices on Pennsylvania Avenue opposite the Treasury, circa 1885. At that time, according to Joseph West Moore, there were fifty-eight people in the Department. Below, diplomats call on the Secretary of State, John Milton Hay, on New Year's Day, 1900. The houses of Hay and Henry Adams, designed for them by H. H. Richardson, shared the corner of 16th and H streets, now the site of the Hay-Adams Hotel. Adams said that he and Hay "had the advantage of looking out of their windows on the antiquities of LaFayette Square . . . on great men, alive and dead."

Charles Pepper, Everyday Life in Washington With Pen and Camera, *1900*

299

"The Centre Market is the largest of the markets, and in many particulars, it is to be considered to be the market, par excellence, of the country. . . . The daily business in and around this splendid structure is simply enormous. During the morning hours there are throngs of buyers of all classes of society, fashionable women of the West End, accompanied by negro servants, mingling with people of less opulent sections, all busily engaged in selecting the day's household supplies. It is a scene of wonderful variety and animation."

　　　　—*Illustrated Washington: Our Capital*, 1890

The Center Market (above) was at 7th Street and Pennsylvania Avenue, now the site of the National Archives building. As one Washingtonian remembered, "The country people, white and black, lined the sidewalk with their old broken wagons and decrepit mules stationed nearby. The colored folk displayed all kinds of herbs and roots guaranteed to cure any ailment and kill bugs and roaches at the same time, all for a dime."

This building, designed by Adolph Cluss and opened in 1873, stood on the site of Washington's original Center Market. It was one of five in the city, described by Hutchins and Moore in 1885 as

> "filled to overflowing with good marketing. The meats are the very best, and they are cheaper than in New York, and fish, game, vegetables, and fruits are to be had in profusion at reasonable prices. . . . The shad and herring caught in the Potomac within sight of the city are noted for their lusciousness. Forty miles down the river are the famous ducking shores, where from November to April vast numbers of canvas-backs, black-and red-heads, and whistle-wings feed on the great beds of wild celery which there abound. The forests of Virginia, within a few miles of Washington, across the Potomac, are filled in the autumn with wild turkeys, which are shot by thousands for the city markets, and the bottom-lands along the river supply great quantities of quail and other game birds. On the upper Potomac the fishing cannot be excelled. No large city is so favored in this respect, and, in consequence, the food supplies are plentiful and cheap."

Today, the name "Market Space" survives on street signs at the site of the Center Market—a reminder that through the 1920s this section was the heart of the city's business life. The only original structure there is an iron-front building where Thomas Hume sold groceries. Two other markets remain: the Northern Market, at 7th and O streets NW, restored in 1975 as the focal point of a new shopping section in an urban renewal area; and the Eastern Market, one of the original markets of the city (it began in 1802), which thrives at 7th and South Carolina Avenue SE.

The Russian minister in 1822 observed: "Washington with its venison, wild turkeys, canvasbacks, oysters, terrapins, etc. furnished better viands than Paris, and only wanted cooks." Later in the century Countess Marguerite Cassini, the daughter of the Russian ambassador, wrote: "Always that terrapin and those bloody red canvasback ducks at Washington dinners! . . . It looked awful and I declined it. Across the table my hostess . . . gave a scream: 'You can't refuse my terrapin! It costs a hundred dollars!'"

"Kennebec Ice" was brought to the Washington wharves by boat from Maine. At right, a cutaway view of the Smith Transparent Ice Manufacturing Company on the Georgetown waterfront. Residents recall Washington winters cold enough that ice could be cut from the Potomac. One such freeze is seen in the turn-of-the-century photograph below.

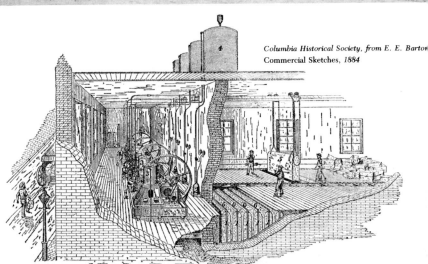

302

"Washington . . . is not a municipality of shopkeepers; it is, and is destined to remain, a place of homes, more truly, perhaps, than any other city of the world. It is not probable that trade will ever intrude to a greater extent than is necessary to supply the wants of the corporation and its immediate vicinity."

—*Harper's*, March 1885

At right, the Greenleaf Coffee and Spice Mills, at Maryland Avenue between 7th and C streets. Below, an 1894 view by Raymond Sawyer shows Washington's financial district, at Pennsylvania Avenue and 15th Street, opposite the Treasury. The square two-storied building at center, earlier the home of the Second United States Bank, here houses Riggs Bank, which is still on the site today, though in a different building. The big building in the background is the National Savings and Trust Company, still the bank's main office. In the distance is the spire of the New York Avenue Presbyterian Church.

MRS E. A. HAINES,
Proprietor.

HAINES

Haines'
FIFTY STORES IN ONE

WHOLESALE & RETAIL.

PENNSYLVANIA AVE. & 8TH STREET S.E.

WASHINGTON. D.C.

THE LARGEST STORE IN THE WORLD, BUILT, OWNED AND CONTROLLED BY A WOMAN.

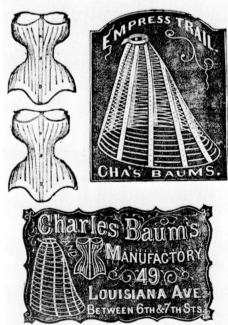

EMPRESS TRAIL.

CHA'S BAUM'S.

Charles Baum's
MANUFACTORY
49
LOUISIANA AVE.
BETWEEN 6TH & 7TH STS.

Hoop Skirts, Corsets and Shoulder Braces
Made to Order and Fit warranted. Also,
always on hand the Largest Stock of
French Corsets, all Sizes and Styles.
CHARLES BAUM,
WHOLESALE & RETAIL MANUFACTURER,

"Washington . . . is not a municipality of shopkeepers; it is, and is destined to remain, a place of homes, more truly, perhaps, than any other city of the world. It is not probable that trade will ever intrude to a greater extent than is neccesary to supply the wants of the corporation and its immediate vicinity."
—Harper's *magazine, March , 1885*

INFANTS' LACE CAPS.

ZEPHYR WORSTED.

EMBROIDERED SLIPPERS.

CHR. RUPPERT
Importer and Dealer in
TOYS AND FANCY GOODS,
403 & 405 7th Street,
Near D St.,   WASHINGTON, D. C.

MERINO CLOAKS.

270   270
J. R. WRIGHT'S
ICE CREAM & OYSTER SALOON,
270 Seventh St., bet. L and M,
(Northern Liberties,)
FAMILIES, PARTIES, &c., &c., SUPPLIED
AT SHORT NOTICE and LOW PRICES.
The Saloon is Closed on Sunday.
NO LIQUORS SOLD.
OYSTERS FROM OCTOBER 1st TO MAY 1st, INCLUSIVE.
ICE CREAM FROM MAY 1st TO OCTOBER 1st, INCLUSIVE.
270   270

MRS. GEO. O. COOK,
DEALER IN
REAL LACES, EMBROIDERIES,
RIBBONS,
Velvets, Fancy Articles, Kid Gloves, &c.
No. 34½ Market Space,
WASHINGTON, D. C.

"All Washington walked abroad in the morning. It was quite a formality: a little note came asking one to 'walk' from ten to twelve. Or perhaps with Nelka Smirnoff, Mrs. Herbert Wadsworth's niece and one of my best friends in Washington, or Helen Hay or Bessie Davis—who later married young Cabot Lodge—or with one of the Warder girls I would go shopping on F Street, followed by our carriage with coachmen and maid. We usually ended up in Woodward and Lothrop's where we bought wrist-length, elbow-length and shoulder-length kid glacé gloves by the dozen and tulle by the mile. The wet greeny stems of the bouquets we carried at dances were ruinous to gloves and by four o'clock in the morning when the ball ended we would be knee-deep in tulle. For such things, gloves, veils, pins, and so forth, girls were made an allowance called 'pin money.' Mine—$500 a month—was never enough. Every month when the bills came I had always a difficult session with my Father."

—Countess Marguerite Cassini, 1956

Advertisements for Washington business establishments are reproduced on these pages. The building below was the brewery of Christian Heurich, who had come to Washington from Germany as a young man. His house at 20th Street and New Hampshire Avenue was given to the Columbia Historical Society by Mrs. Heurich and now serves as the Society's headquarters. The dancing academy of Professor L. G. Marini, advertised at right, is described in an 1884 account as being

"patronized by the *elite* of the city, for indulging in what has been aptly called the 'poetry of motion.' Here congregate during the winter season the very *creme de la creme* of Washington society, the wives and daughters of cabinet ministers, the diplomatic corps, Senators, and members of Congress, and here the young children are taught their first lessons in waltzing with 'the light fantastic toes.' Concerts are also given in the ball room, which has a seating capacity of six hundred and fifty persons."

Lillian Russell, the American comic-opera singer and burlesque actress, is seen at left in a role she played at the Lafayette Square Opera House during the 1890s—that of Florello in *The Brigands*. The Lafayette, later known as Belasco's, was one of three houses that regularly presented idols of the theater world to Washington audiences. The others were Albaugh's, also known as Poli's, and the National. Below is the front page of one of the National's 1888 programs.

The National Theatre, at E Street near 13th, is the city's oldest, having first opened its doors in 1835. Destroyed by fire numerous times, it has occupied a succession of structures, all on the same site. "All fashionable Washington" was at the opening of the fifth or New National Theatre in 1886, reported Carp: "The beaux appeared in their claw-hammer coats, the belles were attired in evening dress. . . . This new theatre is the talk of the town, the verdict being that it is one of the coziest, prettiest, and best appointed houses in the country."

306

Lewis, Samuel and Nathaniel Carusi operated the Assembly Rooms, a popular music and dance hall at 11th and C streets that had been founded by their father, Gaetano Carusi, the leader of a group of Sicilian musicians brought to Washington at Thomas Jefferson's request to improve the quality of the Marine Band (see page 99).

German-born Hugo Worch was a successful Washington music dealer, piano builder and music publisher for over sixty years, operating a music store at 1110 G Street NW. Here he demonstrates a late-nineteenth-century piano-harp—one of over 175 keyboard instruments of the Worch Collection donated in 1914 to the Smithsonian Institution.

A musical evening at the Capitol grounds is seen in the engraving above, based on a drawing by T. H. Nash. Opposite, John Philip Sousa and his Marine Band of 1891. No one did more to develop the band's musical reputation than Sousa, composer of "The Stars and Stripes Forever," "The Washington Post March" and other popular marches. The son of a band member, Sousa enlisted in the band in 1868 at the age of thirteen to learn music. He served seven years, then left to pursue a musical career outside Washington. In 1880 he returned as leader of the Marine Band. As he wrote in his autobiography, *Marching Along:*

"The Commandant had impressed upon me the necessity of a complete reorganization of the band. The men were dissatisfied with the present state of affairs, and to use the Commandant's words, 'The band gives me more trouble than the rest of the corps put together.'

"I found its music-library limited, antiquated and a good deal of it poorly arranged and badly copied. There was not a sheet of Wagner, Berlioz, Grieg, Tschaikowsky, or any other of the modern composers who were attracting attention throughout the musical world. I immediately selected some first-class compositions from the leading catalogues of Europe and proceeded

with the most rigid rehearsals, in order to bring that band up to modern requirements.

"The small pay received by the musicians and the impossibility of getting a discharge from the service except through disability or bad conduct, developed in the band a perpetual grouch. It bothered me so much that I went to the Commandant and explained to him the condition of affairs, and my diagnosis of the case; I suggested that he grant a discharge to any member of the band who applied for a release with my approval. . . .

"By the end of the first year the band was reduced to thirty-three men and even the Commandant was a little alarmed; but I gradually gathered about me an ambitious and healthy lot of young players, and the public performances of the band were such that it began to attract very favorable attention from Washingtonians and visitors to the National Capital.

"From a motley mob of nurses and baby carriages and some hangers-on, the audiences at the White House Grounds concerts grew into the thousands and the Saturday afternoon concerts at the White House became a social event. Thursday concerts at the Barracks were splendidly attended and Wednesday concerts at the Capitol drew large audiences, although we suffered from the noise of street cars and carriages passing."

Kindergarten children inspect a vegetable garden in the photograph above, by Frances Benjamin Johnston. Kindergartens began in Washington in 1898.

"The Educational Ladder"

Public and private education expanded rapidly in the last decades of the nineteenth century. Up to that time public schooling had stopped at the eighth grade. "The educational ladder is not only too narrow but too short for its purposes. Both ends should be extended. The Kindergarten should be added below and the High School above," declared Superintendent of Schools J. Ormand Wilson in 1877. (Describing his role as superintendent, he also said: "An office of this kind is never a sinecure. Its occupant does not embark for a pleasure voyage upon a summer sea.")

Many schools built in the 1870s still stand. On MacArthur Boulevard NW there is a one-room wooden schoolhouse built in 1874 and used for classes until 1928. Sumner, at 17th and M streets NW, was designed by Adolph Cluss and erected in 1871. It was the headquarters of the black school system and is now a District landmark. Stevens, at 21st and K streets NW, has been in use since 1878.

The city's first high school for either race was Dunbar, which began in 1870 as Preparatory High School, a college preparatory school for

blacks. Starting out in the basement of the 15th Street Presbyterian Church, it moved in 1916 to First and N Streets NW and was renamed Dunbar after the black poet, Paul Laurence Dunbar. Its earliest principals included the first black woman to receive a college degree in America and the first black man to graduate from Harvard. Its faculty held many advanced degrees, vocational opportunities other than teaching being scarce for highly educated blacks. In 1899 Dunbar students scored higher in citywide examinations than the students of either white high school. They achieved this record in a school system rated nationally among the top two or three. Much later a 1936 Dunbar graduate, Massachusetts Senator Edward W. Brooke, recalled in a *Washington Post* interview: "Dunbar . . . had an intellectual elite. We enjoyed our own company, and almost never got out of it. We were not aware of the stigma. We were not aware of what we were missing because of segregation." Black students were free to come to Dunbar from all over the city. In 1955, with school desegregation, Dunbar was turned into a neighborhood school, no longer geared specifically to college preparation.

310

From Picturesque Washington, *by Joseph West Moore, 1886*

The Franklin School, at 13th and K streets NW, was designed by Cluss as part of the white school system and was considered the finest school building in the city. The design won prizes in Vienna, Paris and Philadelphia. Finished in 1869, during a period of runaway inflation, the building exhausted the city's school-building fund for the next four years. School Superintendent J. O. Wilson wrote, however, that the school

> "richly repaid its cost in lifting the public school system to its proper place in the estimation of the public. The pernicious idea of charity schools for poor children, on which the sytem was founded . . . disappeared at once and forever. Applications for admission to the Franklin School, including those from the wealthiest and most aristocratic classes, from the day of opening were received far beyond its capacity."

Among those who attended Franklin School were the children of Presidents Andrew Johnson and Chester A. Arthur. The school still stands on Franklin Square and is designated a District landmark.

In the F. B. Johnston photograph below, children of the 7th Division School make leaves for pen wipers, circa 1900.

311

Posture exercises at the 4th Division school, circa 1900.

A typing class at the Business High School, 1899. About this time Frank Carpenter was writing:

"It will not be long now before every government clerk will have to know how to use the typewriter, and no doubt there will be a special civil service examination to prove his skill. For the typewriter is rapidly coming into use. In nearly every department you will hear it clicking as you pass along the aisles. In the Department of Justice alone there are twenty machines; I suppose all told there are as many as a thousand in use in the city."

At right, the Western High School chemistry lab in 1900. Below, the machine shop at one of the city's technical high schools. Industrial and manual training programs were started in 1873 and led to the founding of two technical high schools, Armstrong and McKinley.

OVERLEAF: A Decoration Day tableau staged by students of Washington's 1st Division Public School.

At left, students of Kendall School (now Gallaudet College), circa 1880. A school for the deaf, Kendall was founded by Amos Kendall, Postmaster General under President Jackson. He founded the school on his estate, Kendall Green (at Florida Avenue and 7th Street NE), after he himself adopted five deaf orphans who had been mistreated in another institution. Kendall persuaded Congress to incorporate the school (formally called the Columbia Institution for the Deaf, Dumb, and Blind) in 1857. He contributed $20,000 to its operation and called young Edward Gallaudet, son of a pioneer in education for the deaf, to run the school. Gallaudet remained for fifty-three years. In 1864 Congress empowered the school to grant college degrees and to be known as the National Deaf Mute College, the first of its kind in the world.

Gallaudet College

Catholic University of America

Georgetown University

Patrick J. Healy, S. J., president of Georgetown University from 1874 to 1882. Father Healy was the first black man to head a major white university and was probably the first black Ph. D. A linguistics scholar and professor of philosophy from 1866, Healy, as president, strengthened the university's academic program, particularly in science, law and medicine. The towers of the Healy Building dominate the Georgetown skyline. In an 1889 photograph (left) the staff of Catholic University poses before Caldwell Hall, the first building on the university campus. The hall was named for the Caldwell sisters, whose philanthropy helped establish the college. Intended to provide for the intellectual development of both clergy and laity, the university was established on land that had been the country seat of Margaret Bayard and Samuel Harrison Smith in the years after the founding of the Federal City. The cornerstone of Caldwell Hall was laid in 1888 by His Eminence Cardinal Gibbons. President Grover Cleveland attended the 1889 dedication.

American University

On the campus of American University, visitors file past the university's first building, Hurst Hall, during ceremonies for the laying of the cornerstone of the second, the McKinley Building, in 1902. The site of the university, at Loughborough Road and Massachusetts Avenue, was chosen by Methodist bishop John Fletcher Hurst in 1890, and ground was broken for Hurst Hall (the College of History) six years later. The university was formally opened in 1914.

Students of Miner Teachers College on the steps of Miner Hall in 1893. The college was started by Howard University in 1873, with funds donated in memory of Myrtilla Miner, a young white woman from New York State who had opened a school for black girls in Washington in the decade before the Civil War. She had been supported by the Society of Friends, Harriet Beecher Stowe, Henry Ward Beecher and Johns Hopkins. Miner, the Washington Technical Institute and Federal City College merged in 1976 to form The University of the District of Columbia.

Prints and Photographs Collection, Moorland-Spingarn Research Center, Howard University

Calvary Baptist (above), among the best-known downtown churches, still stands at 8th and H streets. Built in the 1860s to Adolph Cluss's design, it was financed by Amos Kendall.

"There are many fine church edifices in Washington and the number is rapidly increasing from year to year. . . . Washington is a city of churches, and even Brooklyn which has for a long time assumed this title, does not now number as many churches in proportion to the population."

—Stilson Hutchins and Joseph West Moore, 1885

Francis Grimké (1850–1937), for fifty years a community leader and pastor of the Fifteenth Street Presbyterian Church, was termed "the outstanding minister of his people in the Capital and one of the most distinguished clergymen of his time." An outspoken critic of racial discrimination, Grimké had been born in South Carolina to a slave mother and a white planter father. He and his brother Archibald (later U.S. consul to Santo Domingo) were taken north for education (Harvard and Princeton) by their father's kin, the celebrated Grimké sisters, abolitionists and reformers.

Founded by slaves and free blacks, the Metropolitan African Methodist Episcopal Church at 1518 M Street was built in 1886—an outgrowth of a church founded in 1850 by the Union Bethel AME Church Society. Now a District landmark, it has served as a center for black social programs, relief, education (the Bethel Literary and Historical Society, founded by Bishop Payne in 1881) and civil-rights efforts. Black high schools and Howard University often held graduations at this church, and President Taft, Eleanor Roosevelt and Mary McLeod Bethune lectured here. Frederick Douglass' funeral was held here in 1895.

The Adas Israel Synagogue, at 6th and G streets NW, was the first building constructed in Washington for use specifically as a synagogue. The original Washington Hebrew Congregation, incorporated in 1856, had held services in a converted church at 8th and H streets NW. The Adas Israel Congregation was formed in 1869 by conservative members of the Hebrew Congregation who were opposed to liturgical changes and the growing reform movement. Their new synagogue was dedicated in June 1876. Simon Wolf, a participant in the ceremony, noted that it was "the first instance in the history of American Judaism that a President and Vice President attended such a consecration service." In 1907 a larger Adas Israel was built nearby, at 6th and I streets. The original synagogue, moved to 3rd and G streets, is now a Jewish museum.

Albert Small, who grew up in the area, recalled:

> "That neighborhood was our whole lives in those days. The synagogue was the focal point. We went to school at Seaton, and we took music lessons in St. Mary's [German Catholic Church], across the street from our house. We used to help in the family stores two blocks away. I did belong to a Herzl Club in the YMHA at 11th and Pennsylvania but that was about the only time we left the neighborhood. . . . "

The movement to build the Episcopal cathedral grew from an 1891 meeting at Charles Carroll Glover's house on Lafayette Square, where he proposed the idea "for the promotion of religion and education and charity." The first choice of a site was Connecticut Avenue west of the zoo; the final choice of Wisconsin and Massachusetts avenues, then considered daringly distant from city life, was made by Henry Yates Satterlee, first Bishop of Washington. The foundation stone was laid in 1907. Services were held regularly in the Bethlehem Chapel by 1912. Prophetic indeed were Bishop Satterlee's words that the cathedral was not to be "a monument to sectarianism but a witness to Christian unity." From the start there have been many efforts to have the cathedral serve as the "National Church" called for in L'Enfant's original plans for the city. The cathedral has been used for services for many faiths, and national heroes of many sects are buried there.

Other denominations have also built great structures in the capital: the National Presbyterian Center, the National Christian Church, the National Catholic Shrine of the Immaculate Conception and, near the city, the recently built Temple of the Church of Jesus Christ of Latter-day Saints. A Buddhist temple, Russian and Greek cathedrals and the largest mosque in North America also stand in Washington.

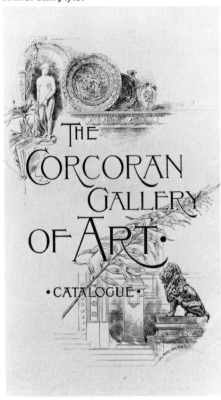

In 1891 a new site was chosen for the Corcoran Gallery of Art: on 17th Street at New York Avenue NW. The new building, designed by Ernest Flagg, was inaugurated six years later and continues to serve as the Corcoran Gallery today.

The man chiefly responsible for the building of the new Corcoran was Charles Carroll Glover (1846–1936), photographed here with one of his grandchildren. Born to a family long connected with Washington, Glover was a financier, civic leader and philanthropist, a trustee of American University and president of the Corcoran from 1906 to 1933. Newbold Noyes of the *Star* credited him with having inspired other philanthropists to give their art treasures to the city. Glover himself also gave the city eighty acres of the tract that became Glover-Archbold Park and two tracts enlarging Fort Dupont Park in Anacostia. He was largely responsible for saving Rock Creek Park.

Art students sketch plaster casts of statues of antiquity at the Corcoran. An 1897 Corcoran catalogue specified that "On Tuesdays, Thursdays, and Saturdays only, persons will be admitted under certain printed regulations, to the privilege of drawing from the casts and copying the pictures."

The monument to Mrs. Henry Adams in Rock Creek Cemetery of St. Paul's Church was sculpted by Augustus Saint-Gaudens in 1890. Charles Moore, in *Washington Past and Present*, quoted Saint-Gaudens as saying of the monument: "Some call it the Peace of God, some Nirvana. To me it is the human soul face to face with the greatest of all mysteries." Moore commented: "He spoke slowly and with feeling. I realized then that to ask for a translation of that statue into words was like asking Beethoven to couch in language what he had expressed supremely in music."

321

"The great nations are rapidly absorbing for their future expansion and their present defense all the waste places of the earth," wrote Henry Cabot Lodge at the turn of the century. "As one of the great nations of the world the United States must not fall out of the line of march." With the Spanish-American War, the United States moved into a stronger role in the Caribbean and the Pacific. John Hay, American minister in London, wrote: "It had been a splendid little war, begun with the highest motives, carried on with magnificent intelligence and spirit, favored by that future which loves the brave."

Among those who marched off to war was Hay's friend, Theodore Roosevelt, who had burst upon Washington in 1890 as a member of the newly formed Civil Service Commission. "The only trouble I ever had managing him," said President

"A Splendid Little War"

At left, the 1st Regiment of D.C. volunteers leaves for its training camp, May 14, 1898. The portrait of Theodore Roosevelt in his Rough Riders uniform was painted by Tade Styka in 1910. Opposite: Those who died in the sinking of the battleship *Maine* are buried with full honors at Arlington Cemetery, December 18, 1899.

Harrison, "was that he wanted to put an end to all the evil in the world between sunrise and sunset." Roosevelt was Assistant Secretary of the Navy when he resigned to lead his Rough Riders against the Spaniards. Three years later he was President. In his whirlwind way Roosevelt was to focus on many of the problems that were to dominate the rest of the century in government, diplomacy and national affairs. The White House had to be enlarged to accommodate his boisterous family, their small menagerie and his athletic, political and social activity. Rudyard Kipling liked to watch him in action with his friends—Lodge, Adams, Hay, Holmes—in the Cosmos Club on Lafayette Square: "I curled up in the seat opposite and listened and wondered until the universe seemed to be spinning around and Theodore was the spinner."

"*Our visit to Panama was most successful as well as most interesting. . . . I kept thinking of the four centuries of wild and bloody romance, mixed with abject squalor and suffering, which made up the history of the Isthmus until three years ago. . . . Now we have taken over the job [the building of the Canal]. The steam shovels, the dirt trains, the machine shops, and the like are all filled with American engineers, conductors, machinists, boiler-makers, carpenters. All of these men are quite as formidable, and would, if it were necessary, do quite as much in battle as the crews of Drake and Morgan; but as it is they are doing a work of much more lasting consequence. . . . Stevens (the chief engineer) and his men are changing the face of the continent, are doing the greatest engineering feat of the ages, and the effect of their work will be felt while our civilization lasts.*"

—Theodore Roosevelt's Letter, November 20, 1906

Above, Walter Reed (1851–1902) as a first lieutenant. The scientific work of Major Walter Reed and Major William Crawford Gorgas in Cuba and Panama led to the control of yellow fever and malaria. William Cline Borden, who was a surgeon during the Spanish-American War and commanded the Washington Barracks Hospital, (left) at Fort McNair, where much of Reed's work was done, realized the need for an Army Medical Center in the Washington area. As a result of his efforts, Congress in 1906 appropriated the money for the purchase of land on 16th Street. The new medical center, seen below in a 1930 aerial view, was named in honor of Walter Reed.

The first American to win the Nobel Prize for Peace, Roosevelt is portrayed in his "morning hours" by A. I. Keller. In this letter of 1905 to his son Kermit, he describes his efforts to mediate the Russo-Japanese War:

"White House, June 11, 1905. . . . On Saturday evening I fried two chickens for dinner, while Mother boiled the tea, and we had cherries and wild strawberries, as well as biscuits and cornbread. . . . During the past fortnight . . . I have been carrying on negotiations with both Russia and Japan, together with side negotiations with Germany, France and England, to try to get the present war stopped. With infinite labor and by the exercise of a good deal of tact and judgment—if I do say so myself—I have finally gotten the Japanese and Russians to agree to meet to discuss the terms of peace. . . . I have kept the secret very successfully, and my dealings with the Japanese in particular have been known to no one, so that the result is in the nature of a surprise."

In another letter he wrote: "the birds have come back . . . a winter wren, purple finches and tufted titmice are singing in the garden." The bird list below was compiled by the President in March 1908.

NIGHT HERON. Five spent winter of 1907 in swampy country about one-half mile west of Washington Monument.
MOURNING DOVE.
QUAIL.
RUFFED GROUSE. One seen on Rock Creek.
SHARP-SHINNED HAWK.
RED-SHOULDERED HAWK.
*SPARROW HAWK. A pair spent the last two winters on and around the White House grounds, feeding on the sparrows—largely, thank Heaven, on English sparrows.
*SCREECH OWL. Steady resident on White House grounds.
*SAW-WHET OWL. A pair spent several weeks by the south portico of the White House in June, 1905.
KINGFISHER.
*YELLOW-BILLED CUCKOO.
HAIRY WOODPECKER.
*DOWNY WOODPECKER.
*SAPSUCKER.
*RED-HEADED WOODPECKER. Nests (one pair) on White House grounds.
*FLICKER. Nests (several pair) on White House grounds.
WHIP-POOR-WILL.
NIGHTHAWK.
*CHIMNEY SWIFT.
*HUMMINGBIRD.
KINGBIRD.
GREAT CRESTED FLYCATCHER.
PHOEBE.
WOOD PEWEE.
HORNED LARK.
*CROW.
*FISH CROW.

*ORCHARD ORIOLE. One pair nested in White House grounds.
BOBOLINK.
RED-WINGED BLACKBIRD.
*BALTIMORE ORIOLE.
MEADOWLARK.
*PURPLE GRACKLE. Nests on White House grounds. Very abundant in early spring.
*PURPLE FINCH.
*THISTLE BIRD. (Goldfinch.)
VESPER SPARROW.
*WHITETHROAT. Sings; this year sang now and then all through the winter.
*TREE SPARROW.
*CHIPPIE. (Chipping Sparrow.) Nests.
BUSH SPARROW. (Field Sparrow.)
*SNOW BIRD. (Junco.)
*SONG SPARROW. Nests.
*FOX SPARROW.
*CARDINAL.
TOWHEE.
*INDIGO-BIRD. Nests.
TANAGER.
PURPLE MARTIN.
*BARN SWALLOW.
TREE SWALLOW.
BANK SWALLOW.
*CEDAR BIRD.
LOGGER-HEAD SHRIKE.
*RED-EYED VIREO. Nests.
*WARBLING VIREO. Nests.
*BLACK AND WHITE WARBLER. Nests.
*BLUE YELLOW-BACKED WARBLER.
*CAPE MAY WARBLER.
*SUMMER YELLOWBIRD. Nests.
*BLACK-THROATED BLUE WARBLER.
*BLACK-THROATED GREEN WARBLER.
*MYRTLE WARBLER.

*MAGNOLIA WARBLER.
*CHESTNUT-SIDED WARBLER.
*BAY-BREASTED WARBLER.
*BLACKPOLL WARBLER.
*BLACKBURNIAN WARBLER.
PRAIRIE WARBLER.
OVEN-BIRD.
WATER-THRUSH.
KENTUCKY WARBLER.
*YELLOWTHROAT.
CHAT.
*BLUE-WINGED WARBLER.
*CANADIAN WARBLER.
*REDSTART. Nests on White House grounds.
PIPIT.
MOCKINGBIRD.
*CATBIRD. Nests on White House grounds.
THRASHER.
HOUSE WREN.
*CAROLINA WREN.
MARSH WREN.
*CREEPER.
*WHITE-BREASTED NUTHATCH.
*TUFTED TIT. Nests on White House grounds.
*CHICKADEE.
*GOLDEN-CROWNED KINGLET.
*RUBY-CROWNED KINGLET.
GNATCATCHER.
*WOOD THRUSH. Nests on White House grounds.
*BLUEBIRD.
*ROBIN. Nests on White House grounds.

(*Denotes a species seen on White House grounds)

At top, the bridge at Pierce Mill on Rock Creek. Linnean Hill (Klingle House), which was acquired as part of Rock Creek Park in 1890, is shown above as it appeared around the turn of the century, when it was the home of a White House guard and zoo keeper. (Those are his children on the lawn.) Built in 1823 by Joshua Peirce (as the name was also spelled), a horticulturist and nurseryman, the house was named in honor of Swedish botanist Karl von Linnaeus. Camellias, newly introduced from the East, were Peirce's specialty. His extensive nursery supplied trees for Lafayette Park and many city streets. Daniel Webster and Henry Clay used to ride out from Washington to enjoy Peirce's gardens and his hospitality. Some of his great trees still dominate the site, which overlooks Porter Street near the intersection of Klingle Road and Beach Drive.

As early as the 1860s proposals were being made for establishing a public park in the area of Rock Creek. As naturalist John Burroughs wrote in 1863: "There is perhaps not another city in the Union that has on its very threshold so much natural beauty and grandeur, such as men seek for in remote forests and mountains. A few touches of art would convert this whole region into a park unequalled in the world." Through the efforts of Charles Carroll Glover, and with the support of Crosby Noyes of the *Star*, the park lands were acquired in 1890.

During his Presidency, Theodore Roosevelt enjoyed making long excursions to Rock Creek Park and other parts of the open country around Washington. One such outing was described by Jusserand, the new French minister, who sent the following dispatch to the Quai d'Orsay:

"President Roosevelt invited me to take a promenade with him this afternoon at three. I arrived at the White House punctually, in afternoon dress and silk hat, as if to stroll in the Tuileries. . . . To my surprise, the President soon joined me in a tramping suit, with knickerbockers and thick boots. . . . On reaching the country, the President went pell-mell over the fields . . . . At last we came to the bank of a stream, rather too wide and deep to be forded. . . . But judge of my horror when I saw the President unbutton his clothes and heard him say 'We had better strip, so as not to wet our things in the Creek.' Then I, too, for the honor of France removed my apparel, everything except my lavender kid gloves. The President cast an inquiring look at these as if they, too, must come off, but I quickly forestalled any remark by saying, 'With your permission, Mr. President, I will keep these on; otherwise it would be embarrassing if we should meet ladies.' And so we jumped in the water and swam across."

Above, ice skating on the duck pond at the National Zoo. Below, an afternoon outing. Washington's zoo historians note that the first gift of an animal was probably a royal jackass, a gift from Charles III of Spain, which was sent to George Washington at Mount Vernon in 1785. Other gifts of state and specimens collected by explorers (including Lewis and Clark's buffaloes) were also brought to Washington. In 1856 the Smithsonian was given charge of the collection. But, having no way of caring for the animals, the Smithsonian farmed out the collection to the Government Insane Asylum as an amusement for the patients and other interested persons. In the 1880s the animals were kept in sheds on the Mall, where they were used for study by taxidermists during the preparation of an exhibit of North American fauna. There the collection attracted such crowds of visitors that Dr. Samuel Langley, then Secretary of the Smithsonian, established a Department of Living Animals as part of the National Museum. The collection was later moved to the new National Zoological Park, which remains an important research center for the study of animals.

328   A picnic party at the lower ford of Rock Creek.

National Zoological Park. Photographed by Frances Benjamin Johnston

Inventors
in Washington

Like Robert Fulton of steamboat fame and Morse of the telegraph and code, inventors continued to come to Washington, being drawn to the capital by the Smithsonian, the Patent Office and the governmental presence, with its potential for subsidies and favorable legislation. Their inventions planted many of the seeds of technological development which, with the rich harvesting of America's natural resources, would create unparalleled wealth. Early in the twentieth century this wealth brought the flowering of chateaux and palazzi that give distinction to Washington today (see following pages).

One of the inventors who transformed modern life, of course, was Alexander Graham Bell; he also left a strong mark on the city. Son and grandson of teachers of speech, Bell came from Boston, where he had been lecturing at the Boston School for the Deaf. In a Georgetown carriage house he continued his research into hearing disabilities. Nearby, using the $10,000 Volta Prize awarded him by the French government for having invented the telephone, he founded the Volta Bureau, dedicated to helping the deaf. At left, Bell with young Helen Keller and her teacher, Annie Sullivan.

Helen Keller was twelve in 1893 when she turned the first spadeful of dirt for the Volta Bureau on 35th Street. Seated below, she holds the shovel. Annie Sullivan is the hatted woman sitting behind her. Mrs. Alexander Graham Bell is the standing woman with striped cuffs; her husband is the tall man at her shoulder. Their daughter Elsie May, seated at far left, lived from 1878 to 1964 and was uniquely connected with the National Geographic Society. Her grandfather, Gardiner Greene Hubbard, was its first president and was one of its principal founders in 1888 (at a meeting at the Cosmos Club). Her father was its second president, and her husband, Gilbert Hovey Grosvenor, was the third president and editor of the magazine from 1899 to 1954. Her son Melville Bell Grosvenor was president and editor from 1954 to 1966. Her grandson, Gilbert Melville Grosvenor, became editor of the magazine in 1975.

330

The photograph above, of Orville Wright flying over Fort Myer in Arlington, was taken in 1908, the year the Wright brothers completed their first airplane for the War Department. This was five years after their first flight at Kitty Hawk, North Carolina. "The great diversion of the late spring and early summer was to go over to Fort Myer to see the Wrights fly," wrote Alice Roosevelt Longworth in *Crowded Hours* (1933). "When the machine actually left the ground and circled the field, a hundred feet or so up, it gave us a thrill that no one in this generation will ever have."

Washington played an important role in the early history of aviation not only because policies and subsidies came from here but because significant inventions were developed here. Samuel P. Langley, Secretary of the Smithsonian, with some funds from Alexander Graham Bell, got a Board of Ordnance and Fortification appropriation to prove that man could fly in a heavier-than-air vehicle. He directed the development of the Langley-Manly-Balzer engine, which, during three bench tests in Washington, ran successfully at full throttle for ten hours. This was well before the Wright brothers flew at Kitty Hawk. Efforts to put this engine in a vehicle and fly it, however, ended in two plunges into the Potomac. The Wrights, having the advantage of previous experience with gliders, knew enough about maneuvering in air currents to build a superior vehicle for their engine to fly.

Dr. Herman Hollerith of Washington was a founder of the Computer Age. Working in a warehouse on the Georgetown waterfront, he invented an electric tabulating machine that read data punched on cards and then tallied up the totals. Used for the Census of 1890, the system revolutionized the census count, making it both rapid and accurate.

Hollerith developed his system after he was appointed in 1879 as Special Agent of the Census Office. As his daughter, Virginia, remembered:

> "This work brought him into contact with Dr. John S. Billings, who had charge of vital statistics in the Tenth Census (1880). . . . Dr. Billings suggested the need for a machine to do the purely mechanical work of tabulating population and similar statistics . . . using cards with the description of the individual shown by notches in the edge of the card and a device something like a type-distributing machine. . . . While traveling in the West Father had once been given a ticket with what was called a punch photograph: when the ticket was first presented to the conductor he punched out a description of the holder—light hair, dark eyes, large nose etc. This, Father said, gave him the idea for making a punch photograph of each person to be tabulated."

Hollerith's Tabulating Machine Company, which gained an international reputation early in the twentieth century, merged with others to form the corporation later known as IBM. In England the cards used in data processing are still called Hollerith cards.

331

The Palace Builders of Massachusetts Avenue

"Dropping cards, paying calls, took hours two or three afternoons a week. The laws of the Medes and Persians governed this ritual. For instance, one had to call within forty-eight hours on a hostess who had entertained one to dinner—the visite de digestion. A note, above all a telephone call, was unheard-of rudeness."

—Countess Marguerite Cassini, 1956

By the time the century began Washington had become home to many members of the new American elite: tycoons who had made their fortunes in mining, publishing, banking, meat packing, shipping, railroads, lumbering and land management. Up and down Massachusetts Avenue rose their stately pleasure domes. Their chosen architects were much under the influence of the Ecole des Beaux Arts in Paris, and the combined work of these men resulted in the creation of a "Period" that the Fine Arts Commission has called "rich, diversified, and flamboyant." The owners of certain of these houses might be said to have fitted the same description.

Most of the little palaces of Massachusetts Avenue were erected between 1900 and America's entry into the First World War. The symbolic end might be said to have occurred with the sinking of the *Titanic* in 1912. Among the victims of that disaster was Clarence Moore, who built 1746 Massachusetts Avenue (now the Canadian Chancery). He was coming home from abroad, having bought for the Chevy Chase Hunt (and sent on another ship) a pack of English hounds, twelve Welsh pony mares and a stallion and eight Irish hunters.

Many of the houses of Washington's *belle epoque* lasted as private homes through World War II, evidence of a life-style that seemed oblivious to rising taxes, soaring costs and shrinking staffs. While Washington still has a substantial number of these houses, many have been demolished for apartment houses and office buildings. Only at Sheridan Circle are there a few blocks where the houses are preserved intact. Those that have been saved—often with great difficulty and at great expense—are headquarters for clubs, organizations and embassies. In their splendid variety they serve as reminders of a unique and brief period of Washington's past.

Massachusetts Avenue at Sheridan Circle, 1911

Martin Luther King Library, Washingtoniana Collection

Above, 1801 Massachusetts Avenue NW as seen from Dupont Circle. Below, a view of the ballroom.

The house "had somehow the shape of a boat," recalled Countess Marguerite Cassini. Fully lighted for a party, with its "prow" headed into Dupont Circle and its sides sweeping back along Massachusetts Avenue and P Street, the house must indeed have looked like a great ship set for "full steam ahead."

The house was built in 1900–1901 for Herbert Wadsworth and his wife Martha (left), the former Martha Blow of St. Louis. Wadsworth owned and managed large agricultural properties in the Genesee Valley of New York State. The architect was probably Frederick Brooke, who later designed the U.S. embassy in London. But according to Countess Cassini, it was Mrs. Wadsworth who "designed and decorated and practically built the huge mansion." Mr. Wadsworth himself declared: "There is only one thing that house lacks. The arch over the carriage entrance should have written on it, in Gothic letters, 'Marfy done it!'" Wadsworth, too, must have been helpful to his wife's project, for he was a trained draughtsman and his hobby was design. He was also a member of the Finance Committee of the Washington Branch of the American Red Cross, to which he and his wife turned over two floors of their home in 1917. In 1918 the Red Cross had entire use of the house. In 1932 the house became the Sulgrave Club.

Irish-born Thomas F. Walsh had come a long way from his native Tipperary when he built his sixty-room mansion at 2020 Massachusetts Avenue NW (below). Walsh, seen at left with his daughter Evalyn, had struck it rich in the gold fields of Colorado in 1896. His Washington house, completed in 1903, cost $835,000—unfurnished. In her memoir, Evalyn Walsh McLean wrote that the house "expresses dreams my Father and Mother had when they were poor in Colorado." Walsh instructed New York architect John Andersen "just what was wanted." For the ballroom there were hangings, chair covers and walls of gold brocade, which also gleamed on the walls of the organ room. The dining table was set with a service of gold made from nuggets taken from Walsh's Camp Bird Mine. The "steamship" stair hall at the center of the house (opposite) was built three stories high, roofed over with glass and adorned with a gracefully curved Art Nouveau mahogany balustrade.

Mr. and Mrs. Walsh enjoyed only a few unclouded years in the house. In 1905 their daughter Evalyn was badly injured and their son Vinson was killed in an automobile accident. Thereafter, Walsh, once a generous host and a contributor to various charitable organizations, became increasingly withdrawn. He died in seclusion in 1910. In 1908 Evalyn eloped with Edward Beale McLean, whose family owned the *Washington Post*. Their first child, Vinson Walsh McLean, was born at the Walsh mansion, and there also they negotiated the purchase of the supposedly unlucky Hope Diamond. Little Vinson was killed by a car in 1919, the McLeans separated in 1930, and Edward McLean was declared insane in 1933.

During World War I, "2020," as the family called it, was used by Washington volunteers to make garments for Belgian refugees. In 1919 it was the scene of a state dinner given by Vice President and Mrs. Marshall for King Albert of Belgium. It is now the Indonesian embassy.

"A noteworthy example of straightforward planning, appropriate to entertaining" was the way *The Architectural Record* of 1901 described the Townsend House, at 2121 Massachusetts Avenue, photographed by Frances Benjamin Johnston in 1915. The house was commissioned in 1899 by Richard Townsend, who had come to Washington after retiring as president of the Erie and Pittsburgh Railroad. The firm of Carrère and Hastings was instructed to build a mansion in the style of the Petit Trianon at Versailles. Because of a superstition that Mrs. Townsend would "encounter evil" if she ever lived in a completely new house, the mansion was to incorporate an already existing house. The instructions were carried out, but the house had no power to ward off sorrow. Soon after the mansion was completed, Richard Townsend died of injuries suffered in a riding accident. His widow and his only child, Mathilde, continued to live in the house, where they entertained lavishly.

In 1901 *The Architectural Record* included this description of rooms on the second or main floor of the house:

> "Those in the front connect with each other, forming a brilliant suite 120 feet in length. When these are all thrown open, the studied planning is revealed in a series of charming vistas in which the color schemes blend warmly and naturally from the heavy, rich green of the Library [below] to the elegant red and gold of the second salon, then the lighter, more delicate silver of the first salon to the festive white and gold of the ballroom."

Downstairs a vast kitchen and various pantries provided for frequent dinners, receptions and supper parties. There was enough china for one thousand guests.

Among the notable events held at the house was Mathilde's marriage in 1910 to Peter Goelet Gerry of New York (the "most brilliant marriage of years," said the *Washington Times*), which was attended by President Taft and which featured music by the Marine Band Orchestra. Early in 1933 President Franklin D. Roosevelt stayed at the house for several weeks as the guest of Mathilde and her second husband, Sumner Welles, who was soon to become Under Secretary of State. Since 1950 the house has belonged to the Cosmos Club.

The house at 2201 Massachusetts Avenue NW is a late example of the Queen Anne and Romanesque revivals, modified by sixteenth-century northern European details. Designed by Washington architect Paul J. Pelz and completed in 1901, it managed to be unique as well as typical. Uniquely, its original plan included an "automobile house," the first in Washington. Typically, it sheltered in luxury a family newly come to Washington: Lieutenant Commander Frederick Augustus Miller (retired), his wife, Alice Townsend Miller, their two teen-aged daughters, Edith (center, left) and Alice (center, right), and their young son, Charles. Charles died as a young man, unmarried; Alice divorced Ashton De Peyster, married Count Boni de Castellane; Edith married Walter Tuckerman—both have descendants in the Washington area.

Having each inherited fortunes, Commander and Mrs. Miller could afford to live anywhere they chose. They chose Washington not for political, diplomatic or business reasons but because the commander believed that the capital would soon be "the most beautiful city in the world" and a mecca for the "culture of the United States." The entire family became active in charitable activities in the capital, and the scrapbooks of the two girls are filled with invitations to other "chateaux," as well as to various embassies and the White House.

As befitting the home of a naval officer (Commander Miller was a veteran of Civil War naval battles at Donaldsonville and Mobile, Alabama), the Miller house abounds with nautical motifs. Stone shells adorn the exterior frieze and bows. In the dining room the mantelpiece is carved with dolphins, Neptune's tridents and more shells. There, too, Miller honored Farragut, his admiral and hero, by installing a stained-glass painting of fish and deep-sea flora: the "Farragut Window," as it is still called. The Miller house is today the Argyle Guest House, with rooms for rent.

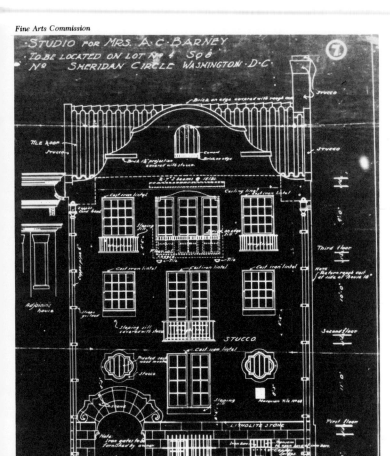

Among its turn-of-the-century neighbors the building at 2306 Massachusetts Avenue is strangely unpalatial. Designed to serve as a studio for Alice Pike Barney (seen above in a 1906 self-portrait), it was built simply as an adjunct to her impressive residence at 2223 R Street—a sort of grownup's playhouse. Born to wealth in 1857 in Cincinnati, Ohio, Alice Pike had married a rich manufacturer of railroad cars, Albert Clifford Barney. Mrs. Barney studied art with Carolus-Duran, Jean Jacques Henner and James Albert McNeil Whistler. ("You are too clever," Whistler told her. "Be careful.")

Mrs. Barney was instrumental in founding the Neighborhood Settlement House on N Street SW, and it was largely through her urging that Congress, in 1917, established the National Sylvan Theatre, where the first plays presented were written and produced by herself. She also staged vast charity pageants and tableaux, in which members of the social and diplomatic set often took part; and she was a skilled portrait painter whose sitters included George Bernard Shaw, Alice Roosevelt Longworth and Ruth St. Denis.

Mrs. Barney's Studio House was filled with ornate Spanish furniture. Besides the studio (below) it had stage facilities and ample provision for servants and party-giving. Today the building serves as headquarters for the Smithsonian Institution's Lending Service. Examples of Mrs. Barney's work are displayed there.

The brownstone house at left, a few steps off Massachusetts Avenue at 21st Street, was built in 1897 by Major and Mrs. D. Clinch Phillips of Pittsburgh, where he, a Civil War veteran, had manufactured glass and where she had been a Miss Laughlin of Jones and Laughlin Steel. After their doctor had advised a climate milder than that of Pittsburgh the Phillipses had been persuaded by friends to try a season in Washington, a "winter watering place." The winter of 1896 was the balmiest in Washington memory (shirt sleeves were seen on front porches in December); so the Phillipses stayed and built their house. It was opened as a gallery in 1920 by their son Duncan and his artist-wife, the former Majorie Acker, who together collected paintings, principally French and American art of the nineteenth and twentieth centuries. The Phillips Gallery of "modern art and its sources" was the first such collection open to the public anywhere. Their highly personal selection now ranges from El Greco to Morris Louis. Some of it is exhibited in a new gallery wing and some in the house, where, as Duncan Phillips wrote, visitors are "welcomed to feel at home with the pictures in an unpretentious domestic setting which is at the same time physically restful and mentally stimulating." An art school was directed there by Duncan Phillips' friend from both Pittsburgh and Yale days, C. Law Watkins, until his death in 1947; it later moved to American University.

The music room of the Phillips Gallery, where free concerts are held on Sunday afternoons.

Fine Arts Commission, photograph no. 66-G-15F-4 in the National Archives

"It seemed here on 21st Street at Dupont Circle there was a leisurely, almost southern village atmosphere, with hurdy gurdies playing and men pushing their carts of fresh flowers or fruits, crying 'stra-a-berries' in loud melodious voices. The hurdy gurdies and the monkeys to pick up the pennies were frequent visitors during the day."

— Marjorie Phillips, *Duncan Phillips and His Collection*, 1970

340

With all its opulence Washington was a small town still, with organ grinders and balloon men and pony rides with Mama down quiet, tree-lined streets. Opposite: New Hampshire Avenue—one of the stately avenues of which Alexander ("Boss") Shepherd had dreamed when, in the 1870s, he launched the most extensive tree-planting program in the city's history.

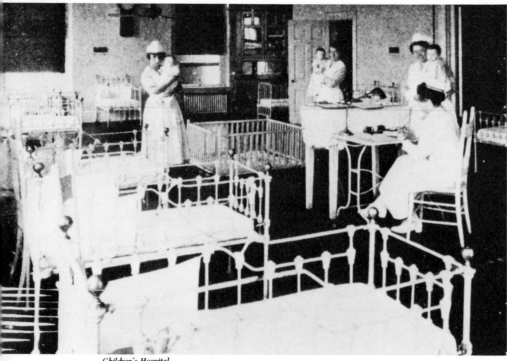

The Infant Ward of Children's Hospital. Jane Gemmill, in her *Notes on Washington* (1884), wrote:

"Even in the most fashionable houses and in the midst of a winter's round of gayety, some time is spared for 'sweet charity.' The Children's Hospital is a notable example of this. Beginning in a small room, rented for the purpose, it has grown to splendid proportions; and now relieves the suffering and administers to the comforts of hundreds of children, in a large well-appointed building reared by the generosity of kind-hearted ladies and gentlemen.

"Congress makes a small appropriation annually, but the greater part of the expense is borne by these persons. The Charity Ball, given each winter for the benefit of the hospital, is usually the most brilliant affair of the fashionable season."

A new building, The Children's Hospital National Medical Center on Michigan Avenue was dedicated by President Carter in 1977.

Children's Hospital

The Charities

Among influential Washingtonians concern for the problems of the sick and the needy has been a tradition since the city's earliest days. An early newspaper notice called for "the ladies of Washington and neighborhood to meet in the Hall of Representatives on Tuesday, October 10th, 1815, to consider the propriety of instituting an asylum for the relief and maintainance of orphans." Thus was founded (and chartered by Congress) the Washington City Orphan Asylum. Mrs. James Madison was its "First Directress." Marcia Burns Van Ness, its "Second Directress," donated a house on H Street near 10th. In 1828 Charles Bullfinch designed a new brick Asylum building.

In 1886 the Asylum, which was to evolve into Hillcrest Children's Center, was one of nearly two dozen asylums, orphanages and charitable institutions listed in the *New Standard Guide to Washington D.C.* The Associated Charities, founded in 1881, was designed to coordinate relief and fund-raising efforts of the District's numerous charita-

ble institutions. The result was organized volunteer groups, better-trained social workers and increased involvement on the part of the local and federal government.

After a Congressional committee reported the existence of twelve governmental and thirty-three private "charitable and reformatory" organizations, the Board of Charities was created by Congress in 1900 and appointed by the President to arrange contracts with private institutions and to supervise "all institutions which are supported in whole or in part by appropriations of Congress."

The Associated Charities and the Board of Charities brought together influential citizen volunteers and professional social workers, who together strove to educate the community about critical social issues. In this atmosphere the Junior League of Washington was founded, prior to World War I, to train volunteers for community service following the model of the first League in New York.

342

The Louise Home (left) was described by *Godey's Magazine* in 1885 as being "a retreat to gentlewomen of culture, who have been reduced from affluence by the Civil War, and other causes, and now need succor in their declining years." The home was founded in 1871 by W. W. Corcoran, who named it after his deceased wife and daughter. The original home was on Massachusetts Avenue between 15th and 16th streets. It is now combined with a similar home, founded by the will of Laura and Abraham Lisner in 1939, on Western Avenue near Wisconsin Avenue.

From Picturesque Washington *by Joseph West Moore, 1886*

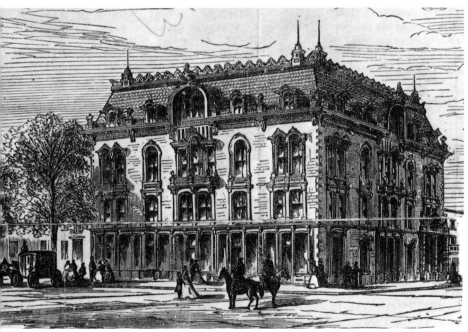

This engraving of the "new" building of the Washington City Young Men's Christian Association appeared in the *Association Monthly* in 1870. Among the many outgrowths of the YMCA was a public library (which formed the nucleus of the Washington Public Library), the Central Union Mission and the YWCA.

Library of Congress, Prints and Photographs Division

American Red Cross

Mabel Boardman (right) described community service as "the rent one pays for one's room on earth." Along with such community commitments as service on the President's Homes Commission, she was for forty-four years a full-time volunteer and a leading spirit of the American Red Cross, which has its national headquarters at 17th Street at the Ellipse. The Red Cross District Chapter continues to be especially active, primarily with the many service families here and the veterans' and service hospitals.

Left and below: alley slums near the Capitol. The distress of the poor has been a constant presence in the city since Washington began. In 1802, 42 percent of the city's revenue went for poor relief. According to the *National Intelligencer* of 1807:

> "The burden of the poor has undoubtedly increased because . . . people came to Washington with hopes of collecting claims against the Government, of getting a pension, or perhaps an office, and then there was a class who had no definite object. Delays, disappointments and failures were the fate of many, and so, with resources exhausted, they were thrown in debtors' prison or became dependent."

The plight of the city's poor was long hidden because for over a century many of the destitute lived in shanties on service alleys. An 1854 *Report of the Board of Health* concerning the high death rate for children declared that "much the larger proportion of these deaths are from among the children of negro, of foreign, and of destitute native parents, who usually reside in alleys." A police survey for the 1897 census recorded 303 such alleys housing one in twelve city residents: 16,828 "colored," 2,150 whites. In 1904 reformer Jacob Riis goaded Theodore Roosevelt into creating the President's Homes Commission, the goal of which was to eliminate alley dwellings. Charles F. Weller wrote in *Neglected Neighbors*, 1909: "There should be no contentment with anything short of a Comprehensive Plan for the steady, progressive, uncompromising elimination of all the evils represented by the alleys, tenements and shanties of the National Capital." The first Mrs. Woodrow Wilson made a deathbed plea for the passage of such legislation. Most alley dwellings finally disappeared in urban renewal upheavals; a few have become mews. Substandard housing remains a major problem.

National Capital Planning Commission; photograph no. 328-M-1B in the National Archives

By 1900 Benjamin Ogle Tayloe's once proud house, The Octagon, down the street from the White House, had deteriorated to the condition seen in the photograph above, taken by Frances Benjamin Johnston. Soon afterward, however, the property was bought by the American Institute of Architects. The house was restored and has served ever since as the showplace headquarters of the A.I.A.

The McMillan Plan

In January 1902 Senator James McMillan of Michigan, chairman of the Senate Committee on the District of Columbia, presented to the Senate a grandly conceived plan for the future development of the capital. A landmark in the city's history, the plan proposed that Washington be treated "as a work of civic art" and called for a return to the planned city envisioned by Pierre L'Enfant.

The plan was the work of the Senate Park Commission, also known as the McMillan Commission, which had been established in response to public alarm over the chaotic development of the rapidly growing city. The commission consisted of architect Daniel Hudson Burnham of Chicago; landscape designer Frederick Law Olmsted, Jr., of Brookline, Massachusetts; architect Charles F. McKim of New York; and sculptor Augustus Saint-Gaudens of New York. Charles Moore, who was Senator McMillan's secretary and himself a prime mover behind the commission's achievements, reported that the commission

> "began with a careful study of the L'Enfant plan as approved by Washington and Jefferson, and thereby they added to their own work the prestige of [the city's] founders. . . . Mr. Burnham, who resembled L'Enfant in seeing things 'in the large,' kept a comprehensive grasp of the entire situation. Mr. McKim took for his special province the orderly development of the Mall and its extensions—the central composition. Mr. Olmsted and the men called from his office gave particular attention to the system of parks, their increase, and the connections among them. Mr. Saint-Gaudens became the arbiter in matters of taste."

The commission's efforts were conducted on a grand scale, with trips to Rome, Venice, Vienna, Budapest, Paris and London being a part of the intensive ten-month effort. They especially drew on the work of Lenôtre at Vaux-le-Vicomte, the forerunner of Versailles.

In dealing with Congress and the public, Burnham, who was ever alert to political realities, emphasized the magnificence of the city's monumental core, which was to reflect America's rank among the nations. By this approach Burnham sought to ensure that there would be sufficient public funds to remake the whole city. Actually, though, the planners intended to limit severely the space devoted to architectural pageantry.

Given the Washington Monument (which was to be surrounded with terraces of American elms), the commissioners planned for only two new monuments: one dedicated to Lincoln and the other a "Hall of the Founding Fathers," which time and politics metamorphosed into the Jefferson Memorial.

Aside from these monuments, the major elements in the commissioners' plans were "fields for the populace." The many Civil War forts that ringed the city would become parks linked by a Fort Drive, so that a great circle of arterial parks would almost enclose the metropolitan area. Between the Washington Monument and the Lincoln Memorial there was to be a canal lined with trees. Beyond the trees there were to be fields for rugby, baseball and polo; and there were to be four baseball diamonds on the Ellipse, with tennis courts tucked in the corners.

The commissioners' vision of the new Washington was water-oriented. They saw the city as a peninsula and made plans for the shorelines from Great Falls around to the headwaters of the Anacostia. Public gymnasia and bathing beaches were to be built along the Tidal Basin. The flats along the shores of the Potomac and the Anacostia were to be dredged and gardens of water lilies would beautify the shoreline. There was to be a commercial Georgetown waterfront, but Roosevelt Island was to be maintained as a natural setting, devoid of artificial monuments and accessible to the people by ferry and walkway from Georgetown.

For all its vision and loving attention to detail, the report of the McMillan Commission did not immediately remake the city. By 1910 the Fine Arts Commission had been established but it took a generation just to move the old Botanical Gardens and forty years to clear the cluttered Mall. But it reaffirmed the L'Enfant concept of a stately and monumental city, defined around its primary axes and untouched by whatever other development might take place within the District or across the river in Virginia. In extending the east-west axis to include Arlington and in recommending the inclusion of a road to Mount Vernon, the commission even carried the concept of the monumental core beyond the original L'Enfant area. It is true that since then there has been a retreat from order in some of the commercial and residential areas lying beyond the monumental park. But the ultimate compliment to the McMillan Commission is that so much of the plan has been carried out and that there has been so little argument over the validity of the basic concept.

"Make no little plans. They have no magic to stir men's blood, and probably themselves will not be realized. . . . A noble and logical diagram once recorded will never die."

—Daniel Hudson Burnham

Library of Congress, Prints and Photographs Division

Library of Congress, Prints and Photographs Division

Library of Congress, Prints and Photographs Division

The need for effective city planning is evident in the 1894 aerial view seen above, taken from the top of the Washington Monument, looking out Virginia Avenue toward Georgetown. Dredging and landfill operations eventually pushed the river's marshy edge from near the monument's base to the seawall-bound shoreline now nearly a mile to the west. Beside the racecourse in the foreground stands the Van Ness mansion, future site of the Pan American Union. The stable in the background remains. At the nearby intersection, facing what had been the Washington Canal, stands the lockkeeper's house (in closeup top left); the lockhouse still stands on the site: now the corner of 17th Street and Constitution Avenue. On the opposite corner is a Bullfinch-designed gatehouse originally on the Capitol grounds (left). One block farther west, in 1883, DeLancey Gill sketched the area near 18th and B streets (bottom), now Constitution Avenue. In the distance, along the river in Foggy Bottom, are the Heurich Brewery, the Naval Observatory and gas storage tanks, which were built in 1858 and stood for nearly a century.

Owned by a descendant of the artist.

The effect of the McMillan Commission was to institutionalize city planning. In the words of President William Howard Taft:

"If General Washington, at a time when his country was a little hemmed-in nation, boasting but a single seaboard, with a population of only five million, and with credit so bad that lot sales, lotteries, and borrowing upon the personal security of individuals had to be resorted to in order to finance the new capital, could look to the future and understand that it was his duty to build for the centuries to come and for a great nation, how much more should we do so now?"

In keeping with this spirit, the Fine Arts Commission was created by Congress in 1910 to review all proposals for government buildings and monuments. A decade later the National Capital Park and Planning Commission was created. Frederick Law Olmsted, Jr., the McMillan Commission's landscape architect, played a major role in both these new commissions.

In subsequent years, other special commissions have been appointed to deal with troublesome areas of city planning. President John F. Kennedy, for instance, appointed a Pennsylvania Avenue Commission for the purpose of making the avenue a magnificent ceremonial way. Like the McMillan Plan, the plans submitted by the new commission were not adopted all in one piece. But they did stimulate debate and increased public participation in the city-planning process.

Below, the Lincoln Memorial rises on land reclaimed from the Potomac. Building went ahead despite "Uncle Joe" Cannon, Speaker of the House, who had declared: "I'll never let a memorial to Abraham Lincoln be erected in that God-damned swamp."

Above, cherry trees on the Tidal Basin, 1923. Instrumental in the development of this reclaimed land as a stylish promenade was Mrs. William Howard Taft, who had delighted in the Manila riverside area, Luneta Park, when her husband was Governor of the Philippines. Below, golf and cricket in Potomac Park.

The Mallside view of the Freer Gallery of Art. Built with Florentine Renaissance solidity, the Freer stands on the south side of the Mall. The gift of Detroit industrialist Charles Lang Freer, the gallery houses his collection of Oriental and Near Eastern art and American paintings by Ryder, Sargent and Whistler. Since its opening in 1923, the collection has been enhanced by additional bequests, including the Oriental art collections of Eugene and Agnes Meyer.

The American Insitute of Pharmacy, on Constitution Avenue at 23rd Street, was described by Senator McMillan's secretary, Charles Moore, as "a vital portion of the frame to the Lincoln Memorial picture." Designed by John Russell Pope and dedicated in 1934, it follows the McMillan Plan tradition of a white classical building in a green setting. It is the only private building on Constitution Avenue.

"In a southern direction from the President's house, and a western one from the Capitol, are to run two great pleasure parks, or malls, which will intersect and terminate upon the banks of the Potomac; and they are to be ornamented at the sides by a variety of elegant buildings, and houses for foreign Ministers."

—John Davis of Salisbury, *Notes on the District, 1801*

Union Station, designed by Daniel Burnham, became the depot for all the city's railroads. Patterned after the Baths of Caracalla in Rome, the building is situated near the Capitol and away from the Mall. A major step toward acceptance of the McMillan Plan came when Alexander Cassatt, president of the Pennsylvania Railroad, agreed to move his line's terminal off the Mall and into Union Station.

Below is a 1913 rendering of the Mall plan recommended by the Senate Park Commission in 1901. In a major shift from L'Enfant's plan, the commission converted L'Enfant's grand boulevard into a grassy, open Mall, thus introducing a new concept in urban design. New government offices were to be built around the Mall and around Lafayette Square. Buildings existing in 1901 and to be retained under the plan included: 1) Capitol; 2) White House; 3) Treasury Department; 4) State, War and Navy Department; 5) Post Office Department; 6) Congressional Library; 7) Naval Hospital. Public buildings for which plans had been prepared by 1913 included; 8) Department of Justice; 9) Departments of Commerce and Labor; 10) George Washington Memorial Hall; 11) Department of State. Public and semipublic buildings undertaken between 1901 and 1913 included; 12) National Museum; 13) Department of Agriculture; 14) Bureau of Engraving and Printing; 15) Municipal Building; 16) Senate Office Building; 17) House Office Building; 18) Pan American Union; 19) Daughters of the American Revolution. Buildings under construction by 1913, or authorized for construction, included: 20) Lincoln Memorial; 21) American Red Cross.

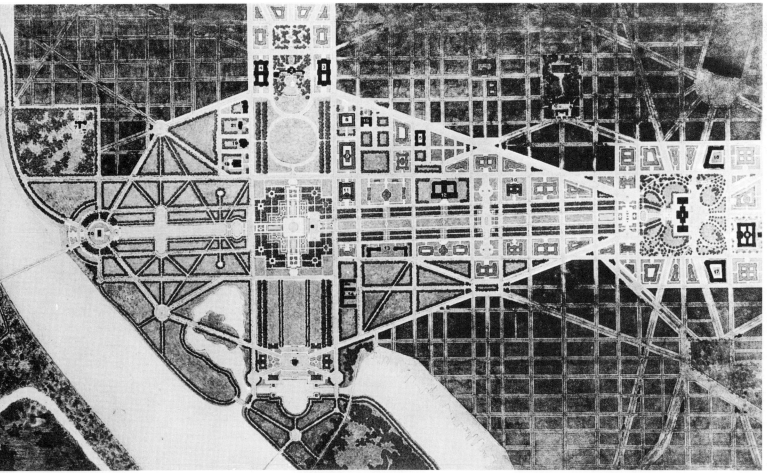

Mobilized
for War

Presidents Taft and Wilson leave the White House for Wilson's 1913 inauguration. In the years before World War I, Washingtonians knew the Presidents as approachable citizens of a small city that still had country charm. President Roosevelt's "morning hours" were informal affairs; President Taft kept a cow on the White House lawn. When President Wilson married Edith Bolling Galt, a Washington widow, the ceremony took place at her house on 20th Street.

In 1917, less than twenty years after trains left Washington carrying troops to fight in the Spanish-American War, local boys were again being mobilized for war. From other parts of the country servicemen and their families came pouring into the capital in great numbers. Volunteers from the District Red Cross provided nursing and social services.

During the World War I, Washington served as a mobilization center for the wealth, manpower and industry of the nation. New agencies sprang up throughout the city. Selective Service gave General Pershing an army within a year, as well as the means of transporting it to Europe. The Council on National Resources and War Industries Board brought prominent businessmen into the government, turning some of them into permanent Washingtonians. The Agriculture Commission, under Herbert Hoover, was responsible for feeding the American Expeditionary Force as well as half of its European allies. Almost 5,000 people worked in the State, War and Navy Building (and twice a day were ordered outdoors for hygienic breathing periods). The typists above were employed in the Warehousing Division of the Department of the Army, in a "temporary" building on Virginia Avenue. (World War I "temporaries" were to remain part of the Washington scene for years, some not being removed until the 1970s.) To handle the growing volume of government business, the Post Office, too, had to be expanded. At left: men whose job it was to keep the mail moving.

353

The World War I Victory Parade, following the traditional parade route down Pennsylvania Avenue from the Capitol to the White House, passes beneath a specially built Arch of Triumph at 15th and Pennsylvania.

Washington and its suburbs in 1923. Half a century ago the city could be mapped quite nicely on a page this size. In the decades that followed, however, the boundaries of the metropolitan area were to spread dramatically.

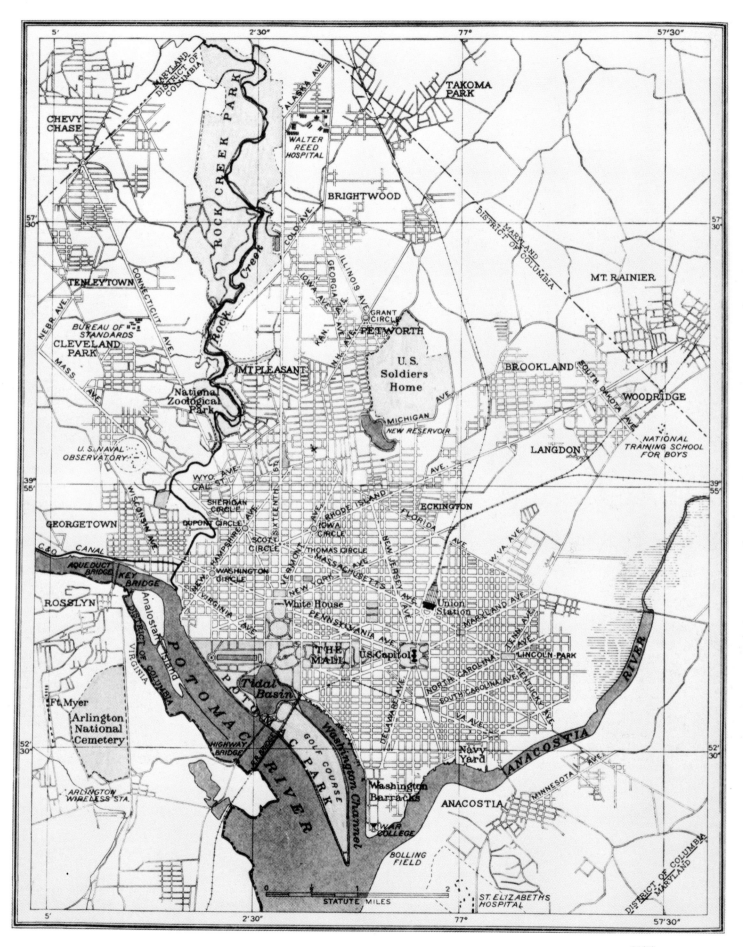

7 Notes on the Modern City

(Downtown, the Mall, Foggy Bottom, Dumbarton Oaks)

"It is a beautiful spot, capable of every improvement, and the more I view it, the more I am delighted with it."

—Abigail Adams, describing
Washington in 1800

Through the 1920s most Washingtonians lived within the Federal City drawn by Pierre L'Enfant: inside the boundaries of the Potomac and Anacostia rivers, Rock Creek and Boundary Avenue (which became Florida Avenue in 1890). There was still plenty of open space on which to build, and most federal buildings and installations were still located inside the city. Distances were short and people walked to work, to school, to markets, shops or theaters, or went by streetcar. But in the 1930s and 1940s, with the government growth that came with the New Deal and World War II, the metropolitan area began spreading beyond the limits of the District of Columbia. Said William Press, executive vice-president of the Washington Board of Trade from 1941 to 1971:

> "Washington's growth has corresponded with governmental emergencies and augmented functions. During the Civil War period 1860–70, D.C. population increased 75.4%. World War I was the main factor in its 32.2% growth to 437,571 at the end of the 1910–20 decade, and the "New Deal" of the 1930's brought the D.C. population up to 663,091 in 1940, a ten year increase of 36.2%. Since World War II and the extraordinary propagation of the Federal government, international economic and social functions which followed have just about tripled Metropolitan Washington's population to about 3 million."

Since limits had been set on building heights (largely as a result of vigorous lobbying by Daniel

Burnham of the McMillan Commission), it was inevitable that the city's growth would be horizontal rather than vertical. As roads improved and city land was built up, most new housing went up beyond the city limits. By 1950 suburban development in adjacent Maryland and Virginia counties covered more ground than the District itself. The great majority of people who considered themselves Washingtonians now lived outside of the District.

The mass flight to the suburbs after World War II was on the whole a white exodus, accelerated by school integration in 1954. Economics and discriminatory real-estate practices in the District and in Maryland and Virginia kept the black population inside the old city. While the racial profile of the metropolitan area has remained quite constant throughout Washington's history (except during the Civil War, when the percentage of blacks doubled), within the city itself the proportion of blacks went from 35 percent in 1950 to more than 70 percent in 1975.

Today's Greater Washington is too large to photograph from the air except by satellite. It now extends twenty miles in any direction from the heart of the old Federal City. "Capable of every improvement" it remains, but much has been accomplished in creating the capital city. Although the capital has been overtaken by explosive growth, Washington's origins and history can still be seen and felt. Its historic center remains.

The sense of the city's past is particularly alive in the four places represented in these, the closing pages of this book. Each place is illustrative of what the city was and is: four focal points telling parts of the story, yet suggesting the whole.

Between the two world wars: the Army Air Corps' Second Bombardment Group flies over the Mall during a training exercise.

357

Downtown

For much of Washington's history the heart of downtown has been the area from 7th Street to the Treasury—a stretch of shops that stops just a block short of the President's House. Laid out along the brow of a hill, F Street in the city's earliest times provided a well-drained route by which stage and mail coaches could avoid the marshy Pennsylvania Avenue lowland between the Capitol and the White House. Architects James Hoban and William Thornton lived on F Street in those days; so did the Baroness Hyde de Neuville and Charles Bird King. The Gales and Seatons lived across the street from Blodgett's Hotel, around 8th and E streets. The Jefferson Stables School was at 14th and G, where Christian Hines described seeing grapevines, blackberries and rabbits. Shops and other businesses, drawn to this center of population, sprang up on Pennsylvania Avenue. Banks clustered near the Treasury.

Above: F Street as it looked before the Civil War, with the columns of the Treasury Building at far right. The Baroness Hyde de Neuville drew the two center houses in 1818 (see page 128). The photograph below, taken in 1911, looks west down F Street toward the Treasury. The Ebbitt House is at near left, on the corner of 14th Street. Once the site of the Forest house (where the Baroness dined, page 129), it later became the site of the National Press Building. Beyond is the Willard Hotel, with its rounded mansard roof. On the right, across from the Willard, is the Wyatt Building, which housed the offices of Western Union.

Local and out-of-town newspapers established offices nearby, making 14th Street, between F and Pennsylvania, the capital's "Newspaper Row." The fashionable Ebbitt House and the Willard Hotel were favored lodgings for Congressmen, Senators, reporters and influence-seekers. In 1883 Frank Carpenter noted:

"F street between the Treasury and the Patent Office has become almost entirely devoted to business, and Henry Clay's old home, just above Thirteenth street, has been torn down, a modern Gothic building of stores and offices standing in its place. The old John Quincy Adams mansion, just above it, is still a boarding house, but offices are all around, and it is sandwiched between a grocery store and a millinery shop, while a physician uses its parlors for his office. Fourteenth street promises to be the great business street of the Northwest, and land almost on the boundary line facing it is worth $1 a square foot. In the vicinity of Blaine's new house on Dupont Circle, where five years ago you could hardly give land away, the prices have risen to from $3 to $5 a square foot."

The engraving (above) depicts Newspaper Row in 1868, on the night President Andrew Johnson narrowly missed impeachment in a Senate trial. Most of the important papers in the country maintained offices in these small buildings. The *Washington Post* was around the corner on Pennsylvania Avenue. The old buildings of the *Evening Star* on Pennsylvania at 11th Street and the *Baltimore Sun* on F Street are still standing. Wrote correspondent Duncan Aikman in *Dateline: Washington* (1949):

"In the late 1860s and early 1870s apparently because it gave easy access to statesmen relaxing in Willard's Hotel bar and parlors, all but a few incurably high-minded correspondents moved into an agreeable rookery of old-fashioned offices on lower 14th Street between Pennsylvania Avenue and F street.

"Here on the site of the present National Press Building a concentrated craft social life developed in an atmosphere of happy anarchy. A continuous round of interoffice visitations went on, flavored with trades in news tips and background information, bottle hospitalities, political arguments and considerable draw and stud poker."

When the National Press Building was erected in 1926, on the site of the old Ebbitt House, it was the city's largest private office building. The Press Club, founded in 1908, occupied the thirteenth floor, and many news bureaus took space in the new building, which became the Newspaper Row of the mid-twentieth century. After World War II the news media—along with other downtown businesses—began moving to new plants and offices in other parts of the city. But the Press Club has remained in the building, and there continues its tradition of providing a meeting place for members of the press corps and a forum for national and world leaders.

In 1912 President Taft's cow Pauline lent a bucolic air to the White House grounds, a block from 14th and F. As commercial development expanded, private houses gradually disappeared. The President's House was one family residence that remained.

General George C. Marshall, the wartime Army Chief of Staff, turns into Pennsylvania Avenue from 15th Street in front of the Treasury during Franklin Roosevelt's Third Inauguration. The historic little Rhodes Tavern is in the background. (The city's oldest commercial building, it dates from 1800–1801 and is seen also in the Baroness Hyde de Neuville's watercolor on page 129.) Pennsylvania Avenue, the route of most of the city's great ceremonial processions, forms the southern boundary to commercial development. At Pennsylvania, downtown ends and the "monumental core" begins.

An elementary-school class visits the Martin Luther King Library on G Street. Designed by Mies van der Rohe's firm in 1972, the District's main library is diagonally across 9th Street from the restored Patent Office, which houses the National Collection of Fine Arts and the National Portrait Gallery. These buildings and the plazas in front of them with their fountains, trees and benches are important parts of the new downtown life.

The Metro Center subway stop in the city's longtime downtown shopping area.

An Indian delegation visits the White House in the early 1900s. The building in the background, formerly the State, War and Navy Building, is now the Executive Office Building.

At right, suffragettes parade down Pennsylvania Avenue. One Washingtonian, Marietta Minnigerode Andrews, left this account of a 1913 march for women's suffrage:

"Then a thin line of resolute women, led by the beautiful Inez Milholland, moved up Pennsylvania Avenue through a dense mob of hostile humanity . . . and many of the leading women of Washington followed her. I was not with them. My husband forbade it, and recreant that I was, I sat upon a balcony with friends, looking on, and eating chocolates! Looking on, but with a thumping heart and guilty conscience, miserably uncomfortable while so very safe and comfortable, as braver women faced a fight!

"The mood of the public was dangerously antagonistic. Police protection was utterly inadequate. Manure was thrown upon the marchers, they were spit upon, every ribald jest and insulting epithet in the vocabulary of the back alleys, was hurled at them. . . . Inez Milholland, leaning from her horse, struck right and left with her riding crop. Mrs. Taft, looking down the Avenue from Fifteenth Street, telephoned to the cavalry from Fort Myer to charge the crowd. . . .

"A police scandal followed, an investigation, and a well deserved dismissal of the Chief of Police because of his flagrant neglect. Thousands of men and women were won, by a natural reaction, to the cause of Suffrage. . . .

"My husband announced that he would have no suffragists in his house; like Horace Walpole, he thought of them as 'Hyenas in petticoats.' "

The scenes at the right and on the opposite page were photographed during the civil-rights demonstrations of 1963.

362

The Mall

Pierre L'Enfant envisioned the Mall as a magnificent avenue; but it was a neglected spot until 1854, when A. J. Downing designed a romantic, tangled bower as a setting for the new Smithsonian. At the turn of the twentieth century the vision of Frederick Law Olmsted and the McMillan Commission determined that the Mall would sweep from the Capitol to the Lincoln Memorial-to-be and established its character as a people's park. The Mall today is lined with galleries and museums of the Smithsonian, half of them opened since 1963, plus the Department of Agriculture, which has been on the Mall's southern edge in one form or another since shortly after the Civil War.

As a rallying point for national issues the Mall assumed unprecedented importance during the 1960s, but of course Washington has always been the soap box where Americans have come to petition or upbraid their government. During recent summers the Mall has been alive with the Smithsonian's Folklife Festival. Today it might be called both a national cultural center and the capital's village green.

In this view of the Mall from the Capitol's West Terrace, taken shortly before World War II, only a few buildings line the Mall, and the Federal Triangle (at far right) has just been built. The domed structure nearing completion in the right foreground is the National Gallery of Art. In the photograph at left, schoolchildren are guided through the Gallery.

The Hirshhorn Museum and Sculpture Garden (below) opened in 1974 as part of the Smithsonian Insitution, whose various cultural and scientific installations dominate the Mall. Besides the Hirshhorn its recent additions include the Museum of History and Technology, opened in 1964, and the Air and Space Museum, opened in 1976. It also includes the museums of Arts and Industries and of Natural History, the Freer Gallery, the National Gallery and, beyond the Mall, the National Collection of Fine Arts, the National Portrait Gallery, the Anacostia Neighborhood Museum and the Zoo. Less visible to the general public are the Smithsonian's Astrophysical Observatory, Radiation Biological Laboratory, Tropical Research Institute, Center for Short-Lived Phenomena, Center for the Study of Man and the Woodrow Wilson International Center for Scholars.

By the 1870s, when the above photograph was taken, the fever-breeding marshlands at the bottom of the Mall were being drained and filled. Constitution Avenue, the broad roadway cutting into the picture from the far right, had been built over the stagnant and long-derelict Washington Canal (roughly along the course of the Tiber Creek), its waters channeled through underground pipes. At left is the mansard-roofed Department of Agriculture, with formal gardens that were the city's pride. Landfill projects begun in the 1870s created the land west of the Washington Monument.

Constitution Gardens (here seen from the top of the Washington Monument) opened during the Bicentennial Year. The forty-five-acre park with its quiet woodland walks lies adjacent to the Reflecting Pool and the Lincoln Memorial. Newly dug lakes take the area full circle back to the time when, in the city's early days, it was under water. Flocks of wild mallards have already settled on the lake.

Washington Post

Foggy Bottom

One of Foggy Bottom's main industries was the glass works of Edwards, Way and Company. Built in 1809, near what is now 22nd Street and Constitution Avenue, it produced window glass and other products for some thirty years. Its wares were shipped by river. Easby's Wharf and Shipyard (see page 168) stood nearby. Later, during the Civil War, a large supply base, a slaughter-house and a horse corral occupied the site. The area is now the site of the Department of State and the National Academy of Sciences.

Foggy Bottom—the words breathe mist, malaria and a touch of farce—is the site of the Department of State, George Washington University, the John F. Kennedy Center for the Performing Arts, the Watergate buildings, the Federal Reserve, the World Bank and more.

Situated between Rock Creek and Tiber Creek, the area that became Foggy Bottom began to take shape in 1768 when Jacob Funk bought a parcel of land there and laid out a little town of 287 lots. Called Hamburg—or sometimes Funkstown—the enterprise did not prosper. Exciting prospects seemed in store for the area nonetheless, for in 1791 George Washington and Thomas Jefferson considered choosing "the highest summit of lands in the town heretofore called Hamburg" as the site for the Capitol. In the end, however, it seemed doubtful that the grandly envisioned seat of the American government could fit between the two creeks. Jenkin's Hill to the east was chosen instead, and thereafter Foggy Bottom fell into years of semiobscurity, its rolling meadows and hill occupied only by the Naval Observatory, farms, a few shipyards and small businesses.

The military barracks of Camp Fry are seen in this 1865 lithograph by Charles Magnus. The view is from Washington Circle to the river, looking down what is now 23rd Street. The flag staff at left stands on the present-day site of George Washington University Hospital. The dome of the Naval Observatory can be seen along the riverbank, just to the right of 23rd Street. At right center is the Camp Fry cavalry depot.

The West Station gas works dominate this Foggy Bottom landscape, painted by Washington artist and teacher Robert F. Gates in 1936. Long home to a diverse population of blacks as well as whites, Foggy Bottom attracted a large number of Irish, German and Italian immigrants after the gas works were built in 1858. Many of these row houses were renovated in the 1950s and 1960s; some were demolished for George Washington University, apartments, offices and freeways. Now glossy apartments and new and restored houses prevail, but a few old churches and houses remain to add interest and variety. The John Marshall house, built in 1825 at 18th and F streets, a block north of the Octagon, survives as the last privately owned in-town mansion, having been brought new distinction by the Robert Low Bacons.

Well situated, Foggy Bottom was ripe for the expanding federal bureaucracy and the international agencies that proliferated after World War II. The State Department's move to 21st and D streets assured the area's prestige and redevelopment. The World Bank and International Monetary Fund now spread over two city blocks on Pennsylvania Avenue, with a dramatic interior court (below) at the center of the complex. Below: the Pan-American Regional Office of the World Health Organization, designed by Roman Fresnedo-Siri of Uruguay, is located diagonally across from the old Naval Observatory and the yellow brick buildings that were the Naval Hospital before its move to Bethesda in the early 1940s.

The Phillips Collection, Washington

World Bank

World Health Organization

Fine Arts Commission

Above: the river at Foggy Bottom, the Lincoln Memorial and the Arlington Memorial Bridge, dedicated in 1932. The steps were planned for ceremonial arrivals by sea—the city's "water gate." (The name, however, is also said to have derived from a nearby Washington Canal lock.) Waterside Drive follows the river upstream and leads into Rock Creek Park. As the road leaves the Lincoln Memorial, it passes under the overhanging terraces of the Kennedy Center and then reaches the Watergate buildings, a complex of offices, shops, restaurants, apartments and a hotel. They are almost at the mouth of Rock Creek, on the northwest edge of Foggy Bottom, near Georgetown. Fishermen still line the banks of the Potomac and Rock Creek when the herring and shad are running in the spring.

The Kennedy Center for the Performing Arts, housing the Eisenhower Theater, the Concert Hall and the Opera House, was designed by Edward Durell Stone and opened in 1971. Providing a permanent base for the city's National Symphony, the facility presents artists and performers from all over the world and has made Washington a major center for music, theater and dance.

The earliest known concert on this spot was only a few yards away from the present site of the Kennedy Center. Commandant of Marines William Ward Burroughs described the ball he gave for "every young lady in Geo. Town and some from elsewhere" atop the hill in Foggy Bottom where his men first camped in 1800:

"The evening was mild. The Moon divine, & the Music the best I ever heard: made up of Wilkinson's and my Band.

"We gave the usual Refreshments to the ladies in the early Part of the Evening after which a cold Collation which the Gentlemen seemed to admire, being ornamented with some of B. W. Morris's best. The Ladies retired about 12, but the young Men kept it up till day light in serenading etc. . . . The Situation of our Encampment is immensely beautiful, and tho' Night, yet the view of the Potomack was solemnly great from the reflection of the Moon. . . ."

Watergate Improvement Associates

John F. Kennedy Center for the Performing Arts

Dumbarton Oaks

Above, the main house at Dumbarton Oaks, showing part of the orangerie at far right.

Dumbarton Oaks

On the heights of Georgetown, the great estate of Dumbarton Oaks has evolved with the nation, mirroring America's growth from an eighteenth-century federal republic to a world power. Once a country house, now a center for scholars and a museum, Dumbarton Oaks, with its splendid gardens, was called "America's most civilized square mile" by planner Carl Feiss. A birthplace of atomic research during World War II, it became internationally famous toward the war's end, the plans for the United Nations originating there. There is no place where the characteristic Washington mix of public affairs and private lives is evoked more strongly than at Dumbarton Oaks.

The land on which the house stands was first owned by Ninian Beall, who named his patent Rock of Dunbarton, after a landmark that rises from the River Clyde, in his native Scotland. ("Coll. Bell's" name is on DeGraffenried's 1716 map reproduced on page 21.) The core of the present mansion was built in 1801 by William Hammond Dorsey of Maryland, who had bought twenty-two acres of the Beall property from Ninian's son, Thomas.

The Beverly family of Virginia, the next owners, added the orangerie.

In 1822 the property was bought by John C. Calhoun, then Secretary of War and later Vice President; he named it Oakly. Later owners remodeled the place to suit prevailing tastes. The house and grounds were bought in 1920 by Foreign Service Officer Robert Woods Bliss and his wife Mildred Barnes Bliss, who spent twenty years raising it to new heights of elegance. On the eve of World War II the Blisses gave the estate they called Dumbarton Oaks—the mansion, the gardens, the libraries and their extensive collection of Byzantine, Medieval and pre-Columbian art—to Harvard University. Lent to the government during the war, the secluded property was used for secret research and meetings. Dumbarton Oaks is now the center of scholarship planned by Mr. and Mr. Bliss, with its museums and acres of gardens open to the public.

From 1829 until 1920 Dumbarton Oaks was owned, successively, by Mackalls, Linthicums and Blounts. The late-nineteenth-century photograph at top shows the house as it looked with mid-Victorian adornments when the Linthicum family owned it. Below is the great music room added by the Robert Woods Blisses, where performances were given by Wanda Landowska, Lucrezia Bori, Igor Stravinsky and Ignace Paderewski. During World War II Allied leaders used the room as a meeting place.

Dumbarton Oaks

The gardens of Dumbarton Oaks encircle the great house and wind down the hillside toward Rock Creek. Mildred Barnes Bliss worked for years with landscape architect Beatrice Farrand making twelve acres of land into terraces, wooded paths, pools, vistas and hidden retreats. Twenty-seven acres of the property were given to the Park Service, linking the property to Rock Creek Park.

In the reading room above, formerly a bedroom, plans were made for the development of the atom bomb. The Los Alamos laboratories and the Manhattan Project were planned here. After the war the first attempt to bring the atom under international control for peaceful purposes—the Acheson-Lilienthal Plan—was prepared during meetings at Dumbarton Oaks. Below: a meeting of the Dumbarton Oaks Conference, which paved the way for the establishment of the United Nations.

Opposite: a room of the museum at Dumbarton Oaks, which was built in 1963. Designed by Philip Johnson, the museum houses the pre-Columbian art collection of Mr. and Mrs. Bliss. Wrote William C. Tyler, Harvard's director of Dumbarton Oaks (from 1969 to 1977):

> "While Dumbarton Oaks has splendid collections of Byzantine and Pre-Columbian art, as well as libraries in these two fields and in landscape architecture and gardening, its major international contribution lies in its role as a scholarly Research and Publication Center.
>
> "Thanks to the distinguished scholars from more than fifty countries in both hemispheres who have come to work there, and to its publications which are to be found in universities and institutions throughout the world, it is understandable —if at times surprising—that Dumbarton Oaks is often better known to people at the far ends of the earth than to residents of Washington, D.C."

At the dedication of Dumbarton Oaks, Mr. and Mrs. Bliss expressed the hope that the house would serve to "clarify an ever changing present and to inform the future with wisdom."

This view of Washington, taken from near the spot where Henry Fleete came to anchor in June 1623, was painted in 1966 by Hereward Lester Cooke, who was at that time the Curator of Painting at the National Gallery of Art. Wrote the artist: "The view looking down the Potomac is one of the world's great city views. The lights, winds, mists, reflections and changing seasons make new combinations every hour. I see this view every day; it is never the same; and I never get tired of it."

HEREWARD LESTER COOKE 1966

"... we came to an anchor about two leagues short of the Falls, being the latitude 41, on the 26th of June. This place without all question is the most pleasant & healthful place in all this Cuntry, & most convenient for habitacon, the aier temperate in somer & not violent in winter. It aboundeth with all manner of fishe.... The Indians in one night... will catch 30 Sturgeons in a place of the river where it is not above 12 fadom broade: And as for deare Buffaloes, beares, & Turkies, the woods do swarm with them and the soil is exceedingly fertile."

—Henry Fleete, 1632

"I believe there are scarcely any places in the world, more beautiful and better situated. . . ."

—De Graffenried, on seeing the hills above the Potomac near Georgetown in 1712

Drawing by Michael Youngblood

ACKNOWLEDGMENTS

To all institutions and people named in our picture credits, our grateful thanks.

Our first words of special appreciation must go to:

Virginia Daiker who introduced us to the Library of Congress Prints and Photographs Division and to the many members of the Division who helped us; Mathilde Williams of the Peabody Room of the Georgetown Public Library; Elizabeth Culpepper of the Washingtoniana Division of the Martin Luther King Library; Perry Fisher, Librarian, and Robert Truax, Picture Curator of The Columbia Historical Society and to all those historians, amateur and professional, whose contributions over the years have made the collections and the published *Records* of the Society invaluable.

In addition to these libaries and to private papers, our principal research was in:

The Library of Congress Manuscript Division: Presidential papers' Peter Force collection, and the papers of Frank Carpenter, Christophe De Graffenried, Henry Fleete, Albert Gallatin, L'Enfant-Digges-Morgan, the McCook family, Robert Mills, Alexander Shepherd, Michael Shiner, Margaret Bayard Smith, Mrs. William Thornton.

The Library of Congress Rare Book Division—in particular the writings of Richard Blome, Tobias Lear, William Tatum, Isaac Weld.

The Antiquarian Society, Worcester; the American Philosophical Society, Philadelphia; the Alexandria Library; the Landmarks Commission; the Maryland Historical Society; the James Monroe Library, Fredericksburg; the National Archives; the National Capital Planning Commission; the New York Public Library; the university libraries of the states of Indiana, Michigan, Wisconsin (Civil War letters); the George Washington University Library, the Wright Collection.

The Christian Heurich Mansion, 1307 New Hampshire Avenue, NW. now the headquarters of the Columbia Historical Society.

We are also indebted to the following people and their organizations:

The American Institute of Architects and The Octagon, their libraries and publications (Jean Butler)

The Corcoran Galley of Art (Linda Simmons)

The Diplomatic Reception Rooms of the Deaprtment of State (Jane Pool)

The Frick Art Reference Library (resources made available through the kindness of Katharine McCook Knox)

Government Services Savings and Loan (Arthur J. Phelan, Kathleen A. Butler)

Howard University, Moorland Spingarn Research Center (Thomas C. Battle)

The Jewish Historical Society (Evelyn Greenberg)

The Kennedy Gallery (Lawrence Fleishman)

The Kiplinger Newsletter (John Hazard and Frances Turgeon)

The National Gallery of Art (William Campbell, Maria Mallus)

The National Park Service (Robert Fenton, Don Heilman)

The National Trust for Historic Preservation, its library and publications (Terry Morton, Diane Maddux)

The Navy Memorial Museum (Captain Roger Pineau)

The Smithsonian Institution (Herbert Collins, James Goode)

The U. S. Capitol, Office of the Architect (Elliott Carroll)

The U. S. Fine Arts Commission, its library and publications (Charles Atherton, Sibley Jennings)

The White House, Office of the Curator (Betty Monkman)

We were grateful for the opportunity to tape the reminiscences of Virginia Murray Bacon, Zachariah D. Blackistone, Charles Carroll Glover, Jr., Perry West, Armistead Peter III, Gladys Hinckley Werpick.

Difficult as it is to single out individuals, our special thanks go to:

Thomas Minor Anderson, Jr.
Wm. Edmund Barrett
James E. Barron
Carroll Marbury Blundon
Mary Bowron
Sally H. Carruthers
Pierre de Viel Castel
Brice McAdoo Clagett
Colby Allen Child
Samuel C. O. Holt
Louisa Catherine Adams Hull
Ernest N. May, Jr.
Charles C. McLaughlin
Mary Mitchell
LeRoy Tuttle Morgan
Dorothy L. B. Porter
Robert Rivoire
Edith Ray Saul
Julie Brès Slavik
Frank Campbell Waldrop

A SELECTED BIBLIOGRAPHY

AIA Guide to the Architecture of Washington. New York, 1965, 2nd ed. 1974.

Adams, Abigail. *Letters of Mrs. Adams.* Boston, 1840.

Adams, Henry. *The Education of Henry Adams.* Boston, 1918.

Ames, Mary Clemmer. *Ten Years in Washington.* Hartford, 1874, 1882. 2 vols.

Andrews, Marietta Minnegerode. *My Studio Window.* New York, 1928.

Arber, Edward. *Travels and Works of Captain John Smith.* Edinburgh, 1910.

Beale, Marie. *Decatur House and Its Inhabitants.* Washington: National Trust, 1954.

The Bladensburg Races. Washington, 1816.

Briggs, Emily Edson. *Olivia Letters.* New York and Washington, 1906.

Brown, George Rothwell. *Washington: a Not Too Serious History.* Baltimore, 1930.

Brown, Glenn. *History of the United States Capitol.* Washington, 1901–1904. 2 vols.

Brown, Letitia Woods. *Free Negroes in the District of Columbia, 1790–1846.* New York, 1972.

Brown, Letitia W., and Lewis, Elsie M. *Washington from Banneker to Douglass, 1791–1870.* Washington, 1971.

———. *Washington in the New Era, 1870–1970.* Washington, 1972.

Bryan, Wilhemus B. *A History of the National Capital . . . .* New York, 1914, 1916. 2 vols.

Busey, Samuel C. *Pictures of the City of Washington . . . .* Washington, 1898.

Cable, Mary. *The Avenue of the Presidents.* Boston, 1969.

Caemmerer, H. P. *Washington, the National Capital.* Washington, 1932.

Carpenter, Frank, *Carp's Washington.* Edited by Frances Carpenter. New York, 1960.

Cassini, Countess Marguerite. *Never a Dull Moment.* New York, 1956.

Clark, Allen C. *Greenleaf and Law in the Federal City.* Washington, 1901.

Clay-Clopton, Virginia. *A Belle of the Fifties.* New York, 1904.

Corcoran, William Winston. *A Grandfather's Legacy.* Washington, 1870.

Dickens, Charles. *American Notes for General Circulation.* London, 1892.

D. C. Sesquicentennial Catalogue. Library of Congress, 1950–1951.

Douglass, Frederick. *Life and Times of Frederick Douglass.* New York, 1893.

Eberlain, Harold, and Hubbard, Cortland. *Historic Homes of Georgetown and Washington City.* Richmond, 1951.

Ecker, Grace Dunlop. *A Portrait of Old Georgetown.* Richmond, 1951.

Elliott, Jonathan. *Historical Sketches of the Ten Mile Square.* Washington, 1830.

Ellis, John B. *Sights and Secrets of the National Capital.* New York, 1869.

Federal Writers' Project. *Washington, City and Capital.* American Guide Series. Washington, 1937.

Gahn, Bessie Wilmarth. *Original Patentees of Land . . . .* Silver Spring, Md., 1936.

Gemmill, Jane W. *Note on Washington.* Philadelphia, 1884.

Goode, James. *The Outdoor Sculpture of Washington.* Washington, 1974.

Green, Constance McLaughlin. *Washington, 1800–1872.* Princeton, 1962.

———. *Capital City, 1879–1950.* Princeton, 1963. 2 vols.

———. *The Secret City.* Princeton, 1967.

Guide books and City Directories from 1822.

Gutheim, Frederick. *The Potomac.* New York, 1949.

Hamlin, Talbot. *Benjamin Henry Latrobe.* New York, 1955.

Harrison, Fairfax. *Landmarks of Old Prince William.* Berryville, Va., 1964.

Hines, Christian. *Early Recollections of Washington City.* Washington, 1866.

Hobbs, Horace, Jr. *Pioneers of the Potomack.* Ann Arbor, University Microfilms, 1964.

Hutchins, Stilson, and Moore, J.W. *National Capital Past and Present.* Washington, 1885.

Jackson, Richard Plummer. *Chronicles of Old Georgetown . . . .* Washington, 1878.

Kimmel, Stanley. *Mr. Lincoln's Washington.* New York, 1957.

Latrobe, Benjamin Henry. *The Journal of Latrobe.* New York, 1905.

Leech, Margaret. *Reveille in Washington.* New York, 1941.

Lockwood, Mary S. *Historic Homes in Washington.* New York, 1889.

Logan, Mrs. John A. *30 Years in Washington.* Hartford, 1901.

Lomax. Elizabeth Lindsay. *Leaves from an Old Washington Diary.* Edited by Lindsay Lomax Wood. New York, 1943.

Longworth, Alice. *Crowded Hours.* New York, 1932.

Maddox, Diane. *Historic Buildings of Washington, D.C.* Pittsburgh, 1973.

Mitchell, Mary. *Divided Town.* Barre, Mass., 1968.

Moore, Gay Montague. *Seaport in Virginia.* Richmond, 1949.

Moore, Joseph West. *Picturesque Washington.* Providence, 1884.

Morrison, Alfred J., editor. *The District in the 18th Century . . .* (As Described by the Earliest Travellers): (Henry) Wamsey, (Francis) Baily, (Issac) Weld, (Duke of) La Rouchefould-Linancourt, (John) Davis (of Salisbury). Washington, 1909.

Nicolay, Helen. *Our Capital on the Potomac.* New York, 1924.

Periodicals, Newspapers and Magazines of the 18th, 19th, 20th centuries.

Pepper, Charles M. *Everyday Life in Washington with Pen and Camera.* New York, 1900.

Phelps-Stokes Catalogue of the Collection in the New York Public Library.

Poore, Benjamin Perley. *Reminiscences of 60 Years in the National Metropolis.* Philadelphia, 1886.

Proctor, John Clagett, editor. *Washington Past and Present.* New York, 1930, 1932. 2 vols.

Records of the Columbia Historical Society. Washington, 1895–1974. 49 vols.

Reps, John W. *Monumental Washington.* Princeton, 1967.

———. *Tidewater Towns.* Charlottesville, 1972.

Roberts, Chalmers. *Washington, Past and Present.* Washington, 1949–1950.

Royall, Ann. *Sketches of History, Life and Manners in the United States.* New Haven, 1826.

Rutland, Robert A. *The Papers of George Mason, 1749–1792.* Chapel Hill, 1949.

Smith, Margaret Bayard. *First Forty Years of Washington Society.* New York, 1906.

Twining, Thomas. *Travels in America.* New York, 1893.

Tayloe, Benjamin Ogle. *In Memoriam.* Washington, 1872.

Trollope, Frances. *Domestic Manners of Americans.* Edited by Donald Smalley. New York, 1949.

Vedder. Sarah E. *Reminiscences of the District of Columbia.* St. Louis, 1909.

Willard-Bradley Memoirs. Privately printed. Washington, 1925.

Warden, David Baille. *A Chorographical and Statistical Description.* Paris, 1816.

Young, James Sterling. *The Washington Community: 1800–28.* New York, 1966.

A recent paperback is recommended for libraries and students:

Fisher, Perry G. *Materials for the Study of Washington: a Selected Annotated Bibliography.* George Washington University.

INDEX